Clinical Empathy

Clinical Empathy

David M. Berger, M.D.

Jason Aronson Inc.
Northvale, New Jersey
London

For my parents, Mordecai and Leah,
and my wife, Marilyn

Library of Congress Cataloging-in-Publication Data

Berger, David M.
   Clinical empathy.

   Bibliography: p. 275
   Includes index.
   1. Empathy.   2. Psychotherapist and patient.
   1. Title.   [DNLM: 1. Empathy.   2. Psychotherapy—methods.
BF 575..E55 B496c]
RC489.E46B47   1987   616.89′14   86-32138
ISBN 0-87668-920-9

Manufactured in the United States of America.

Contents

Part I: Concepts of Empathy

v

Chapter 11. Empathic Interventions   185

The Structure of Interventions: Questions and Answers/ Enhancing the Patient's Self-Understanding/The Qualities of an Intervention: Simplicity, Allusiveness, and Indirectness/ Inexactness, Subjectivity, and Conflict/The Dialogue/The Perfect Intervention/Clinical Illustrations

Chapter 12. The Emergence of Empathic Understanding   201

Theory and the Clinical Setting/The Empathic Process

Chapter 13. Empathy as a Curative Factor   217

Historical Background/Insight and Working Through/Relationship Factors/The Accuracy of an Intervention/Insight versus Relationship Factors in the Clinical Setting/The Therapist's Attitude in the Clinical Setting/Heuristic Issues/ Sharing the Patient's Perspective versus Interpreting/Longstanding Improvement

Chapter 14. Empathy in Psychotherapy Supervision   237

The Conflictual Component of Learning/Learning the Principles of Psychotherapy/Supervision versus Psychotherapy

Chapter 15. Epilogue: The Fate of Empathy at
Termination   259

The Fate of the Therapeutic Relationship/The Fate of the Narrative/Introspection, Fascination, and Curiosity/Summary: The Book as Metaphor of Psychotherapy

It is easy to cloathe Imaginary Beings with our own Thoughts & Feelings; but to send ourselves out of ourselves, to think ourselves in to the Thoughts & Feelings of Beings in circumstances wholly & strangely different from our own . . . and who has achieved it? Perhaps only Shakespere . . . a great Poet must be implicite if not explicite, a profound Metaphysician. He may not have it in local coherence, in his Brain & Tongue; but he must have it by Tact/for all sounds, & forms of human nature he must have the ear of a wild Arab listening to the silent Desart, the eye of a North American Indian tracing the footsteps of an Enemy upon the Leaves that strew the Forest; the Touch of a Blind Man feeling the face of a darling Child.

Samuel T. Coleridge (1802)

If the historian will submit himself to his material instead of trying to impose himself on his material, then the material will ultimately speak to him and supply the answers.

Barbara Tuchman (1979)

Acknowledgments

A complete list of contributors to this volume would include hundreds of teachers, colleagues, students, and patients; the many authors whose works, ranging from *Treasure Island* to the *Interpretation of Dreams*, influenced my thinking at various junctures in my life; and my parents, who from the beginning taught me to doubt and to be curious in ways intended and not intended. Indeed, help and encouragement came from many quarters. Closer to the task at hand, however, a few individuals deserve special mention. As the chapters were written, Professor Donald Carveth, Dr. David R. Freebury, and Dr. Gordon Warme went over them one by one. Their advice was invaluable. Dr. R. C. A. Hunter reviewed the manuscript as a whole, and Dr. Alan Kindler provided a helpful critique of Chapter 3. These teachers and colleagues were chosen not because their views on psychotherapy necessarily coincided with mine but because I respected their judgment. Ms. Rhea Tregebov improved the organization and grammar of the text, Mrs. Blanche Stuart provided every secretarial need an insecure author required, and Ms. Thelma Law was a virtuoso on the word processor.

The book has its own unique history. A talk on the therapeutic usefulness of puzzlement and multiple perspectives given in Toronto by Dr. Leston Havens in 1982 prompted me to write an article on empathy. Several months after its publication, I received a phone call from Dr. Jason Aronson, who encouraged me to expand the article into a book. Both he and Ms. Joan Langs vetted this venture. Dr. V. Rakoff, professor and chairman of the Department of Psychiatry at the University of Toronto, and my colleagues at the Mount Sinai Hospital, Toronto, made it possible for me to take a six-month sabbatical leave. My empathic and practical wife, Marilyn, not only helped with the manuscript but also made it possible for me to take a sabbatical from my duties at home. My children, often taken aback by "Mr. Empathy's outbursts of temper," as they ironically called them, were models of tolerance.

Although the thoughts expressed in this book have been brewing in my mind for many years, it was not until I reexamined the cases under my care that I was able to appreciate the significant facets of what I consider to be empathic understanding. In the process of writing, I discovered many things I didn't know that I knew or, more correctly, many therapeutic principles I didn't know that I followed. The case material is the foundation of the book. Although the patients' narratives have been fictionalized for the purpose of confidentiality, the significant core of each story has been preserved. Indeed, the major themes outlined in the text have emerged from the narratives—in the same surprising and labyrinthine fashion that characterizes a course of dynamic psychotherapy.

Part One

Concepts of Empathy

Chapter One

Knowing the Patient

Empathizing with the patient is the therapist's major function in most forms of psychotherapy. It is no surprise, therefore, that empathy as a therapeutic modality has attracted thoughtful attention from a number of divergent schools of psychotherapy. The opinion that empathy is clinically useful has received support from the existential point of view (Frank 1978), client-centered therapists (Bachrach 1976), a recent evaluation of the work of H. S. Sullivan (Havens 1973, Margulies and Havens 1981), and therapists whose clinical approach is practical and reality oriented (U'Ren 1980). Recently, efforts have been made to study the empathic process in psychotherapy quantitatively and to examine its relation to the outcome of treatment (Bachrach, Mintz, and Luborsky 1971, Deutsch and Madle 1975).

In dynamic or psychoanalytic psychotherapy, the therapist empathizes not only with the patient's present state of mind and concerns but also with warded-off contents and conflicts, and defensive operations such as repression, denial, and regression. Indeed, Freud (1921) and Ferenczi (1928) considered empathy an essential therapeutic modality. Others, however, approached the concept with caution, claiming that it was un-scientific and vague, and that it might compromise the basic rule of neutrality (Hartmann 1927, Reik 1948). In recent decades, greater therapeutic attention to borderline and narcissistic personality disorders and the work of Kohut (1977) and other members of the self psychology school have refocused attention on the central importance of empathy. Self psychologists are critical of the traditional psychoanalytic approach, claiming it to be mechanistic and lacking in empathy. Classical psychoanalysts are skeptical that self psychologists have anything new to offer.

The extent to which empathy is felt to contribute to the curative process also varies according to the different schools (Havens 1982a). Self psychologists believe empathy provides a growth-promoting experience that had been lacking in an individual's childhood (Ornstein and Ornstein 1977). Traditional therapists, on the other hand, consider it a stepping-stone on the road to insight: here the curative factor is felt to be an enriched understanding of oneself. These points of view are not mutually exclusive. Many therapists consider empathy to be one of several factors that contribute to the curative process.

That there are differences of opinion about the meaning of the term is self-evident. Researchers, such as Truax (1966), who measure empathy by auditing tapes of patient–therapist interactions are probably not measuring the same entity that psychoanalysts refer to as empathy. Truax concluded that a therapist's empathy can be meaningfully studied without hearing what the patient has to say. His conclusion highlights the disparity between quantifiers and clinicians. The accrued clinical wisdom of psychoanalytically oriented therapists would indicate that the term *empathy* does not describe a set of responses but, rather, an intrapsychic process; its accuracy can be assessed only in the light of an understanding of the patient. It is unsettling, however, that different schools of psychoanalytic therapy, notably self psychology and the traditional school, each claiming to be guided by empathy, can arrive at differing views of the patient and the therapeutic process. With these differences in mind, this book will explore and develop the psychodynamic concept of empathy and its clinical application in a way that employs useful contributions from both schools.

THE DEFINITION OF EMPATHY

The term *empathy* is a relative latecomer to the English language. Although it is likely that in common usage the term made its appearance several decades earlier, the *Supplement* to the *Oxford English Dictionary (OED)* records that the term first appeared in a literary context in 1903 as the English equivalent of the German *einfuhlung*. *Einfuhlung*, "to feel into" or "to feel within," had been used by Lipps to describe the capacity for aesthetic appreciation (Szalita 1976, Post 1980).

In everyday usage, the term has acquired a number of meanings. The adjective *empathic* is frequently used to describe an individual who is sensitive to the needs and feelings of others. Behavior that is tactful, altruistic, sympathetic, or indulgent is often designated as empathic. However, if one adheres to the precise definition, the term *empathy* embraces a more specific and neutral meaning.

Empathy is defined as "the power of entering into the experience of or understanding objects or emotions outside ourselves" *(OED)* and "the capacity for participating in the feelings or ideas of another" *(New Merriam–Webster Dictionary)*. Two terms occasionally confused with *empathy* are *sympathy* and *insight*. *Sympathy* is defined as "the capacity of entering into or sharing the feelings of another," specifically "being thus affected by the suffering or sorrow of another; a feeling of compassion or commiseration" *(OED)*. *Insight* denotes "sight or seeing into a thing or subject" *(OED)*. Although the terms clearly overlap, from these definitions it might be reasonable to infer that empathy occupies an uncertain middle ground in relation to the object, not so far removed as is implied by the term *insight*, yet not as involved as is implied by the term *sympathy*.

EMPATHY IN PSYCHOANALYTIC PSYCHOTHERAPY

In the setting of psychoanalytic psychotherapy, the meaning of the term *empathy* undergoes a number of subtle alterations that are not immediately apparent in its definition. The definition put forward by Moore and Fine (1968) in *A Glossary of Psychoanalytic Terms and Concepts* is in keeping with the preceding definitions and is not significantly at variance with the descriptions of other schools of psychotherapy:

> *Empathy:* A special mode of perceiving the psychological state or experiences of another person. It is an "emotional knowing" of another human being rather than intellectual understanding. To empathize means temporarily to share, to experience the feelings of the other person. One partakes of the quality but not the quantity, the kind but not the degree of the feelings.
>
> The capacity for empathy is an essential prerequisite for the psychoanalytic therapist. Usually a preconscious phenomenon, it can be consciously instigated or interrupted. It can also occur silently and automatically and may oscillate with other ways of relating to people. The essential psychic mechanism is the analyst's partial and temporary identification with the patient.
>
> Both empathy and intuition, to which it is related, are means of obtaining quick and deep understanding. Empathy establishes close contact in terms of emotions and impulses; intuition does the same in the realm of ideas. Empathy is a function of the experiencing ego, while intuition seems to be a function of the observing ego.

The sense has been retained that empathy denotes the capacity to know emotionally what another is experiencing from within the frame of reference of that other person, the capacity to sample the feelings of another or to put oneself in another's shoes. The definition put forward by Moore and Fine relies heavily on Greenson's contribution to the subject (1960) and is presented here as an approximate starting point from which to begin our discussion.

Empathy, which has been incorporated procedurally in psychoanalytic and nonpsychoanalytic treatment, is also a common experience in daily interaction. Understandably, setting plays a role in its nature and manifestation. In the setting of psychoanalytically oriented therapy, the therapist's stance is characterized by neutrality, abstinence, and attentiveness to the patient's verbal and emotional expressions, the last encompassing empathy (Basch 1983a). Neutrality describes the therapist's ability to sample the patient's thoughts and feelings with nonjudgmental equanimity. Abstinence describes the therapist's capacity to withhold responding to the patient when it is in the interest of promoting insight to do so. The four steps in the therapist's work are (1) listening, (2) inwardly experiencing, (3) comprehension (cognition), and (4) interpretation (Thomson 1980). Empathy is an ingredient of the second step, but the degree to which the third step, cognition, is intentionally or unwittingly involved in the process of inwardly experiencing is difficult to assess. Although the term *empathy* is generally not applied to the communication of an interpretation itself, it is self-evident that the quality of the empathic experience will influence the tone and the expression of the therapist's communications.

Basch (1983b), in agreement with Kohut, has stated that the empathic capacity is a value-free function; the use to which it is put may be harmful or selfish as well as beneficial: ". . . much of the time we are empathically attuned to the affective state of others primarily to fulfill our own needs and to spare ourselves pain . . . some of the world's greatest scoundrels have been exquisitely and unerringly attuned to grasping the significance of the unconscious or unspoken affective communications of others and have used that knowledge to achieve base aims" (pp. 119–120). Nevertheless, in psychoanalytic therapy, empathy is always associated with the specific intent of broadening the patient's self-understanding and ability to cope. Indeed, Schafer (1959) has suggested that the mature empathy employed by the psychoanalytic therapist should be labeled "generative empathy" (i.e., growth-promoting empathy) in order to distinguish it from other forms of empathy.

The therapeutic situation is not an unbiased field. The therapist anticipates that the data he will uncover will be congruent with the theories he has gathered from teachers and textbooks, as well as the informal lessons of life. Because the four steps in the therapist's work occur almost simultaneously, it is next to impossible to determine the extent to which theoretical knowledge has contributed to the therapist's understanding. Conversely, it is equally difficult not to be influenced by one theory or another when attempting to formulate retrospectively the events that have led up to a brief span of empathic understanding.

The following discussions of the inexactness of theory, the use of metaphor, and the dilemmas inherent in the human condition stem from a need to place empathy in the setting of the psychoanalytic therapies. In this setting, the definition of empathy seems at first hardly altered. The term *empathy* is used to describe an intrapsychic process in the therapist by which an understanding of the patient, particularly an emotional understanding, a capacity to feel what the other is feeling, is enhanced. Situated somewhere between listening and interpreting, empathy serves as a precondition for both. The role and nature of empathy, however, cannot be easily separated from the bias of the therapist's orientation. For example, the dynamic psychotherapist will surely set his empathic understanding to a task different from that of the client-centered therapist, with the latter's emphasis being on the here-and-now aspects of the patient's life.

THE INEXACTNESS OF THEORY

Despite their differences, the psychoanalytic paradigms (classical theory [Brenner 1973, 1982], object relations theory [Segal 1980], and self psychology [Kohut 1977]) have much in common. The gathering of data takes place in a nonjudgmental setting. Patients are encouraged to let their minds wander, to be unrestrained by the conventional rules of syntax and order, and to voice their thoughts uncritically. The therapist listens with evenly hovering attention, attending to associations and feelings (one's own as well as the patient's) that will reveal elements of the stories behind the story or that will relate past occurrences to present-day events. Each theory asserts that there is a hierarchical layering of emotionally charged memories, or stories, and that the less-conscious stories originating in the individual's childhood are couched in more archaic or unconventional modes of cognition. The more deeply layered stories are actively defended against, yet they somehow surface in disguised form and play a role in character formation and symptoms. Invariably, the cast of these less-available stories is comprised of the patient's parents and siblings; the protagonist is the patient. Whether the emphasis is on castration anxiety (classical theory), envy (object relations theory), or a sense of fragmentation (self psychology), the archaic, less-available emotions are predominantly painful. In each theory there is a recognition that aspects of the self and other can be confused and interchanged, whether one employs a transference–countertransference model in which parent imagos are transposed onto the therapist or focuses on the projection of introjects or on the selfobject use of the therapist.

The depth psychologies exhibit a number of similarities in the design and aim of the treatment. The patient's past, in somewhat altered fashion, is recapitulated in the narrative and in the therapeutic interaction. Two factors propel the treatment forward: The therapist's interpretations bring to light the ways in which the therapist is being acted upon as a character from the past, and second, the therapist's availability as a new object provides the opportunity to alter the older patterns adaptively (Loewald 1960). The now-remembered events are worked over by a more mature cognitive system that had been unavailable at the time these events had occurred. The memories that had contributed to the individual's sense of self are reviewed, with the beneficial effect that the urgency for the patient to repeat outdated patterns is diminished.

There are also differences among the psychoanalytic theories. The differences in the central paradigms of each theory (i.e., of the oedipal triangle in classical theory, of splitting and projection in object relations theory, of the self-selfobject configuration in self psychology) are immediately apparent.

A number of sources contribute to the disagreements in psychoanalysis. It is often difficult to fit the patient's material neatly into a theoretical framework, understanding (including empathic understanding) is never entirely accurate (a fact insufficiently noted), and the capacity to communicate complex ideas in words is often limited. Language, fashioned by the social group and by the individual's passage from simple to increasingly complex forms of cognition, is most effective in the middle range of thinking (Basch 1976). At the most complex levels, language has to be modified and supplemented in order to accommodate more elaborate abstractions. Unfortunately, as a means of characterizing an archaic preverbal period, the words and terminologies developed by psychoanalysis are necessarily adultomorphic approximations.

It is possible that, at least in some instances, one model is more congruent with the data than a second as, for example, in the claim that the self psychology model is superior to other models for an understanding of narcissistically disturbed individuals. The issues involved in this debate include the manner in which data are gathered—and empathic understanding is at the center of the controversy. The tendency of theory to become increasingly elaborate and abstract over time often makes it difficult to tease out false elements, that is, elements based on incorrect assumption. The proposition, for example, that "at the age of four, boys regard their fathers as rivals," is clearly at a different, more experience-near level of abstraction than is the later proposition that "structure formation by means of identifications and anti-cathexes explains theoretically the decline of the oedipal complex" (Rapaport and Gill 1959). The usefulness of reexamining a theory and its data base, particularly in the light of significant advances in related disciplines, is illuminated by Basch's endeavor (1976) to bring Freud's views on cognition in line with the newer paradigms of Piaget and Vigotsky. The present-day debates among classical psychoanalysts, self psychologists, proponents of an "action language" (Schafer 1978), and object relations theorists has prompted a vital reexamination of psychoanalytic theory, its data base, and the means of data gathering in the clinical situation. Therapists exhibit a preference for one theory over another. A few of the many reasons for a therapist's preferences will be considered in the following sections.

THE USE OF METAPHOR

Metaphor and imagery are inherent in language and in paradigm building (Rubinstein 1972). When a neurologist asserts that a neuron fires twelve times per second, what exactly the neuron is doing is here being usefully compared to the firing of a rifle. Undoubtedly, a future neurologist, better equipped to study the data, will recruit a more suitable metaphor.

Freud said that "to explain a thing means to trace it back to something already known" and Nietzsche defined explanation as "the expression of a new thing by means of signs of something already known."* Progress in understanding is a process in which inexact models are replaced by less inexact ones; their inexactness necessitates the therapist's consideration of the role of metaphor in scientific creation.

The analogy in which mental functioning had been compared to a system of lenses, one of Freud's earliest metaphors (1900), has lately been supplanted by the metaphor of the modern computer. Another illustration of the intentional use of metaphor is Freud's comparison of the therapist to a surgeon, a mirror, and a telephone receiver (1912). Through this sequence of metaphors Freud acknowledged the inexactness of his concepts and left the field open for further study. Freud's regular use of contrasting metaphors contributed to the rich texture of his ideas.

Misunderstandings surface not from the intentional use of metaphor but from the failure to consider that every theory is a nidus for metaphor and imagery. Language itself is strewn with so-called dead metaphors: words and phrases that have been around for so long that their allusive origins have been gradually forgotten (e.g., the "legs" of a table). It is clear that a paradigm containing both live and dead metaphors may subtly trigger a different set of personally relevant images in each individual. The sinful hero of classical theory, the (projected) overpowering mother of object relations theory, and the delicately mirrored

---

*Freud and Nietzsche are quoted in Eissler (1968, p. 167).

crystal prone to fragmentation in self psychology represent only a few of the possible images that the theories may evoke. In a different vein, Edelheit (1973) has suggested that the self psychologist's merger model may represent a sentimental reverence for a primal empathic state visualized as a preverbal Garden of Eden. These descriptions, intentionally hyperbolic, are necessarily subjective. Their purpose is only to indicate the evocative potential of a theory and the possibility that the preference for one theory over another may be a reflection of the imagery generated in the observer and its personal relevance to him.

THE ANTITHETICAL
ESSENCE OF THE HUMAN CONDITION

The aim of the psychoanalytic theories to faithfully explain facets of the individual's mental functioning necessitates a discussion of the context within which the theories are presented: the human condition. Of particular relevance is the ubiquitous presence of antithetical issues. The most poignant and irreducible antithesis is that the individual, wanting nothing less than eternal well-being, is nevertheless faced with mortality (Becker 1975).

Paradox is inherent in the infant's first steps away from the mother: the tension between the drive toward autonomy and change on the one hand and the yearning for repetition and sameness on the other. The infant's joy of accomplishment is tempered by the fear of separation. The proper gleam in the mother's eye may attenuate the conflict, but it can never completely eradicate it.

The bridge between the infant's early creaturely needs and fears and the mature individual's concern with mortality has been tentatively formulated in such concepts as the "transitional object" and "paradoxical creativity." Winnicott's concept of the transitional object (1958, 1967), the first object that is both "me" and "not me", is felt to be replaced at a later stage in life by culturally relevant and aesthetically evocative symbols. The individual's developing capacity to meaningfully reach out to religion or art in order to cope with impermanence has been labeled "paradoxical creativity" by Steingart (1983).

The intimate connection between the earliest fears of annihilation, fragmentation, castration, or guilt and later concerns about mortality has been demonstrated in literature, philosophy, and psychotherapy, particularly in the overlapping nature of the symbols that these fears evoke. The earliest annihilatory fears are propelled forward by the dawning recognition of the human condition, and rage about one's mortality, rage at God, or rage at one's parents create a nidus for guilt. The transience of the human condition is a central dilemma in the minds of the parents who provide (or fall short of providing) the child's earliest needs. Procreation is linked to immortality. The child's needs are set against the parents' need to have children. The mother's failure to respond to the child is fueled not only by her own childhood history of poor mothering but by a history of having coped unsatisfactorily with the dilemmas inherent in the human condition. The tension that embodies the two interacting subjectivities of parent and child, two separate centers of drive and initiative, is set against this background.

The psychoanalytic theories (including Freud's concept of the life and death instincts) have attempted to embrace the antithetical essence of existence. The recognition of impermanence and the sense of guilt and responsibility that is fueled by this recognition is apparent in every patient's question: "Am I or are others responsible for my symptoms?" Adler's statement, "All neurosis is vanity" (Becker 1975, p. 158), proposes that neurosis signifies a failure to use, in a guilt-free yet responsible fashion, the sustaining illusions of the larger group in order to cope with impermanence.

Freud's early theoretical shift from a belief that his patients had suffered actual sexual trauma at the hands of their parents (or the household help) to a belief that neurotic symptoms emanated from the oedipal wishes of childhood is an illustration of the influence of paradox in theory building (Schimek 1975). Expressed in its starkest form, the shift from an emphasis on actual events to fantasied wishes as the generative source of neurosis shifted the responsibility for symptoms from the parent to the patient. One wonders whether underlying this shift was Freud's struggle with the antithetical nature of responsibility.

In an existential sense, the individual is innocent and guilty, victim and agent. Each psychoanalytic model conveys the antithesis differently. In classical theory, the guilt of Oedipus is set against the realization that Oedipus had been abandoned as a child. The object relations view raises the question of whether the child's projected badness onto the mother emanates from inherent instinctual anger or failures in parenting. In self psychology, the relevant question is whether the parent is intended to serve as a sustaining selfobject for the child, or (as Erasmus might have asserted [Thompson 1965]) the child as a sustaining selfobject for the parents.

These questions are a rewording of the philosophical controversy that sets the notion of an inherently sinful child whose instincts need taming against the representation of an innocent newborn corrupted by society. In the arena of child rearing, it is apparent that the questions that stem from this controversy have been answered differently by different investigators.

Clinically, it may be tempting to operate from a framework that excludes from consideration such philosophical dilemmas as freedom versus determinism or innocence versus guilt (e.g., the concept of the child as a *tabula rasa*). This may seem to be the case in a situation, for example, in which rage and guilt toward a parent can be traced back to an early painful case of colitis in an individual's childhood. But is this explanation sufficient? It is true that the human condition can be used as a central focus by patients to defensively ward off addressing relevant events of their childhood. An illustration of this is the case of a young woman, a sociology major, who insisted for months that her only problem was that she had been born into the wrong era. However, despite assertions that guilt and responsibility are irrelevant because every parent had parents, or that to describe a 1-year-old child as inherently guilty would be ludicrous, or that the psychoanalytic theories are better imbedded in the apparently firmer bedrock of neurophysiology, the larger human issues simply cannot be dismissed. Behind the specifics of an individual's story is the unceasing presence of the human condition with its unceasing influence on human development. Conflict and paradox are integral to the ways in which we think and experience. A framework that attempts to ignore paradox is simply taking one side and neglecting the other.

The psychoanalytic theories do not address themselves to the issue of paradox evenhandedly. Although each makes room for dilemma — and issues such as responsibility versus victimization may be seen to vary from case to case — the classical theory with its emphasis on the mature Oedipus seems to tilt the balance in favor of the view that the individual is responsible for his neurosis (Freud 1930). Self psychologists view the parents' mishandling of the child as the source of the difficulty for the later adult (Wolf 1976). Those theories that attempt to elegantly bypass the dilemmas of life (e.g., the concept of a mismatch between parent and child, of improper cueing, or of a state of tension between two centers of initiative) are only putting aside the question (Stolorow, Brandchaft, and Atwood 1983, Schwaber 1980).

Guilt, responsibility, tragedy, and victimization are inevitable components of the stories that patients relate to their therapists, and therapists are morally developed individuals. It is their moral nature and the degree to which their unresolved conflicts prohibit them from appreciating antithetical issues that skew their capacity to empathize with some states of mind better than with others. A narrative that embodies feelings of deprivation, for example, may be easier to empathize with than one that embodies murderous wishes. It is desirable that the therapist have an appreciation of the antithetical essence of existence in order to empathize with the widest possible array of emotions and stories. This ideal position is mitigated by the fact that the therapist may be inclined for personal reasons relating to unresolved conflicts to be less available to one set of stories than another.

THE DIMENSION OF TIME

The recognition that theories are inexact metaphorical frameworks and that progress, in its most benign description, proceeds over time like an asymptotic curve moving closer and closer but never quite touching or encompassing the baseline of the human condition is necessary in order to appreciate that moods and assumptions are specific to an era.

In the present day, empathy is regarded as a positive therapeutic attribute. Therapists vie with one another to present themselves as empathic, and patients expect this quality in their therapists. References to the term *empathy* in the psychoanalytic journals have increased sharply in the last fifteen years (Shapiro 1974, 1981). This new interest in empathy has been attributed to such factors as the failure of psychoanalysis to deal with a broader spectrum of patients (perhaps a new era of patients), the recent reexamination of the psychoanalytic setting as a "holding" environment (Modell 1976), and the introduction of new therapeutic approaches such as self psychology, believed to be the outcome of empathic immersion. Although historically clinicians have been more kindly disposed to the concept than have been theoreticians, the sharp rise in the use of the term suggests that empathy has not always enjoyed a position of prominence in psychoanalysis.

Shapiro (1981) has proposed an explanation for the recent interest in empathy: He argues that, having failed to narrow the gap between psychoanalysis and the physical sciences, psychoanalysts have flocked in the opposite direction. Empathy, their new receiving instrument, now serves as a marker to distinguish the two sets of disciplines and confers upon psychoanalysis the status of "equal but different."

Two major concerns pertinent to the renewed interest in empathy have been voiced:

1. In the treatment situation, the distinction between the common usage of the term *empathy* (e.g., indulgence, sympathy) and its technical meaning (e.g., the capacity to experientially comprehend the thoughts and feelings of the patient) may become blurred.

2. The desire that a mutually satisfying experience of emotional togetherness be achieved may be used defensively to ward off recognizing an unpleasant state in the patient or the therapist.

Some psychoanalysts contend that empathy is not the central receiving instrument of psychoanalysis. Others argue that paradigms other than that of self psychology are the proper end result of accurate empathic immersion. Unfortunately, the shortcomings of departed theorists are less elusive than our own. It is likely, however, that the extent to which today's therapists consider themselves or wish to be considered empathic will influence the preference for one theory or another.

AN OUTLINE OF THE TEXT

The preceding overview anticipates and prepares the ground for the discussion of empathy in the ensuing chapters. The first section will present a review of the concept in the psychoanalytic literature, its historical background, and the controversies that surround it. Because there are major differences of opinion concerning empathy between the self psychology school and other schools and because self psychologists regard their model as having been arrived at by empathic immersion, a separate and detailed outline of this model will be presented.

In the second section, clinical illustrations will be used to demonstrate that focusing on the patient's imagery rather than on theory promotes the therapist's empathic responsiveness and that empathic understanding is the end result of an open-ended process, consisting of interaction and dialogue, that is promoted by the therapist's using multiple perspectives, that is, by alternating or oscillating freely between paradoxical or conflicting positions along a number of axes. These positions include experiencing and observing, appreciating the incidents the patient reports from both the patient's perspective and that of an external observer, in terms of the patient as both agent and victim, and in terms of both the patient's and the therapist's conflicts. As well, the therapeutic process needs to be viewed as both a reconstruction of the patient's past and a breakdown or analysis (literally, a deconstruction) of present-day convictions and stories. The view that empathy is enhanced by attention to the patient's imagery and by the use of multiple perspectives makes it possible to include useful contributions from both traditional psychoanalysis and self psychology. That conflict and dilemma are central in human experience underpins this approach.*

The final chapters in this section will summarize in a practical way some general issues that surface in the clinical illustrations, notably the relationship between empathy and theory, empathy as a curative factor, its role in psychotherapy supervision, and its fate at termination.

---

*In this book, the view of conflict as central in human experience is grounded in dilemma, not in a mechanistic drive–defense model.

Chapter Two

The Traditional Concept of Empathy

In the traditional view, empathy is regarded as the inevitable outcome of free-floating attention; its clinical usefulness has been taken for granted without, until recently, close critical attention to the concept. Theodore Reik (1948) remarked that the word *empathy* "sometimes means one thing, sometimes another, until it does not mean anything at all" (p. 357). Thirty-five years later, Basch (1983b) expressed the opinion that psychoanalysts were still undecided as to whether empathy should be considered "an end result, a tool, a skill, a kind of communication, a listening stance, a type of introspection, a capacity, a power, a form of perception or observation, a disposition, an activity or a feeling" (p. 102). In his list of unresolved questions, he included such issues as the difference between empathy and intuition or countertransference, the degree to which empathy represents a mature or a regressive function, and the degree to which affect, cognition, projection, and identification contribute to the process.

Nevertheless, moments of uncommon and instantaneous intuneness with the inner thoughts or images of their patients have been reported by many therapists. The following clinical vignette reported by Beres and Arlow (1974) is typical of such descriptions:

> A patient reported the following dream: He was alone in a house in the country. It was not yet dark, but it was no longer light. The patient called out "Peter" and somebody in a joking voice called back "Joey."
>
> At this juncture the therapist suddenly found himself having a visual fantasy of standing at an airport terminal. The passengers, having disembarked at a distance from the terminal, were being transported in a bus. Among the passengers on the bus, the therapist recognized his dead father. The therapist remembered having made a journey to the city of his father's youth and he suddenly felt as if he were in a twilight zone between life and death. He imagined that the patient might also be feeling in a twilight zone and he remembered that the names Peter and Joey were names that the patient and his uncle who had been a father surrogate had called each other. As the therapist emerged from his fantasy he heard the patient say "Last night I was watching television. The show was the 'Twilight Zone' . . ." and the therapist understood the dream to represent the patient's wish to be reunited with his uncle. (p. 38)

Freud used the word *einfuhlung* on fifteen occasions (Wolf 1983b). His English translators, however, did not always use *empathy* in its place. Freud (1921) described empathy as "the process . . . which plays the largest part in our understanding of what is inherently foreign to our ego in other people" (p. 108). In 1921 he wrote: "A path leads from identification by way of imitation to empathy, that is, to the comprehension of the mechanism by means of which we are enabled to take up any attitude at all towards another mental life" (p. 110). In Basch's opinion (1983b), the phrase "any attitude at all" stems from an inaccurate translation of the German word *uberhaupt* (i.e., *mainly*). As it stands, instead of conveying Freud's emphasis on the usefulness of empathy, the translation gives the misleading impression that the empathizer is free to attribute whatever he chooses to the patient.

At first, reports in which patients were felt to have grasped an apparently uncommunicated state of mind in the therapist captured the imagination of psychoanalysts. Such empathic perceptions based on very little information were considered quasi-telepathic. Helene Deutsch (1926) described such an experience: In a session a patient reported a dream about a childless couple celebrating their eighth wedding anniversary. This material prompted the therapist to remember that the very subject of the patient's dream, childlessness and an upcoming eighth anniversary, had distracted the therapist (but had not been communicated to the patient) in the preceding session.

The early optimism that transference and countertransference would someday explain telepathic phenomena quickly waned (Simon 1981). Psychoanalysis was grounded in neurophysiology, and psychoanalysts were not prepared to consider the presence of supernatural forces between therapist and patient (as Sullivan [1953] might have done) or to place the notion of relationship ahead of the internal workings of the mind.* Empathy, however, as an intrapsychic process in the therapist, triggered by the patient's communications, continued to hold their attention.

Helene Deutsch (1926) contributed to an initial understanding of the process: "The affective psychic content of the patient, which emerges from his unconscious, becomes transmuted into an inner experience of the analyst, and is recognized as belonging to the patient (i.e., to the external world) only in the course of intellectual work" (p. 136). Deutsch felt that the catalyst was the therapist's momentary identification with the patient.

Deutsch also described the basic (and somewhat paradoxical) components of the therapist's position in the empathic process, an oscillation between the position of close emotional harmony with the patient's inner life (with the patient himself or his ob-

---

*In Brice's opinion (1984), Buber's emphasis on relationship rather than the individual contributed to differences between psychoanalysis and existentialism with regard to a developmental model of empathy.

jects) and that of intellectual evaluation, experience distant objectivity. In order to make use of the empathic process, Deutsch felt that the therapist had to master the roles of participant and observer. She did not clarify, however, whether these divergent positions could be experienced simultaneously, that is, whether a therapist could experience a moment of merger yet maintain a dim perception of separateness from the patient.

Deutsch's assertion that empathy originated in identification was soon disputed. Reik (1948) stated that the therapist became as the patient but that identification did not bring about this state. Fliess (1942) and Furer (1967) introduced the modified concepts of trial, or transient, identification and partial identification. And Greenson (1960) excluded identification on the grounds that the therapist "partakes of the quality but not the quantity, the kind but not the degree" of the patient's inner life (p. 418).

In his discussion of the origins of the empathic process, Fenichel (1953) emphasized that imitation contributed to empathy. He asserted that, whether contrived or automatic, delicate or gross, imitative posturing through which the therapist assumed the facial expressions and bodily attitudes of the patient enhanced the therapist's capacity to sample the patient's experiential state. The taking over by the subject of the object's inner state represented a narcissistic identification. Fenichel felt that because the therapist permitted the patient's inner state to enter and activate his own, empathy was a form of submission that reflected a masochistic, or feminine, tendency. Fenichel's concepts received support from later comparisons between a therapist's empathizing with patients and a mother's empathizing with her child, and by descriptions of the clinical setting as a situation of safety, or a holding environment.

Fliess (1942) added to the discussion by addressing the subject of the therapist's altered state during an empathic experience. He proposed that during an empathic experience the therapist's superego and ego underwent a regression, relaxing their hold on the therapist's unconscious. The therapist's unconscious was thus permitted to resonate freely with the patient's unconscious. Fliess felt that the therapist experienced the patient's inner state from within. This useful regression on the part of the therapist was considered the counterpart of the therapeutically useful regression (i.e., "regression in the service of the ego" [Kris 1950]) recommended to patients.

Annie Reich's contribution to the subject (1966) stressed the immediacy of an empathic experience and examined the relationship between empathy and countertransference. Reich observed that a momentary empathic experience commonly came as a surprise to the therapist; this surprise indicated the presence of unconscious derivatives. As Sawyier (1975) later put it, it was as if the therapist suddenly recognized right then and there that something had happened to him. Reich believed that empathy was an ego activity whereas countertransference was a breakthrough of id derivatives or a defense against such a breakthrough. She asserted that overly intense impulses or defenses in the therapist interfered with the transition to consciousness essential for empathic experiencing. For example, if a patient evoked sexual feelings in the therapist, the therapist's acting upon them (an id activity) or denying them (defensive activity) would interfere with his recognition that the feelings were pertinent in therapy (an ego activity). Inherent in Reich's formulations was the view that certain conditions (e.g., self-awareness) could enhance the capacity to empathize. Later writers added that the capacity to empathize required stamina (Schafer 1983) and could be prolonged (Schwaber 1983b).

Only a few of the many psychoanalysts who have contributed to the literature on empathy have been mentioned. In the sections that follow, the issues raised in this overview will be examined in terms of (1) levels of empathy, (2) the communication of affect, (3) attention to the therapist's inner state, (4) developmental issues vis-à-vis the merger model, (5) the role of the mechanisms of defense, (6) the role of countertransference, and (7) a conceptual model of the patient.

LEVELS OF EMPATHY

Empathy in dynamic psychotherapy differs from empathy in other settings. A therapist's empathic appreciation of a patient's inner state is more than a sharing of feelings; it is directed at unconscious conflicts. Schafer (1959) spells out this assumption: The therapist is expected to empathize with "a hierarchic organization of desires, feelings, thoughts, defenses, controls, superego pressures, capacities, self-representations, and representations of real and fantasied personal relationships" (p. 345).

The complexity of the therapist's aim is illustrated in the following clinical vignette:

> Early in therapy, a patient reported that his infant had awakened in the night with an ear infection. The patient, who was a physician, had ignored the child, despite his concern. Although puzzled by the patient's inaction, the therapist felt he could to some degree appreciate the paralyzing effect of the patient's anxiety. A few sessions later, the patient recounted an event in which his parents reportedly had failed him when he had been ill as a child. The therapist, remembering the earlier session, attained a more complex appreciation of the patient's sense of helplessness and rage.
>
> Many months later in therapy, the therapist was pressured by the patient to give advice with respect to a career change. Aided by the patient's associations, the therapist realized that he was briefly experiencing vis-à-vis the patient the same indecision that the patient had experienced with his child—and that the patient's parents had experienced with him.

At each stage of therapy, the therapist's oscillating between the roles of participant and observer contributed to his understanding of the patient. At first it was difficult to participate in the patient's perspective because it was difficult to empathize with the neglect of a sick child. It became easier to participate when the therapist discovered the incidents in the patient's history that underlay such inaction. Later in therapy, the therapist recognized retrospectively that feelings of paralysis had been evoked in him.

The therapist attempts to appreciate currently relevant, unrecognized emotions and conflicts (originally preconscious or unconscious) in a historical context. Because an appreciation of a patient's inner state is enhanced by a knowledge of the patient, and because this knowledge accrues only as therapy progresses, empathy becomes more accurate toward the middle and terminal stages of therapy than it is at the outset (Olinick 1969). Although the therapist's role as participant (not observer) at every stage of interaction might be considered empathic, in the psychoanalytic literature the term *empathy* is used to describe a complex array of experiences. The impossibility of specifying the accuracy of an empathic experience and the failure to acknowledge a hierarchy of experiences or to recognize that empathy becomes more complex and accurate as therapy progresses often makes it difficult to compare and contrast empathic experiences reported in the psychoanalytic literature.

THE COMMUNICATION OF AFFECT

Attunement to one's own emotions is considered to be an accurate indicator of the patient's inner state. Freud (1921) postulated an "original archaic method of communication between individuals" that "in the course of phylogenetic evolution . . . has been replaced by the better method of giving information with the help of signals," yet that may "put itself into effect under certain conditions—for instance, in passionately excited mobs" (p. 55).

More recently, Basch (1976, 1983b) proposed that affect represents an early mode of cognition developing from the fixed action patterns that appear at birth. These neurologically encoded autonomic reactions are felt to have both a private and a public function, preparing the infant to respond with attraction to or avoidance of an external event and, at the same time, serving as highly visible messages to alert the caretakers tuned in to them. An infant's cry of hunger, for example, is private in that it evokes affect and prepares him for feeding, and it is public in that it alerts the parents to remedy the hunger.

Affect is transmitted instantaneously. Basch (1983b) has suggested that "because their respective nervous systems are genetically programmed to respond in like fashion, a given affective expression by a member of a particular species tends to recruit a similar response in other members of that species" (p. 108). An affect signal evokes in the observer an automatic, albeit imperceptible, imitation of the sender's movements and postures. An observer, for example, automatically cringes when he encounters a person in pain.

This form of communication, labeled "co-enesthetic communication" by Spitz (1965) and "affective resonance" by Buie (1981) facilitates interaction between mother and child. In Basch's opinion, a mother's attention to a child's messages follows two routes: Consciously, she evaluates them and unconsciously she experiences an immediate imitative affective response (i.e., she feels for the infant). A conflictual state interferes with the capacity to properly appreciate signals. Although infants appear to be attuned to their parents, such attunement is felt to be the outcome not of a capacity to reflect but of imitative autonomic responsiveness, pattern matching skills, and complex perceptual abilities.

The preceding description of the communication of affect neglects the communicative function of such uniquely human factors as reflection, conflict, and the use of symbols. The description does, however, add a useful dimension to an understanding of the empathic process.*

ATTENTION TO THE INNER SELF

Freud (1913) advised patients to say whatever came to mind even if they considered their thoughts unimportant, irrelevant, or nonsensical or feared experiencing embarrassment or distress at revealing them. This fundamental rule for patients represents a requirement that is rarely if ever fulfilled.

---

*Recently, the application of sociological and social-psychological concepts to physiological studies has formed the basis of a new field of inquiry, termed *sociophysiology* or *interpersonal physiology*. Through this field, such concepts as social sanction and empathy have been examined in a physiological context. Kaplan and Bloom (1960) have written a review of selected experimental studies in this new field.

Freud's advice to physicians (1912) is contained in the following:

> He should withhold all conscious influences from his capacity to attend, and give himself over completely to his "unconscious memory". . . . The most successful cases are those in which one proceeds as it were without any purpose in view, allows oneself to be taken by surprise by any new turn in them. . . . The correct behaviour for an analyst lies in swinging over according to need from the one mental attitude [free floating attention] to the other [intellectual evaluation], in avoiding speculation or brooding over cases while they are in analysis . . . the doctor must put himself in a position to make use of everything he is told for the purposes of interpretation and of recognizing the concealed unconscious material without substituting a censorship of his own . . . he must turn his own unconscious like a receptive organ towards the transmitting unconscious of the patient. He must adjust himself . . . as a telephone receiver is adjusted to the transmitting microphone. Just as the receiver converts back into sound waves the electric oscillations in the telephone line . . . so the doctor's unconscious is able, from the derivatives of the unconscious which are communicated to him, to reconstruct that unconscious, which has determined the patient's free associations . . . he [the doctor] may not tolerate any resistances in himself which hold back from his consciousness what has been perceived by his unconscious; otherwise he would introduce into the analysis a new species of selection and distortion. . . . (pp. 112–116).

The therapist's state of evenly hovering attention was later addressed in Isakower's description of the "analyzing instrument" (Balter, Lothane, and Spencer, Jr. 1980). This instrument is made up of a semiautonomous subset of ego functions that the therapist employs while analyzing the patient. The therapist's state is slightly less regressed than, but complementary to, the patient's state of near-reverie. The regressive pull of the patient's uncritical attention to inner thoughts and sensations is tempered by the need to put these thoughts into words. The regressive pull of the therapist's uncritical attention to inner thoughts and sensations is tempered by the need to attend to the patient. The meeting of these two inner states facilitates a deeply revealing interaction.

Isakower's formulation highlights how the quality of the therapist's attention changes at deeper levels of communication. At a more discursive level, the oscillating attention required of the therapist is a relatively simple undertaking. A willed flexibility is usually sufficient to appreciate the narrative both from the patient's perspective and from that of an external observer. During periods of regression, however, the therapist's task is more difficult. During these periods it is easier to listen as an observer or outsider to the patient's associations than it is to listen as if from within the patient. Listening as if from within requires paying attention imaginatively and actively, as well as passively, to one's own personal imagery, inner feelings, and visceral sensations (i.e., one's inner state). It also presumes that unrecognized elements in the patient's inner state will activate and resonate with elements in the therapist's inner state.

Unfortunately, a therapist's inner thoughts contain a mixture of messages, and the sources of the messages are not easy to distinguish. Some stem from vibrations in harmony with elements in the patient. Others originate from the therapist — as a separate individual or as an individual interacting with the patient.

A second difficulty arises from the varying nature of the communication. At more superficial levels, language is mainly discursive, couched in the secondary process. At deeper levels, it becomes less discursive and is characterized by a greater use of imagery and symbolism. To listen to the patient's free associations, the therapist needs to rely on unconscious functions. It is not surprising that at this level of communication empathy is experienced as an instantaneous event, recognized only retrospectively.

The capacity to read messages that emanate from within is enhanced by the therapist's own analysis and by an ability to bear with "muddle" (Thomson 1980) and endure a confusion of unfamiliar inner thoughts (as is experienced in a state of artistic creation) (Beres 1957, 1960, 1962, Arlow 1963). The capacity to resist needing to know permits inner thoughts to remain a subliminal part of one's perception until a fragment of meaningful experience emerges (Havens 1982b, Margulies 1984).

THE MERGER MODEL OF EMPATHY: DEVELOPMENTAL CONSIDERATIONS

Two complementary proposals have been outlined: that affective resonance between two members of a species is a genetic given and that empathy is enhanced by a regressed state. These proposals have fostered the opinion that empathy is an archaic faculty that wanes as later forms of cognition are superimposed. Ferreira (1961) has compared empathy to an umbilical cord between mother and fetus. Burlingham and Olden's descriptions of attunement and lapses in empathy between mother and child have contributed to the impression that empathy represents a capacity to penetrate the deepest, most archaic recesses of another's mind (Burlingham 1967, Olden 1953, 1958).

Buie's more cognitively anchored approach (1981) takes issue with these notions. Although he acknowledges the possibility that resonance contributes to the communication of affect between individuals, he argues that empathy is grounded in ordinary perception and that to ascribe to it the unique qualities of a special sensory mode would be scientifically unsound.* He considers the proposal that therapists merge with patients (much as mother and child are felt to be at one) to be based on an illusion. The infant's presumed sense of merger reflects a neuropsychological incapacity to differentiate self from other. The child's attunement to its mother is a less integrated capacity than the mother believes it to be. Therefore, Buie believes, the concept of merger provides a shaky foundation upon which to base an adult's capacity to empathize. He suggests, rather, that ordinary perception leads to inference and that inference about another person's state of mind is often inaccurate. For the therapist, con-

---

*In this context, Shapiro (1981) has questioned the capacity of a blind man, for example, to empathize with the inner state of another person in the absence of verbal communication.

stant checks are necessary in order not to create a fiction of the patient.

Empathic experiences are retrospectively recognized in the context of the therapist's awareness that he and the patient are separate and autonomous. There may indeed be some validity to the notion that empathy represents a capacity to recapture elements of an earlier mode of relating. However, several essential ingredients of mature empathy are *not* available at birth: An infant's sense of self is not clearly defined, its ability to hold an image without perceptual reminders is limited, and the capacity to decenter, to view events from another's perspective, is felt not to be acquired until the latency period (Piaget 1954, Furer 1967).

Although a capacity for regression may contribute to empathy and parental attunement to a child's earliest needs may foster the development of a sense of self sufficiently cohesive and elastic to tolerate the requirements of empathy, empathy does require such uniquely adult functions as an ability to decenter within the framework of an integrated sense of self and a capacity to imaginatively manipulate symbols.

THE ROLE OF THE MECHANISMS OF DEFENSE

The mechanisms commonly associated with empathy are *identification* and *projection*.

In *A Glossary of Psychoanalytic Terms and Concepts* (Moore and Fine 1968), *identification* is defined as follows:

> An automatic unconscious mental process whereby an individual becomes like another person in one or several aspects. It is a natural accompaniment of maturation and mental development, and aids in the learning process (including the learning of speech and language), as well as in the acquisition of interests, ideals, mannerisms, etc. An individual's adaptive and defensive reaction patterns are often attributable to identification with either loved or admired persons or feared ones. By means of identification with a needed person, an individual can often provide for himself the satisfaction of the needs

desired from the person. Separation from a loved person becomes more tolerable as a result of identification.

Although a therapist's capacity to identify with patients has often been equated with empathy, and improper distancing between therapist and patient has commonly been attributed to a tendency to over- or underidentify, many clinicians are reluctant to consider identification an essential component of empathy. Identification is generally considered to play a role in the acquisition of new psychic structure and to function as a defense. These qualities are not fundamental to empathy. A therapist empathizing with a patient may change slightly (Brown 1984). However, the therapist uses psychic structure that is already present. Empathy does not contribute significantly to the therapist's mental development. In addition, because therapists actively tolerate the empathic position, their empathy is not defensive. Given the current definition of identification, many clinicians believe that other mechanisms such as affective resonance and inference play a more fundamental role in the generation of empathy than does identification (Buie 1981, Basch 1983b).

Projection has also been equated with empathy. The belief that therapists are able to project themselves into the patient's situation is predicated on the assumption that individuals are sufficiently similar that, given similar circumstances, similar emotions and attitudes will be generated. However, the role of projection in the empathic process is vulnerable to the same concerns raised earlier in the discussion of identification. To project one's attitude onto a patient may serve as an unconscious defense against unacceptable conflicts and may interfere with an accurate understanding of the patient. The therapist may, in addition, fail to take individual differences into account.

Basch (1983b) believes that, with reference to empathy, the term *projection* has been confused with the more appropriate term *generalization*. Generalization is a nondefensive function similar to affective resonance and inference (Novick and Kelly 1970). An individual who, for example, projects his sexual feelings onto another denies such feelings in himself. Moreover, the projected feelings may be altered; the love may be turned into hate. In generalization, an individual attributes feelings to an-

other without denying them in himself and without transforming them in the process.

For some the term *projection* (and the related term *projective
identification*) refers to a mechanism by which a therapist attempts to impose his own traits on the patient. For others, on the
contrary, it represents a process by which a therapist empathizes with feelings that really exist in the patient but that also
exist in the therapist (Gedo 1981, Tansey and Burke 1985). Many
clinicians are intentionally inexact about the mechanisms contributing to empathy, suggesting, for example, that it originates in
the early introjective-projective matrix (Low 1935, Knight 1940).
Is it altogether necessary to exclude the possibility that mechanisms of defense contribute to empathy, albeit in a minor capacity? It is a common observation that a therapist's retrospective
recognition of defensive behavior in himself often *adds* to an understanding of the patient. In the discussion of countertransference following, the contribution of the mechanisms of defense to empathy will be further examined.

COUNTERTRANSFERENCE AND EMPATHY

Originally, the term *countertransference* denoted only those unconscious feelings evoked in the therapist by the patient's compulsion to repeat an archaic relationship (in slightly altered fashion) with the therapist (Orr 1954). The therapist's aim was to
interpret, to reflect back to the patient the manner in which the
patient attempted to misuse him. Any unwitting or unrecognized emotion was attributed to a therapist's unconsciously assuming the role of a parent or sibling, or defending against it.
The therapist was expected to serve only as an accurate mirror
for the patient. Therapists were advised to purge themselves
(through personal analysis or through careful self-scrutiny) of
hidden conflictual feelings that, stirred by the patient, interfered
with therapy.

The impossibility of attaining such a pristine state and the difficulty in distinguishing whether a therapist's feelings were a reflection of or a reaction to a patient's state of mind, or whether

they emanated from the therapist's own experiences (conflictual and nonconflictual) fostered inconsistencies in the definition of countertransference (Balint and Balint 1939). Some psychoanalysts currently favor a broad definition that embraces the therapist's total response to the patient (Little 1951, 1957). Others favor the older, more stringent, definition. Most psychoanalysts occupy a middle ground in this debate.*

This state of uncertainty makes it difficult to answer the following questions: To what extent is countertransference therapeutically useful? If it can be a help *or* a hindrance (as most psychoanalysts have come to believe), are there ways of distinguishing the two forms of countertransference? Should countertransference feelings (e.g., rage or passionate feelings toward a patient) be communicated to the patient?

Gitelson (1952), M. Cohen (1952), and A. Reich (1950a) have attempted to examine the ways in which countertransference interferes with therapy. There is agreement that in order for countertransference to be transformed into a useful function, its presence needs to be recognized by the therapist. To attempt to define empathy with respect to such an ill-defined concept as countertransference, however, is an almost impossible task. Where does empathy leave off and countertransference begin? Both terms denote an emotional state in the therapist. Empathy is felt to be therapeutically useful. Unless it is recognized, countertransference is felt to be detrimental. Whereas empathy is felt to guide a therapist's communications, there is no agreement concerning the manner in which a therapist's countertransference feelings should be communicated to the patient. The following example, reported by Arlow (1963), illustrates the difficulty in distinguishing the two concepts:

A young therapist had earlier reported to his supervisor a case in which a patient had barged into his office unannounced. The therapist himself later repeated this action with his supervisor.

---

*Sandler, Dare, and Holder (1973) attribute the confusion concerning countertransference to the fact that for many years countertransference had been considered detrimental. Not until 1950 did publications that proposed that paying attention to countertransference contributed to an understanding of the patient begin to appear.

The therapist had missed the significance of the patient's actions. Arlow presented this case as an example of countertransference. The patient's behavior had stirred up conflicts in the therapist that had to be defended against. Would the therapist have empathized with the patient's inner state if he had recognized the significance of his behavior?

Two distinguishing characteristics have been proposed to differentiate countertransference from empathy:

1. An emotional state experienced by a therapist mutually with the patient as *subject* should be labeled empathy; an emotional state experienced mutually with an *object* in the patient's inner world (e.g., a parent's harsh strictures) should be labeled countertransference (Fliess 1953, Meissner 1971, 1972).

2. Empathy originates in the unconflicted sector of a therapist's personality whereas countertransference originates in the conflicted sector (Thomson 1980).

With respect to the first distinction, it is often impossible to determine which of the two possibilities is at work. For example, in a session in which a patient reports a memory of being beaten as a child by a drunken father, a memory that evokes feelings of helplessness and rage in the patient, the therapist's empathic appreciation of the patient's emotional state may stem from a number of sources: the father's anger, the patient's sense of helplessness in reaction to the father, or a similar event in the therapist's past. The roots of emotional experience are inextricably intertwined. This problem is compounded by the complexity of emotions, their subliminal nature, and the blurring of boundaries between self and object that occurs at archaic levels of experience. If the aforementioned therapist is particularly attuned to anger, he may choose to define his experience as a countertransference state; if attuned to helplessness, an empathic capacity. If the patient angrily turns on the therapist the way the patient's father had once turned on him (role reversal), the therapist's apparently empathic experience of helplessness will have been arrived at in reaction to—rather than in harmony with—the patient's inner state.

The difficulty in distinguishing whether an experiential state originates in the conflicted or unconflicted sector of the therapist's personality is illustrated in the following vignettes:

In a session, a therapist informed his patient that he sensed in her a feeling of abandonment. The patient withdrew into silence. At the end of the session she said, "You're right, but it makes me feel painfully invisible when you say it." Although her statement confirmed the accuracy of his communication, the therapist wondered whether his statement had been motivated by a defensive need to appear omniscient. The therapist's empathic perception appeared to have threatened the patient's sense of self. It may have been that in empathizing with one aspect of the patient's experience, the therapist had failed to empathize with a more salient aspect (Book 1984).

In a second example, during a session a therapist's mind had wandered to a daydream about a tropical beach. From previous experience, the therapist knew that his fantasies harbored an uncared-for feeling. His attention was realerted by the patient's mention of a similar tropical setting. He listened further. The patient began to talk about the fact that her parents had holidayed often, leaving her behind with incompetent nursemaids. The therapist realized retrospectively that he and the patient had either shared a moment of separateness or that they had simply withdrawn from each other. Did this event represent a moment of empathy or a defensive maneuver?*

These examples illustrate that there is no simple formula that determines the effect on the therapist of a patient's emotional state. A male therapist is not invariably transfigured into an oedipal father. Empathy and countertransference are often indistinguishable. The therapist's unconscious needs may spill over and merge with empathy. These contentions are supported by Greenson's speculation that depressive therapists make the

---

*In a detailed case report, Bennett Simon (1981) pursues in depth the issues raised by this example.

best empathizers (1960) and E. S. Wolf's list of the pathways leading to empathy (quoted by Basch [1983b]). The list includes only two categories.

1. Spontaneously occurring mental states of introspective awareness that one's own mental state had been evoked by (a) a similar state in the patient, (b) a state in reaction to the patient's mental state, or (c) a state that one might have expected but had not been evoked.
2. Deliberately constructed thought experiment.

The factors that make it difficult to define countertransference also make it difficult to distinguish countertransference from empathy; the two states often appear to merge. Therapists invariably fall into states of countertransference. Retrospectively recognized, such states contribute (as do empathic experiences) to an appreciation of a patient's inner state, and they prepare the ground for an empathic understanding of the patient.

A CONCEPTUAL MODEL OF THE PATIENT

Blum (1972) has suggested that the therapist, situated within the patient's psychic world, operates with the materials of the patient's reality and within the framework of the patient's universe of discourse. This metaphor complements the more prevalent model characterized by the statement that the therapist constructs a mental model, or a "hologram," of the patient. Everything the therapist has learned about the patient, the patient's fears, desires, and defensively altered stories, is contained in this structure. The preference among clinicians for the hologram model may reflect a desire to create models compatible with the paradigms of neurophysiology.

Isakower used the term *analyzing instrument* to depict a subset of ego functions. There are, however, similarities between his concept and the hologram model concept. Both describe a temporary structure occasionally assembled for specific purposes. The semiautonomous nature of these structures suggests that they may be disassembled or stored away in the patient's absence. Occasionally, the model of the patient may spring to mind in the patient's absence, triggering a moment of enlightenment (Hamilton 1981).

Attempting to retrospectively reconstruct the events that precede a momentary experience of empathy, Greenson (1960) reported the following sequence: In a session, a patient described a party she had attended. The sadness expressed by the patient puzzled the therapist. He retraced his steps, this time taking along the model of all that he knew about the patient. He attended the party, so to speak, from within the model of the patient. This maneuver permitted him to experientially comprehend the patient's emotional state.

Buie (1981) proposed that the conceptual model of the patient is constructed from varying external and internal referents. Guided by the patient's emotional state, one listens, observes, makes inferences about the patient's inner state, and tests them against what one knows about oneself and others and, when necessary, imaginatively contrived events. A variety of referents contribute to a model's composition.

In Basch's description (1983b), empathy initially is rooted in affective resonance and generalization. Set in a progressively more complex matrix of cognition, it can be depicted as a spiral of ever-increasing understanding. The therapist may enter the spiral at any point. The steps may appear to be immediate, unstudied, and intuitively surprising. However, over a period of time the therapist comes to have an empathic understanding of the patient's communications through a painstakingly constructed model of the patient.

The therapist's appreciation of a patient's inner state is the end result of information accrued and integrated from various positions and various modes of cognition. The common aim of these varying formulations is to graphically depict the complex relationship between empathy and understanding.

A GENERAL FORMULATION OF EMPATHY

The preceding sections offer a composite description of the processes felt by traditional therapists to play a role in empathy. The therapist's aim is to appreciate (albeit with reduced intensity) a meaningful aspect of the patient's inner state. The functions and events can be summarized as follows:

The basis of the empathic process is an evenly focused attention to the patient from within and from without (that is, as participant and observer). Emotional and ideational, as well as conscious and unconscious, factors contribute to the process at every stage.

At deeper levels of interaction, the therapist pays close attention to inner experiences on the assumption that personal imagery, emotions, and visceral sensations have been activated by the patient's inner state. The therapist reaches for unavailable aspects within—for archaic, painful, and usually unrecognized emotions and conflicts.

Occasionally, the therapist may experience a state of merger with the patient. The therapist may experience aspects of self to be interchanged with aspects of the patient. The capacity to resist needing to know during such experiential states contributes to empathy. The concept of regression in which the therapist's ego and superego have relaxed their hold on the id has been implicated in such states.

Occasionally, the therapist, moving unwittingly into defensively generated states of countertransference, may become overly sympathetic or draw back from the patient. The tempo of oscillation is altered. In an overly sympathetic state, the therapist may be drawn into a prolonged identificatory position. In an intellectually distant state, the therapist may attend to the patient's communications only as an outside observer. The difference between a nondefensive state of empathy and a state of countertransference may be that in the latter state the therapist's appreciation of an inner experience is delayed. Some psychoanalysts prefer to restrict the term *empathy* to nondefensively generated states characterized by emotional resonance. It needs to be stressed, however, that retrospective recognition of a countertransference state can indeed contribute to an understanding of the patient. In this context, projection and identification, for example, may be considered therapeutically useful.

Empathic experiences are recognized retrospectively by the therapist. When this occurs, the therapist no longer experiences a sense of merger with the patient.

The multiplicity of events that contribute to the empathic process do not occur in any particular order. The therapist may be drawn into the process at any point. Intellectual insights (for example, the recognition that an upcoming vacation may upset a patient) may set the process of empathic understanding in motion. The greater the variety of contributing modalities, the richer and more complete the therapist's understanding will be.

The various empathic experiences are integrated into a conceptual model of the patient that becomes increasingly complex over time. As therapy progresses, the possibility of examining the patient's communications from within an increasingly complex model facilitates a more accurate appreciation of the patient's inner state.*

The likelihood of error and inexactness makes it necessary to check and recheck the accuracy of an empathic experience against the patient's experience and against what the therapist has already learned about the patient. Whether or not a therapist's empathy is limited to events experienced (as Schafer [1959] suggests) is uncertain (Basch–Kahre 1984). This issue may be addressed by the Roman dramatist Terence's statement: "I am a man; nothing human is alien to me."

AREAS OF UNCERTAINTY

The confusion generated by the term *empathy* stems partly from the fact that a simple noun is often employed to denote one or several functional elements of an elaborate and painstaking process or to denote the process as a whole. Schlesinger (1981) has recommended that the noun *empathy* should be replaced by the adjective *empathic* or the adverb *empathically*. A retrospectively recognized appreciation of a patient's inner state might

---

*Such a model will be shaped by the therapist's theoretical preferences. It may be assumed that a classical therapist will imbed an empathic experience in a conflict model of the patient. However, the traditional psychoanalytic literature on empathy does not address directly the subject of the influence of theory on the therapist's empathy.

then be designated an empathic experience, a prolonged state of evenly focused attention might then be designated empathic immersion, and an interpretation informed by an empathic experience might be termed an empathic communication.

Schlesinger's proposal provides only a partial solution. For example, there is no way to designate the accuracy or complexity of an empathic experience. In addition, given that so many varied functional elements contribute to the empathic process, it is difficult to speak of a single capacity to empathize. Should the capacity to empathize refer to a capacity to resist needing to know or to a capacity to examine the significance of a state of countertransference? Although the various capacities are not significantly different, it is likely that different therapists follow slightly different routes to arrive at understanding and that some patients are better approached from one direction than from another.

Some of the difficulty in defining the concept stems from the fact that the functions, capacities, and experiences that contribute to the empathic process merge imperceptibly with other functions, capacities, and experiences. A brief empathic experience, for example, is not merely a momentary appreciation of a patient's feelings. Because it embraces the almost simultaneous task of incorporating information into an elaborate model of understanding, the empathic process contains an important cognitive component as well. Similarly, a therapist's state of attunement occasionally slips into a countertransference state. How does one differentiate between an empathic experience and understanding, or between empathic immersion and countertransference? To attempt to be overly exact would be to overreach, and the end result would be a reified inaccurate description of a complex, dynamic process.

Chapter Three

Empathy in Self Psychology

Self psychologists view the traditional approach as mechanistic and unempathic. They assert that their model has been derived by the clinical use of empathy and that using their model facilitates empathic understanding (Schwaber 1980, Wolf 1980). Is their concept of empathy different from the traditional concept? Lichtenberg (1983, p. 233) demonstrated the application to therapy of the self psychology model with an example summarized here.

In the middle phase of an analysis, a number of sessions were characterized by the therapist's drifting off as he listened to the patient. Careful self-scrutiny failed to reveal a conflictual cause for the inattention. In one session the therapist found himself comparing his state of remoteness to the way he felt when he sat with his children watching a television program that didn't particularly interest him: He would attend to the program intermittently, only to be able to talk with them about it; otherwise he would occupy himself with his own inner thoughts. At this juncture he heard the patient begin to talk about television. The patient described coming home in the evening, turning on the television set, preparing dinner, and then letting the evening drift away without getting to work on his long-overdue tax refund claim. The television set provided a background noise that only intermittently captured his attention. At first his behavior had irritated his girlfriend; later she became accustomed to it. The therapist cued in to the association between his own inner thoughts and the patient's narrative, and in time he was able to relate the patient's behavior to the latter's use of alcohol and the need to interact with another person in a state of remoteness.

Lichtenberg's example, in which the therapist employed his reverie to tune in to the patient's sense of himself and to understand the patient's experience of the therapist, is strikingly similar to the clinical vignette reported by Beres and Arlow (1974) presented at the beginning of Chapter 2. The claims self psychologists make are not immediately apparent in a clinical example; indeed, they necessitate a full examination of their model. In the sections that follow, an outline of the origins and tenets of self psychology and a critique of its formulations will precede a discussion of the different usage of the term *empathy* by self psychologists and traditional therapists.

THE ORIGINS OF SELF PSYCHOLOGY

Two articles by Heinz Kohut on empathy and narcissism prepared the ground for the theoretical constructs of self psychology.

Empathy

In 1959 Kohut proposed that it was the method of data gathering that distinguished psychoanalysis from disciplines dedicated to investigating external events. Assisted by refined instruments (the microscope, for example), the natural sciences relied upon the sense organs; the data accumulated were integrated into theory by what Kohut described as a series of "conceptual thought bridges." He used the word *introspection* to define the distinguishing operational mode of observation in psychoanalysis. The analysis of one's own inner state required introspection; in Kohut's opinion, sensory organs did not contribute to self-observation. He believed that Freud's noteworthy discoveries (dream analysis, for example) were the outcome of introspection.

Kohut designated the method of comprehending the inner world of another person as "vicarious introspection," or "empathy." Empathy and introspection were considered essential for comprehending the psychological state of another and were often linked and amalgamated with other methods of observation. Kohut believed that the scope of psychoanalysis was limited by its essential methodology, that is, by the scope of empathy or vicarious introspection. For example, vicarious introspection could inform an observer whether a subject experienced a sense of freedom or drivenness, but it could not resolve such philosophical issues as the debate between free will and determinism. Kohut believed that there were several areas in psychoanalysis in which theory had unwittingly been overextended beyond what could be accurately observed by means of vicarious introspection. For example, an infant's state of mind (or the archaic component of a patient's behavior) was not easily accessible through empathy. In Kohut's opinion, to apply such conceptually advanced notions as conflict and drive to an infant's inner state was to obtrude adultomorphic projections that had not been arrived at empathically but by other methods. He believed that such constructions led to a lifeless and incorrect understanding of a childhood state; they therefore had to be questioned. Because a therapist could only empathize approximately with a childhood state, Kohut recommended the use of such terms as *regulation* and *deregulation* to capture the approximations more accurately than terms such as *conflict* and *drive*.

Narcissism

Kohut's 1966 paper on narcissism examined a neglected facet of development. Kohut believed that psychoanalysts had focused their attention on the manner in which narcissistic libido (i.e., that component of the sexual drive that was invested in the self) was transformed into object love. Although he agreed that narcissistic libido contributed to an individual's capacity to love, he stated that an early bifurcation in the developmental road of the libido had been insufficiently addressed. Psychoanalysts had failed to pay sufficient attention to the libido, which remained invested in the self (i.e., which remained narcissistic) and which continued to play a role in the individual's sense of self. He attributed this lack of attention to the negative connotation the term *narcissism* had acquired.

Kohut described the first stage of infancy, characterized by an inability to distinguish self from other, as being followed by a second stage in which the young child oscillates between a sense of merger with the mother and a sense of separateness from her. During the early stages, the child's sense of control over the mother and her ministrations parallels more closely the sense of control over one's own mind and body that an adult has than it does the sense of control over others that an adult has. The mother's proper attunement facilitates the forward progression toward a separate and individuated sense of self. The mother's ministrations contribute to the child's healthy narcissism. The child experiences its narcissistic supplies to emanate sometimes from within itself and sometimes from an external source.

The narcissistic supplies that perfuse the child's nuclear self contribute to its desires and ambitions. The second source of narcissism, contained in the child's internalized image of the parents, contributes to its ideals. The continuing tension between ambitions and ideals influences an individual's narcissistic equilibrium, that is, one's sense of cohesiveness and self-worth. The need for narcissistic supplies never ceases. Kohut proposed that the function of narcissistic regulation was later subserved by every object relationship.

It has been suggested, in light of Freud's informal definition of mental health as the capacity to love and to work, that Kohut's contribution represented an attempt to redress an imbalance. Earlier psychoanalytic theory had overemphasized the developmental road culminating in the capacity to love. Kohut directed his attention to the developmental road culminating in self-esteem and the capacity to be productive (Goldberg 1974).

Empathy and Narcissism

Kohut (1966) proposed an affiliation between empathy, narcissism, and parental attunement. He believed that the feelings, actions, and behavior of the mother are included in the infant's self. This prepares the ground in the child for the recognition that others experience states similar to our own. According to Kohut, empathy belongs to the innate equipment of the human psyche and remains associated to some extent with the primary process.

With development, nonempathic forms of cognition attuned to objects dissimilar to the self are felt to become increasingly superimposed over the original mode of reality reception. The operation of empathy is thus impeded. Outside the realm of psychology, empathic modes of observation lead to faulty conceptions. Nonempathic modes of observation, on the other hand, are not attuned to the experiences of other people. If such modes are employed in psychology, they lead to a "mechanistic and lifeless conception of psychological reality" (p. 263). Proper narcissistic development, fostered by adequate parental attunement, contributes to the capacity to know the inner state of another person.

THE PSYCHOLOGY OF THE SELF

The psychology of the self is an outgrowth of Kohut's early formulations (Kohut 1971) and is derived from Kohut's and others' use of vicarious introspection or empathy in the clinical investigation of narcissistically disturbed individuals. Such individuals are characterized by a grandiose sense of self-importance, fantasies of unlimited success, a constant need for attention and admiration, overreaction or complete indifference to criticism or defeat, feelings of entitlement, exploitativeness, and a lack of empathy (American Psychiatric Association 1980). According to self psychologists, in the course of the treatment of these patients the use of vicarious introspection revealed a reactivation of early narcissistic needs. The exigency that these patients exhibited suggested that an archaic need for admiration and confirmation had not been met and led to the hypothesis that an early phase of normal grandiosity was essential for proper development.

As the theory evolved, Kohut's original formulations were revised and expanded, and some of the tenets of the new theory clashed with the tenets of the older psychoanalytic theories (Kohut 1977). Among self psychologists, references to libidinal drives and energies disappeared (Kohut and Wolf 1978, Wolf 1980). The classical concept that the infant's forbidden instinctual needs had to be contained by the ego was replaced by the concept that archaic narcissistic needs had to be met by an appropriately receptive other in order for the self to develop. The concept of drive was relegated to a secondary position; for example, clinical manifestations of pathological aggression previously attributed to a primary aggressive drive were felt to be the response of a vulnerable self to narcissistic injury.

A new terminology was created. Kohut's fluid description of the developmental course of narcissism in terms of libido theory was replaced by the concept of functional units of experience that were labeled *selfobjects*. The overriding composite structure to which the new theory addressed itself was the self. The concept of the selfobject was considered distinct from the concept of the internalized object of traditional psychoanalytic theory. The term *selfobject* referred to any function that enhanced the sense of self or its development and that contributed to such capacities as tension regulation, self-integration, and self-confirmation. Values, ideals, the use of transitional objects (Winnicott 1958), and every object relationship provided selfobject needs. Although selfobjects might appear to be located externally, an individual experienced selfobject functions as coextensive with the sense of self. There were several kinds of selfobjects: Mirroring selfobjects confirmed or reflected back an innate sense of vigor, greatness, and perfection to the child; idealized parental imagos were selfobjects that the child could look up to and with whom the child could merge as images of calmness and omnipotence; and twinning selfobjects provided an experience in which parent and child shared a sense of perfection.

The earliest selfobject functions are provided by the parents. Because the young child experiences itself as being merged with the mother, the parental selfobject functions are perceived to emanate from within the child's body and mind. An early developmental stage in which the child's mirroring and idealizing needs are met is considered the prerequisite of a firm nuclear self. The self (the core of the personality) is considered to be comprised of various constituents acquired in the interactions between parent and child. A harmonious synchrony between mother and child results in optimal gratifications and optimal frustrations. The formation of structure occurs in the wake of minor nontraumatic parental failures to mirror the child or to be available as an idealizable other. Such optimal failures lead to the child's gradually acquiring the functions provided by the parents. This process has been labeled *transmuting internalization*. The resultant self is not a replica of parental selfobjects; the functions are assimilated according to the program of the child's nuclear self. Kohut and Wolf (1978) compared this process to the ingestion and rearrangement of foreign protein as it entered and became integral to the recipient's body.

The self is considered to represent the outcome of the interplay between parental expectations, often present before birth, and the infant's innate equipment. A firm self resulting from optimal experiences of the parents as selfobjects consists of two cohesively integrated groups of functions depicted as poles. One pole contains the basic strivings for power and success. The second pole harbors the basic idealized goals. These poles derive from but are not identical with the selfobject functions that the parents formerly provided. The individual's basic talents and skills occupy an intermediate area, and the interrelationship between the three components (i.e., ambition, talent, and ideals) describes a tension arc. The self could be damaged in any one of its three constituent areas. Depending on the parents' attunement to the child, the adult self emerges in varying states of cohesion ranging from fragmented to firm, in varying states of vitality ranging from enfeebled to vigorous, and in varying states of functional harmony. A firm self is felt to contribute to a realistic sense of self-esteem resilient to setbacks, and it engenders such attributes as creativity, humor, empathy, and wisdom.

PSYCHOPATHOLOGY IN SELF PSYCHOLOGY

In the spectrum of the disorders of the self, the narcissistic disorders occupy a middle range. They lie between the more severely disturbed schizophrenic and borderline states and the less severely disturbed neurotic disorders.

Schizophrenic disorders are characterized by a seriously fragmented self with no compensatory structures to cover over the defect. The disintegration may be due to an inherent biological tendency, to an absence of even minimally effective mirroring in infancy and childhood, or to a marked disparity between biological capacities and parental expectations. The origins of the enfeebled, disordered, and fragmentation-prone self of the borderline state has been described as follows: "At the very point . . . when the nascent self of the child required the accepting mirroring of its independence, the selfobject because of its own incompleteness and fragmentation fears insisted on maintaining an archaic merger" (Kohut and Wolf 1978, p. 415).

Neurotic disorders, on the other hand, are characterized by a sense of self sufficiently well integrated that states of narcissistic depletion do not surface. They can therefore be safely overlooked in therapy.

The narcissistic disorders, which lie in the middle ground of the spectrum, do reveal a reactivation of unmet narcissistic needs in the course of treatment. Unlike schizophrenic or borderline patients, however, patients suffering from narcissistic disorders *can* tolerate such a reactivation without protracted fragmentation. This makes it possible for them to benefit from an insight-oriented approach.

As self psychology has evolved, the range of patients felt to benefit from a self psychological approach has been extended beyond the narcissistic disorders on both sides of the spectrum.

This territorial expansion has transformed the psychology of the self. What was originally a complementary paradigm particularly useful for the management of difficult patients has become a competing paradigm in relation to other dynamic theories.

The various ways in which narcissistically disordered individuals cope with self deficiencies has given rise among self psychologists to a rudimentary typology: Mirror-hungry personalities thirst for selfobject others to confirm and admire them; ideal-hungry personalities search for selfobject others whom they can admire; alter ego personalities seek selfobject others with whom they can conform; merger-hungry personalities need to control their relationships and use the selfobject other to provide essential structure to their lives; and contact-shunning personalities avoid social contact in order to ward off conflicts pertaining to narcissistic needs. That the manifestation of symptoms varies in narcissistically disordered personalities implies that there is a hierarchy of stage-appropriate needs and that the parents may have failed to meet one or several of them.

Most narcissistically disordered patients do not fall clearly into one category or another, nor are their symptoms simply the present-day expression of an earlier normal selfobject need. Because of the intensity of their needs and the conviction that their needs will not be met, the nuclear self is repressed or split off. This formulation, which echoes Winnicott's concept of the true and false self (1965), takes into account the presence of compensatory mechanisms and defensive structures. The defenses of the self against selfobject failures have been described by Kohut (1977). Shame and fragmentation anxiety are the predominant affect states that mobilize defenses and that generate resistance in therapy. Selfobject needs are disavowed (vertical split) and repressed (horizontal split). Defenses against under- or over-stimulation by selfobjects, merger fears (with loss of self), and fears of rejection or contempt are common components of character pathology. The presence of defense mechanisms is most apparent in the description of contact-shunning personalities. Self psychologists consider defenses to be instituted against selfobject failures whereas traditional psychoanalysts consider defenses to be instituted against wishes or drives. Both self psychology and traditional psychoanalysis contain the notion of conflict; however, self psychologists consider deficiency (that is, selfobject failures) to be a more basic issue than conflict.

THE PSYCHOTHERAPY
MODEL IN SELF PSYCHOLOGY

The self psychology paradigm alters the therapist's position vis-à-vis the patient (Goldberg 1973, 1974). In this section some of the differences in the therapist's position will be discussed. The related topics of neutrality and abstinence, the concept of cure, and the subject of empathy will be examined in separate sections. Criticisms of self psychology will be summarized in the section, "A Critique of Self Psychology."

In self psychology, such behavior as a patient's clamoring assertiveness or the failure to consider the therapist as a separate individual with unique aims and needs represents not the recrudescence of a forbidden or conflictual wish but the reactivation, in slightly altered form, of unmet selfobject needs. As the narcissistic transference unfolds, the therapist becomes a selfobject for the patient, providing esteem and cohesion to the patient's vulnerable self. The therapist does not actually mirror or offer himself as an omnipotent other but examines the patient's free associations within a framework that considers such needs.

Because in self psychology patient and therapist are considered part of a contextual unit, the therapist accepts as a phase-appropriate transference need the patient's need to have the therapist serve in a selfobject capacity. The therapist's failure (actual or perceived) to serve as an empathic selfobject is the focus of the interpretive work; that is, the therapist's function as a selfobject is included in the therapist's field of observation. If an inexact interpretation, a canceled appointment, or an ambivalent greeting on the part of the therapist evokes an excessively angry response in the patient, an interpretation is presented from the patient's frame of reference. Interpretations may include when appropriate an acknowledgment of the therapist's perceived or actual failures. Interpretations in which, for example, a patient's rage is linked with the recapitulation in therapy of an early parental failure may appear more compassionate and palatable to a patient than interpretations in which the rage is felt to represent a defense against envy or forbidden desires.

The patient in turn is regarded both as a separate entity and as a selfobject for the therapist. Countertransference difficulties are felt to stem from a therapist's inappropriate selfobject needs (e.g., a therapist's need to be constantly admired).

The therapist's appreciation of the patient's selfobject needs is felt by self psychologists to create a therapeutic environment in which pathognomonic regression can occur. In this environment, the more primitive and unconscious selfobject needs can be experienced, expressed, and ultimately interpreted in the transference. It is as if the nuclear self, less certain that its needs will be rebuffed, is slowly flushed from its hiding place. As the defenses (splitting and repression) are overcome, the narcissistic or selfobject transference unfolds, and the therapist's interpretations are informed by a progressively more complex level of understanding. A deepening selfobject transference reveals a hierarchical organization corresponding to developmental stages. For example, a selfobject need for idealizing may give way to a previously unconscious mirroring need. This may be followed by the appearance of merger needs, often at the preverbal or sensorimotor level.

Classical therapists, guided by a conflict model of the mind, analyze or dissect the patient's narrative into meaningful segments and elements that reveal varying levels and aspects of conflict. Because the overriding structure in the self psychology model is the self, self psychologists take a more holistic approach to the patient's stories and dreams. The self psychologist asks, "What does this story or dream reveal about the patient's sense of self in relation to its selfobjects?" The classical therapist asks, "What elements or symbols are contained in the narrative that provide clues to the underlying conflict?" In the self psychology casebook (Goldberg 1978), for example, a patient, Mrs. A., makes the following statement about her mother: "In any comparison with Jack [her brother] that my mother made I got the short end of the stick" (p. 247). The phallic imagery of the

phrase "the short end of the stick" might have alerted a classical
psychoanalyst to a condition of penis envy in the patient. The
self psychologist who reported the case, presumably because he
considered sexual conflicts to be secondary to underlying
selfobject failures, understood the patient's statement to reflect
a persistent unmirrored state.

Self psychologists believe that their interpretations are
experience-near: The self psychology model is consistent with
the natural propensity to regard oneself as whole rather than as
a composite of disparate elements. The issue of whether a theory
is experience-near or experience-distant, however, is clouded by
the fact that every theory of psychoanalysis is at some level formulated by abstraction. In classical theory, for example, the concept of drive is more abstract and more experience-distant than
the concept of wish. In Chapters 4 and 5 these issues will be examined in greater detail.

NEUTRALITY AND
ABSTINENCE IN SELF PSYCHOLOGY

The concept of the therapist's neutrality originates in clinical
theory (Shapiro 1984). Freud (1915) wrote about the concept
of neutrality with specific reference to transference-love,
advising the therapist to guard against the impulse to emotionally gratify the patient or himself—that is, to guard against
countertransference.

The therapist's abstinence permitted the patient's yearnings
to persist and to serve as a force impelling the patient to work.
The proper course of therapy lay between the Scylla of over-
gratifying the patient's needs and the Charybdis of excessively
inhibiting them.

As an ideal, the term *neutrality* came to embrace a number of
features: a nonjudgmental or value-free attitude; open attention
to every aspect of the patient's communications and actions, as
well as to one's own thoughts and fantasies; an equidistant
stance regarding the patient's superego, ego, and id (A. Freud
1946); and attention to the patient both as an empathic partici-

pant and as a cognitively positioned observer. Contained in this description are the therapist's non-self-serving availability to the patient and respect for the patient as a unique individual (Leider 1983, Poland 1984).

Freud's reported behavior with patients was much more human than one might have expected from his published instructions, and in practice psychoanalysts reveal themselves to be far from unresponsive. Nevertheless, the introduction of such concepts as the therapeutic and working alliance and the real relationship (Zetzel 1956, Greenson 1965a) suggest that it was necessary to clarify that the therapist was more than a mirror or a surgeon.

Self psychologists favor the recommendations of Zetzel and Greenson. The contributions of Winnicott (1971), Modell (1976), and Mahler, Pine, and Bergman (1975), which emphasize the patient's basic need for object-relatedness in the clinical setting, are also congruent with the self psychology model. However, although classical therapists feel that such concepts as the real relationship and the therapeutic alliance are natural heirs of the positive nonlibidinal relationship described by Freud (Friedman 1969), self psychologists consider them to be revisions of classical theory necessitated by the traditional model's neglect of the patient's relational needs in the analytic setting. Self psychologists feel that such concepts as the therapeutic alliance are not necessary for them because the patient's relational needs are an intrinsic feature of self psychology. Within the self psychology framework, the danger of a therapist's behaving coldly (a misuse of the concept of neutrality) is lessened because the patient's selfobject needs constitute the central transferential configuration. Furthermore, self psychologists claim that their model alerts the therapist to a wider spectrum of understanding: A patient's announcement of a recent job promotion, for example, may be seen to contain elements of oedipal rivalry (as in classical psychoanalysis), but it may also represent a legitimate or phase-appropriate need to be mirrored. Self psychologists take issue not with Freud's views on the subject of neutrality but with psychoanalysts who interpret Freud's statements too rigidly in order to justify a silent and nonresponsive posture (Wolf 1983a).

THE CONCEPT OF CURE IN SELF PSYCHOLOGY

In classical psychoanalysis, it is the therapist's alternating role as an old and a new object that propels the treatment forward. As an old object, the therapist takes on the character of a patient's parent imago in attitude or action and reenacts an archaic scenario with the patient. As a new object, the therapist recognizes the patient's transference before or shortly after taking part in the scenario and interprets it to the patient.

Self psychologists examine the patient's free associations within a framework that highlights the state of integration and vitality of the patient's self. This framework is also used to examine the manner in which the patient's experience of the therapist affects this state. The therapist's interpretations are dictated by this framework. The therapist interprets to the patient the patient's selfobject needs of the therapist, and the therapist's perceived or actual successes and failures in meeting these needs. The patterns that emerge are used to reconstruct the patient's past in terms of archaic selfobject failures.

Although interpretation is considered the major vehicle for cure in self psychology, self psychologists believe that an interactional pattern characterized by minor nontraumatic failures and optimal gratifications provides a necessary atmosphere for effective interpretation (Kohut and Seitz 1963). This interactional pattern is similar to the optimum growth-promoting behavior of the parent with respect to the developing self of the child.

A CRITIQUE OF SELF PSYCHOLOGY

In order to examine the concept of empathy in a manner that highlights the differences between traditional psychoanalysis and self psychology, it is necessary to articulate the controversial aspects of self psychology. Many of the criticisms of self psychology by other schools of psychoanalysis have been anticipated in the preceding sections.

A number of inconsistencies have been noted. The term *self* is not clearly defined. As a result, statements about the self sometimes give the impression that the self is a creature or homunculus with its own aims and drives. It is not clear whether the term *nuclear self* is synonymous with the term *self* or whether it represents a substructure of the self. The term *selfobject* is used sometimes to refer to a parental function, sometimes to an internalized function. Self psychologists recognize the inexactness and apparent inconsistencies of their theory but claim that it is in a nascent stage.

Kohut's descriptions of the therapist's countertransference with respect to narcissistic patients is generally considered to be a useful contribution. Notwithstanding this contribution, classical analysts feel that self psychology is original in its emphasis but not in its substance and question whether a new paradigm is necessary (Rothstein 1980). As this chapter demonstrates, self psychologists write differently and use a terminology different from that of other psychoanalysts. Many clinicians (e.g., Annie Reich [1953]) have written about narcissism in a vein similar to that of self psychologists without suggesting the need for a new terminology. Classical psychoanalysts claim that many concepts of self psychology can be embraced by the older terminology. The *idealized parental imago* is considered similar to the older *ego ideal*. *Transmuting internalization* is felt to be similar to the older concepts of *introjection* and *projective identification*. Many revisions that have moved psychoanalysis closer to the self psychology model have been successfully embraced by the traditional theories: the recognition of the importance of the developing therapeutic alliance, of the observer's role in altering the field of observation, and of the impossibility of the therapist's maintaining an unbiased and reality-anchored position; the application to therapy of Mahler's observations of mother–child interactions (Mahler, Pine, and Bergman 1975); the description of the treatment setting as a holding environment; and the recognition that deficits may provide a nidus for drives (Racker 1957). The object relations school has been able to move away from the tripartite model of id, ego, and superego without having to set up a competitively exclusive theory. The object relations school's description of projected idealized and persecutory objects is felt to have anticipated Kohut's concept of the therapist serving as a selfobject for a patient's fragmenting self.

Self psychologists are critical of the object relations school's use of adultomorphic concepts such as envy and guilt to describe the vicissitudes of infancy. As a rule, however, their criticism is aimed at classical theory. Classical clinicians, however, maintain that self psychologists have set themselves in opposition to an outdated version of classical theory and practice. Furthermore, instead of limiting the many possible stories in a patient's psyche to the monolithic theme that pathology arises from parental deficiencies, the older theories embrace a wide array of possible formulations. Self psychology, with its emphasis on the patient as victim, neglects the rich interplay of paradoxical stories. It does not address such potential sources of pathology as envy, parental strife, sibling rivalry, differences in input from mother and father, and actual parental abuse. For example, classical therapists suggest that narcissistic needs may vary at different developmental stages. A patient's exigency may represent a need to maintain the illusion of an oedipal triumph or a defense against envy. The so-called fragmentation of the self may in fact represent a maneuver to contain or to ward off anger. Self psychologists often neglect anger and sexual feelings.

Traditional psychoanalysts claim that interpretations made by self psychologists are not necessarily more holistic than interpretations made by other psychoanalysts. In a properly conducted analysis, an interpretation concerning a conflictual *element* in a patient's story (for instance, an element that may alert a therapist to a conflict pertaining to penis envy) is never formulated without first taking into consideration the patient's psychological state *as a whole.*

The debate concerning whether or not self psychology is a form of psychoanalysis centers on the definition of psychoanalysis. For Brenner (1982), Gray (1973), and Arlow (1985), psychoanalysis is essentially a theory and a treatment method based on the concept of conflict. Although self psychologists acknowledge the role of conflict in the splitting off and repression of archaic unmet selfobject needs, at heart self psychology is a deficiency theory. For Greene (1984), psychoanalysis is by definition a treatment in which the curative factor is insight. Self psychologists do consider insight by way of interpretation to be the major vehicle for cure. Greene, however, believes that self psychologists provide compassion and avoid confronting anger. Unfortunately, because the factors that facilitate change or improvement in any form of psychotherapy are not known at the present, a debate concerning curative factors is premature.

The debate between traditional psychoanalysts and self psychologists has centered around which theory provides the therapist with a deep and accurate understanding of a patient's difficulties. It is important to recognize, however, that the difference between the two models stems from differing structural cores: conflict versus deficiency.

EMPATHY IN SELF PSYCHOLOGY

It is difficult to compare and contrast the use of the noun *empathy* by self psychologists with its use by other psychoanalysts. Theoreticians and therapists do not fall neatly into opposing camps, nor does each group speak with a unified voice on the subject. The contributions of Basch, who supports the self psychology school, are consistent with and augment the classical descriptions of empathy. Lichtenberg's example of a momentary empathic experience is viewed from the self psychological perspective, yet it is similar to the "aha" experiences of classical psychoanalysts such as Greenson, Beres, and Arlow. Kohut's statement that empathy (presumably the *capacity* for empathy) originates in the primary empathy between mother and child, his inattention to the contribution of ordinary perception, and his use of the phrase *vicarious introspection* as a definition for empathy without his having provided a detailed examination of the process may have given the unfortunate impression that he had discovered a unique experience founded on a unique mode of perception. In fact, Kohut claims that empathy is a mode of observation and not a unique mode of perception. The term *mode of observation* can refer to a method by which perceptions are centrally received or filtered.

Both schools of psychoanalysis agree that the empathic process contains conscious and unconscious components and emotional and cognitive elements. Self psychologists do not advocate a heightened attention to emotion as opposed to ideation.

Some of the controversy stems from the fact that the noun *empathy* is used by the different schools to describe different facets or stages of the empathic process, a process that is complex and not easily delimited. Classical psychoanalysts commonly use the noun *empathy* to denote a momentary empathic experience that is imbedded in a conflict model of the patient. Although empathic experiences are felt to contribute to an understanding of patients, and understanding is felt to contribute to empathic experiencing, the relationship between empathy and understanding has not been clearly defined by traditional psychoanalysts.

Self psychologists commonly use the noun *empathy* to denote a capacity or vantage point that is essential for understanding another person's experience. Self psychologists claim that the hallmark of empathic understanding is the capacity to comprehend the other's state of *self* (including such characteristics as vitality, cohesion, and fragmentation), especially the other's experience of the observer. By contrast, classical therapists recommend the position of evenly hovering attention and are often surprised by a momentary empathic experience. In classical descriptions of empathy, a momentary empathic experience is often recognized only in retrospect. Empathy appears to be a more studied and prolonged state in the therapist in the clinical reports of self psychologists. In a posthumously published book edited by Goldberg and Stepansky, Kohut (1984) suggested that the therapist experiences himself to be simultaneously merged with and separate from the patient.

It is apparent that, although traditional psychoanalysts may agree that empathy is essential for understanding another person's experience, self psychologists use the term *empathic* to refer to the self psychology model itself. Self psychologists claim that their theory is empathic because the field of observation encompasses the patient's experience of himself as a whole (or the patient's experience of himself in a state of fragmentation against the normative parameter of wholeness) within the context of the therapist's regulatory effect on the patient's sense of self. Although classical theory may not appear to encompass such a vantage point, classical psychoanalysts state that their model is also holistic. Their use of the term *empathy*, however, is less closely aligned with the use of a particular theory.

Both schools view empathy and understanding as interacting. Understanding is achieved by observation, experiencing, and cognition. However, self psychologists use the phrase *empathic vantage point* as if it were synonymous with the self psychology model. Indeed, self psychologists claim that their theory was derived from the clinical use of empathy and that their model provides an organizational framework that enhances one's capacity to appreciate the patient's experience of the therapist.

Clearly, the differing use of the term by the two schools and the self psychologists' use of it to justify or explain the configuration of their model makes it difficult to compare the concept without comparing the theoretical models themselves.

Chapter Four

Factors Contributing
to the Debate on Empathy

There are a number of differences between traditional psychoanalysts and self psychologists concerning the subject of empathy. A major difference is that self psychologists often introduce the word *empathy* into discussions of the various theoretical formulations. Self psychologists claim that their framework offers therapists an empathic vantage point whereas traditional models (a term that includes the classical tripartite model of id, ego, and superego, and the object relations paradigm) do not. They argue that the self psychology model is more accurate than traditional models because it was arrived at by the clinical use of empathy. Is the self psychology model less mechanistic and therefore more empathic than other models? In order to answer this question and to expand on the issues underlying this debate, it is necessary to examine the nature of paradigm construction. This subject will be considered in the present chapter in terms of (1) historical background, (2) factors contributing to theory formation, (3) the present-day climate in science, (4) the use of metaphor, (5) antithetical issues in the human condition, and (6) the role of empathy in the debate.

HISTORICAL BACKGROUND

The present-day controversy between traditional therapists and self psychologists originates in a particular philosophical debate that began almost 60 years ago. In a 1927 paper titled "Understanding and Explanation," Heinz Hartmann, a proponent of psychoanalysis, took issue with opinions earlier expressed by Wilhelm Dilthey (1894), an eminent German philosopher. Although some of the terms of the debate are unclear, it is presented here in order to place Kohut's claim regarding the accuracy of vicarious introspection in a proper historical context.

Dilthey had put forth the proposal that the natural sciences and the psychological sciences differed from one another in their methods. In a natural science, the data observed could be explained; in psychology they could only be understood. The former was a science of explanation; the latter a science of understanding.

In Dilthey's opinion, explanation was the result of an observer's intellectually analyzing or breaking down the data. Explanation applied to causal connections as they pertained to the natural sciences (i.e., physical and biological events). Psychological understanding, on the other hand, was achieved through empathy, and empathy entailed an appreciation of all the data. As a result, psychology was able to generate descriptive formulations but could not generate meaningful formulations about the causes of psychological disorders.

Hartmann disagreed with Dilthey's assertions. He believed that Freud's discoveries had indeed made it possible to explain a patient's symptoms and personality traits. The discoveries of psychoanalysis, he believed, had erased any difference between psychology and the natural sciences. Freud's discoveries had made it possible to state that a symptom in an adult had in fact been *caused* by a series of childhood events and had extended psychological knowledge beyond what could be empathically understood about another person. For example, in Hartmann's opinion, empathy alone could never have uncovered the relationship between anal retentiveness and pedantry. An observer might empathize with anal retentiveness or pedantry, but the series of mechanisms that knitted the two attributes together, the mental apparatus, could never be experienced. Although Hartmann's argument against the primacy of empathy was raised in the context of a debate concerning scientific methods, it can be assumed that in therapy as well he would have relegated empathy to a secondary position.

Eissler (1968), who also supported the concept of a mental apparatus, proposed that the events that an individual felt he could empathize with would change from era to era as the tenets of psychology entered the public domain. He differentiated the terms *explaining* and *understanding* by assigning to the first term a quality of objectivity and to the second a quality of subjectivity.

Dilthey's distinction between the methods of the natural sciences and the methods of psychology traces once again the age-old attempt to delineate the differences between animate and inanimate matter. Handelman (1982) locates the origins of the debate between Hartmann and Dilthey in the conflict between the Jewish tradition of interpretation (explanation) and the German Protestant tradition of inspiration (understanding). Despite Handelman's assertions, however, Dilthey did not use the term *empathy* in reference to a mystical form of intuition.

Self psychologists state that traditional, or classical, interpretations are lifeless, whereas interpretations organized by the use of their model provide patients with a feeling of being empathically understood. Kohut (1977), for whom empathy and introspection are the essential methods of psychology, argues that the affinity between anal retentiveness and pedantry (although it had served therapists for years) is incorrect, precisely because this affinity had not been arrived at empathically. Basch (1983b), in agreement with Kohut, contends that recent advances in our understanding of affect and cognition have made it possible to study the vicissitudes of empathy itself. Classical psychoanalysis is accused of having created mechanistic formulations that extend beyond what is knowable. Self psychologists follow in Dilthey's footsteps in the conviction that the methods of observation of the natural sciences differ from those of psychology, in their claim that empathy is the essential receiving and organizing instrument of the latter discipline, and in their holistic approach to the patient's narrative. Although traditional psychoanalysts may be in agreement with self psychologists regarding the importance of empathy, they do not agree that use of the self psychology model is essential for empathic understanding.

FACTORS CONTRIBUTING
TO PARADIGM CREATION

Kohut's claim that Freud's great discoveries were arrived at purely by introspection is contradicted by Eissler's account of the factors contributing to Freud's discovery of the Oedipus complex. In Eissler's account (1968), Freud was influenced in his discovery by a knowledge of Greek mythology and of literature (including an interest in Shakespeare's *Hamlet*), by interactions with patients, by correspondence with colleagues, and by his disappointment with his earlier hypothesis that neurosis was caused by parental sexual abuse. It is ironic that although Kohut attributed Freud's discovery of dream interpretation to introspection, self psychologists have deemphasized Freud's method of parsing out the symbolic elements of a dream in favor of examining the dream as a whole.

Although he praised Freud's use of introspection, Kohut (1959) tempered his praise with the criticism that, under the influence of a Newtonian vision of the world, Freud's discoveries had been extended into inaccurate, lifeless, and mechanistic abstract structures by the unwarranted use of conceptual thought bridges. It is indeed reasonable to assume that Freud's formulations were influenced by the assumptions of his era, nor is it difficult to conceive of the mental structures and energies that he postulated as having an almost palpable quality. It is, however, evident that the paradigms of both traditional psychoanalysis and self psychology are based on an abstract imagery of configurations or structures. For example, in classical psychoanalysis, the relationship between anal retentiveness and pedantry is described in terms of such abstract concepts as id, ego, and superego. The countervailing drives are described by such terms as *cathexis, countercathexis,* and *mental energies.* In self psychology, pedantry and anal retentiveness stem from an unmet need for self-affirmation. However, these two attributes are also described in abstract terms such as *selfobjects* clustered around *poles* and knitted together by a process labeled *transmuting internalization* and by a *tension arc.*

Kohut himself attempted to moderate the view that the traditional theories had been formulated differently from the self psychology paradigm. In his posthumously published book, Kohut (1984) acknowledged that the self psychology model was in fact configurationally organized and that it had been arrived at by conceptual thought bridges. Theory formation necessitates the use of abstractions precisely because it represents a move from the particular to the general, from the singular to the plural. Because both the traditional and the self psychology models were formulated by modes of cognition not limited to vicarious introspection, a variety of sources knowingly or unwittingly have contributed to their formulation.

The claim that one set of configurations is less accurate than another needs to be tempered by the recognition that the very aim of creating a generally applicable set of orderly relations imbues every theory with the quality of inexactness; the unique aspects of the individual case are lost in the orderly rule. In their desire to formulate a set of orderly relations, theoreticians necessarily overreach. Browning's statement ". . . a man's reach should exceed his grasp, Or what's a heaven for" is particularly applicable to scientific creation.* Kohut's accusation that the drives and structures of classical theory were lifeless and mechanistic was presumably directed against the propensity among some classical analysts to define as actual and measurable structures that were not simply inaccurate but nonexistent. Given that classical theory evolved under the influence of Newtonian physics, Kohut's statement may have some validity. On the other hand, paradigms are not of necessity mechanical and lifeless. That a paradigm is perceived as such may reflect the manner in which it is appreciated. Concepts evoke imagery in an

---

*From *Andrea del Sarto* (Browning 1895).

individual; the nature of conceptual imagery varies from person to person. The manner in which we picture such concepts as libidinal drive or selfobject function colors our understanding of a theory. Scientists at present are tentative about the relationship between a theory and the events it describes. Given this climate, it is not surprising that the present-day therapist has a greater appreciation than the therapist in Freud's day of the fact that the theoretical schema of Freud's theories (or Kohut's, for that matter) are approximate signposts of a useful but limited set of orderly relations.

Every theory is a set of approximate configurations derived from many sources by various modes of cognition (including abstract thinking). The significance a paradigm has for the beholder may account for the qualities felt to be intrinsic to it.

Empathy and Intuition in Theory Building

Before focusing on the role of empathy in paradigm creation, it is necessary to look again at the concept of empathy in self psychology and traditional psychoanalysis, and because empathy has often been contrasted with intuition as a tool for understanding patients, to distinguish these two modes of comprehension.

Kohut (1984) did not believe that self psychology uncovered a new form of empathy. He described two modes, or levels, of empathy. The first mode pertained to a studied positioning of oneself within the patient's frame of reference; the second pertained to an immediate and deep appreciation of the patient's state of mind. This description conforms with the traditional view that there are levels of empathy. Kohut's description of the second mode of experiencing empathy is similar to modes reported by classical psychoanalysts. His posthumously published statement that the therapist maintains a position of objectivity while simultaneously experiencing an aspect of the patient's inner life is not significantly different from classical descriptions of the stage of retrospective recognition.

Kohut believed that self psychologists could properly claim

that the self psychology model enhanced the therapist's capacity to take an empathic position. This statement makes it possible to entertain the opinion that the unique configuration of the self psychology paradigm evolved because its originator had employed empathy in therapy more consistently than had other therapists.

Because empathy is commonly contrasted with intuition, it might be inferred that the conceptual differences between classical or traditional psychoanalysis and self psychology stem from Kohut's having used empathy to a greater extent clinically than he had used intuition.* In the first chapter, Moore and Fine's definition (1968) was introduced in order to distinguish the two concepts:

> Both empathy and intuition to which it is related are means of obtaining quick and deep understanding. Empathy establishes close contact with the patient in terms of emotions and impulses; intuition does the same in the realm of ideas. Empathy is a function of the experiencing ego while intuition is a function of the observing ego. (p. 43)

In the preceding definition, empathy and intuition have been compared along two axes: emotions versus ideas and experiencing versus observing. Although an adequate theory of emotions and affects is lacking in psychoanalysis, there is agreement that affect and ideation always act in concert (Brenner 1974, Noy 1982). There is no thought so pure as to be devoid of affect, and there is no affect so pure as to be devoid of ideation. Basch (1976) has suggested that affect and ideation are two interacting forms of cognition. Affect, a developmentally earlier mode anatomically linked with the paleocortex and the autonomic nervous system, is an immediate form of cognition. Ideation, a developmentally more advanced mode anatomically linked with the neocortex and the voluntary nervous system, is a delayed form

---

*The distinction between empathy and intuition, which was first mentioned in Chapter 1 and is here examined in terms of theory building, will be considered again in Chapter 5 in terms of the therapist's clinical use of imagery.

of cognition. Classical psychoanalysts and self psychologists do not disagree on the nature of affect and ideation or on the fact that the two forms of cognition intertwine; they also concur that their respective paradigms have not been derived from the use of significantly different proportions of affective and ideational cognition.

Nor does the second distinction between empathy and intuition—experiencing versus observing—introduce a clear-cut difference between the ways in which the traditional and self psychology models were developed. Here one can discover a difference only in *perspective*. Traditional therapists experience and observe from the perspective of free-floating attention. Self psychologists, on the other hand, experience and observe with special attention to the patient's experience of the therapist, particularly the latter's effect on the patient's sense of self. Indeed, the preceding discussion emphasizes that these different perspectives did not arise from different sources or forms of cognition. Furthermore, it is questionable whether the altered perspective of self psychology could in itself have accounted for the significant differences in configuration and terminology between the two models. In the sections that follow, several factors will be considered that, though they are unrelated to empathy, do appear to have contributed significantly to the self psychology paradigm and to the debate between traditional therapists and self psychologists.

THE PRESENT-DAY CLIMATE IN SCIENCE

In his early paper on empathy, Kohut (1959) questioned the use by traditional psychoanalysts of the concepts of drive and conflict. He felt that these concepts were adultomorphic and too precise to describe a childhood state of mind. Because a therapist could empathize only approximately with a childhood state, Kohut used the terms *regulation* and *deregulation* to capture the *inexactness* of a therapist's empathy. How had he arrived at these terms? It is interesting to consider Kohut's choice of terminology in the light of remarks by Galenson, which were reported in a review of a panel on infancy research (Sander 1980):

> She pointed out that the symposium papers represent studies which are remarkably different from the bulk of infancy research 15 or 20 years ago. Although they employ many of the same scientific criteria . . . the issues they address are different from earlier studies and the differences are addressed differently. . . . The words rhythmic, *regulation* [my italics], recurrence, etc. occur in each study description. Established psychoanalytic theories regarding psychosexual development do not provide for many of the new research data. (p. 191)

Was it simply fortuitous that infancy researchers, by observing infants, and Kohut, by the clinical use of vicarious introspection, had hit upon the same word? Had infancy researchers been influenced by Kohut? Had Kohut been influenced by infancy researchers? Or were there other overriding factors at work that had influenced the direction of both?

Kohut and other self psychologists believed that the clinical application of empathy provided them with a view from which the analytic ambience became itself an object for analytic interpretation. In a similar vein, Galenson is reported to have said that in present-day infancy research the infant is considered as part of an "interactional system" (Sander 1980). It is noteworthy that similar concepts had also been articulated by such traditional psychoanalysts as Kris (1956) and Loewald (1970).

The sudden appearance of similar concepts at a similar period in history among infancy researchers and traditional therapists makes one question the notion that Kohut's formulations had been arrived at by empathy alone. The concepts of inexactness, regulation and deregulation, and the notion that a dyadic relationship is an interactional unit profoundly affected by each member of the unit (i.e., a field theory)—all these elements of theory are remarkably congruent with the tenets, prevalent in the culture at large, of present-day nuclear physics. It is likely that infancy researchers, traditional psychoanalysts, and Kohut alike had been influenced (as has been every thoughtful individual) not only by the climate of uncertainty introduced by two world wars, an economic depression, and the possibility of nuclear annihilation, but particularly by a scientific revolution that has shattered our earlier conceptions of energy and matter. Two related concepts introduced by nuclear physicists are remarkably similar to the concepts introduced by infancy researchers and by Kohut: the principle of uncertainty and the recognition of the inexactness of theory. The first concept is elucidated in the following quotation from Margenau (1949):

> Empirically, the effect of a measurement upon the state of a system is extremely complicated, sometimes slight, sometimes . . . destructive to the identity of the physical system. It is difficult to make a simple theory about the dynamical fate of a system during measurement. (p. 265)

The second concept is contained in the following quotation from Wheeler (quoted in Begley, 1979) an eminent physicist and colleague of Einstein:

> What is so hard is to give up thinking of nature as a machine that goes on independent of the observer. . . . [our conception of reality] is a few iron posts of observation with papier-mâché construction between them that is but the elaborate work of our imagination. . . . for our picture of the world, this is the most revolutionary thing discovered . . . (p. 62)

In the present day, the concept of objective reality as a knowable state has come into question.

The many references to the physical sciences in Kohut's publications is testimony to the influence the physical sciences had on his thinking. Schwaber (1980, 1983a, 1983b) claims that the accuracy of the use of vicarious introspection can be demonstrated by the congruence between the findings of Kohut and other self psychologists and those of infancy researchers. This is circular reasoning. The theories of both Kohut and infancy researchers have been influenced by a social climate in which the prevalent view of the nature of objective reality has been profoundly altered by major scientific discoveries.*

THE USE OF METAPHOR

Although numerous sources of imagery (including art and literature) appear to have contributed to psychoanalytic theory, at an abstract level it is the imagery derived from neurophysiology and the physical sciences that has influenced the formulation by classical psychoanalysts of the principles of mental functioning.

As a physician with a keen interest in science, Freud (1900, 1912) was fascinated by and employed in his metaphors such scientific instruments as the lens and the telephone receiver and such functional structures as the reflex arc. His hope that the physical sciences would one day discover the underlying origins of mental illness and his struggle to place his theoretical formulations in the apparently firmer bedrock of neurophysiology shaped the concepts he proposed. The metaphors Freud used may also be considered to provide evidence that he was influenced by the Newtonian vision of objective reality. Freud's theories contained relatively enduring functional structures such as the id, ego, and superego. These structures acted upon each other and were affected by forces and drives that resembled the configurations of the physical and biological sciences of his day. Freud's recognition of the inexact and descriptive nature of his configurations, however, permitted him to alter them or leave them in a state of incompleteness when they failed to serve their purpose.

---

*Major scientific discoveries do not play an unassisted role in affecting a society's views concerning the nature of objective reality. Such cultural phenomena as the appearance of cubism in art and the use of atonal scales in music are influenced by and in turn influence such views. The emergence of a new technology also influences and alters the way we think. For example, the development of the computer has had a profound effect on the manner in which neuropsychologists conceptualize mental functioning. The influence of science, art, and technology on the way we think, however, is a complex subject beyond the scope of this book.

It is obvious from the many references to nuclear physics by Kohut as well as other self psychologists that they were familiar with the tenets and assumptions of modern science. The scientific principle that the observer alters the field of observation has been described earlier in the chapter as being remarkably similar to the principle that the therapist's presence has a profound regulatory effect on the patient's sense of self. But has more than a principle crept into Kohut's thinking? Is it possible that Kohut derived the unique configuration of the self psychology model from the paradigms of nuclear physics? Examined within the framework of this premise, the conceptual scheme of the self reveals a number of striking similarities to that of the atom or molecule.

The self and the atom both have a core. The self is occasionally referred to as a nuclear self. The self is felt to be the overriding composite structure in self psychology. Like the atom, however, it is felt to be too inexact to be clearly defined. Its stability is highly dependent on the surrounding field. Like stable and unstable atoms and molecules, the self exists in varying states of fusion and lack of cohesion. An unstable self is intimately affected by a therapist's behavior just as an unstable atom or molecule is intimately affected by scientific observation. The stability of the self is affected by the relationship of the nuclear self to its selfobjects just as that of an atom depends on the interaction of its nuclear particles with orbiting electrons. Selfobjects are not necessarily contained within the self but are experienced as coextensive with the self. As such, they occupy a territory very similar to the territory occupied by electrons in the structure of an atom. Just as electrons contribute to the characteristics of an atom and its nucleus, selfobjects contribute to the harmony, cohesion, and vitality of the nuclear self.

The uncertain positioning of selfobject functions or units parallels in the self the inexact boundaries of the atom. Similarly, Kohut's tension arc (1977) is evocative of the bonds that hold together an atom or a molecule. The process by which the self develops, the process of transmuting internalization, has been explicitly compared by Kohut and Wolf (1978) to the rearrangement of a protein's molecular structure. It is interesting to compare Kohut's description of the two *poles* of the nuclear self, the pole of ambitions and the pole of ideals, to Wheeler's description of reality: "What we conceive of as reality is a few *iron posts* of observation with papier-mâché construction between them that is but the work of our imagination" (italics mine). Perhaps the image at the center of the self psychology model was derived not from a delicate vase (as suggested by the phrase "delicately mirrored crystal" in Chapter 1) but from a crystal of sugar or salt examined under an electron microscope.

Issues pertaining to metaphor and imagery do in fact play a role in the debate between classical theorists and self psychologists. For example, self psychologists see the Freudian model as being based on an outdated science; that their model is shaped by the concepts of nuclear physics is not acknowledged. In their belief that their theory gets to the heart of the matter, psychologically speaking, self psychologists assume that undertaking a microanalysis of the basic substructure of the self makes it unnecessary to examine the more grossly fashioned elements of a patient's narrative. Such arguments have the flavor of a physicist's argument that inspecting the shape and luster of a diamond is superficial compared to an examination of its molecular structure.

One paradigm is better than another to the degree to which it accurately conveys a more *useful* set of relations or principles. The failure to acknowledge the import of issues of metaphor contained in the debate has led to a confusing polarization of the two schools of psychoanalysis.

DILEMMA IN THE HUMAN CONDITION

In the first chapter, the therapist's preference for one theory over another was linked to whether or not he felt an individual was responsible for his condition. This question was shown to be handled unevenly by the models of classical psychoanalysis and self psychology. In classical theory, the concept of the individual's wish to possess one parent and destroy the other tilts the balance in favor of ascribing responsibility to the patient.* In self psychology, the balance is tilted in favor of ascribing responsibility to parental failures. In classical psychoanalysis, the patient is seen as warding off conflictual drives. In self psychology, the patient is seen as suffering a deficiency.

The unevenness of these positions has been carried over into the treatment setting. Classical therapists often focus on the patient's resistances to examining conflictual wishes. Self psychologists, on the other hand, often focus on the patient's experience of the therapist and on the therapist's real or perceived failure to meet the patient's selfobject needs.

Neither theory is in fact completely one-sided. In classical theory, deficiency is reflected in the concept of the child's unrequited oral needs. In self psychology, the child is held responsible for its failure or incapacity to use the parent as a selfobject or to serve as a selfobject for the parent. Conflict, too, is recognized in the patient's need to ward off the wish to be understood.

Within their respective schools, a number of clinicians have raised issues that could serve to bridge the gap between the two communities. Among traditional psychoanalysts, Racker (1957) has emphasized need as opposed to drive. Kris (1956), Winnicott (1971), and Modell (1976) have all emphasized the therapist's role in providing the patient with fundamental relational needs. Among self psychologists, Newman (1980) has emphasized the role of conflict in the patient's defending against the wish to be mirrored because such a wish is felt to be shameful. Wolf (1980) has stressed that the self psychology paradigm needs to be expanded to account for a stage-appropriate hierarchy of narcissistic needs. With only a few exceptions, however, therapists have proclaimed the supremacy of one theory over the other.

---

*At a more abstract level of theorizing, classical psychoanalysis introduced the concept of a *genetically programmed drive* to possess one parent and destroy the other. Although such a concept suggests that the patient is a victim of a genetic condition, Freud believed that the individual had an obligation to go against his nature. This view in turn emphasizes responsibility and conflict (Freud 1930, Kline 1972, p. 96).

In this context, the description of dissonance in therapy as tension at the junction of two subjectivities or centers of initiative is of particular interest (Schwaber 1980, Stolorow, Brandchaft, and Atwood 1983). This is a more evenhanded approach than the classical formulation in which patients are described as "resisting" or the self psychology formulation in which the patient's needs occupy center stage. The difficulty with this formulation is that it may leave the impression that antithetical issues have been resolved or eliminated. Although one theme may be more prominent than others, the antithetical elements of victimization versus guilt are invariably present in a patient's narrative.

An additional antithetical issue surfaced in the dialogue between Hartmann and Dilthey. Should the individual be considered as a sum of parts or as a totality? This issue as well has been perpetuated in the debate between classical theorists and self psychologists.

Clearly, individuals oscillate in self-regard, sometimes perceiving themselves as whole and sometimes as a sum of parts, sometimes as integrated and sometimes as fragmented. Classical psychoanalysts have emphasized analyzing the elements of a patient's conflicts, bringing the conflictual elements to consciousness. The ultimate purpose of this endeavor, however, is to permit the patient to integrate discordant aspects (i.e., unrecognized conflicts) into a cohesive sense of self. By focusing on the therapist's actual or perceived failure to serve as an empathic selfobject for the patient, self psychologists have emphasized the integrative aspects of therapy. Lichtenberg (1981) has recommended as a possible middle road that the therapist should adopt an oscillating stance, regarding the patient as a sum of parts contained within an integrated whole. The different emphases of the two schools may be partly attributable to the fact that self psychology arose from the study of more disturbed patients than did the classical model. Despite the difference in emphasis, however, both schools do consider therapy to be a process of breakdown and reassembly, analysis and synthesis.

The tilt of their respective models toward one side or another on such antithetical issues has contributed to the polarization of traditional therapists and self psychologists. This polarization is

exemplified by Kohut's statement (1982) that traditional psychoanalysts emphasize the story of "guilty man," whereas self psychology emphasizes the story of "tragic man." The tendency to
take one side or another on antithetical issues is an age-old phenomenon. In ancient Greece, physicians argued vehemently
over the treatment of hysteria. Some recommended the compassionate method of luring the womb back to its proper position
with sweet-smelling salts applied to the vagina; others, the
harsher method of driving it back with foul-smelling salts applied to the mouth (Berger 1971).

THE ROLE OF EMPATHY IN THE DEBATE

At the level of rhetoric, empathy has played a central role in the
debate between the two schools of psychotherapy. One model is
felt to have evolved from the empathic process; the other by
unwarranted abstractions. One school claims to be empathic;
the other is not. The preceding discussion has attempted to put
this rhetorical posturing into perspective by a close examination
of the wider philosophical, social, historical, and metaphoric issues that in fact contributed to each model.

Kohut's theories, like all theories, were derived from the complex of the foregoing list of factors and not through the empathic
process alone. Particular emphasis has been laid in this
discussion on Kohut's borrowings from scientific imagery – the
imagery of nuclear physics in particular. It is important to note,
however, that Kohut's borrowings have not simply produced
new imagery; they have produced new and valuable concepts.
They have allowed us to conceive of the self as an entity having
uncertain boundaries, an entity whose state of cohesion and vitality is dependent on its surroundings.

Self psychology's challenging of classical theory has forced
the psychoanalytic community to acknowledge and examine the
inexactness of theory in general. This has benefited the community as a whole. It must be pointed out, however, that Kohut's
theoretical model is not exempt from this principle. Useful as it
may be, the self psychology model deemphasizes the very issue

that is stressed in traditional models: the paradoxical nature of the human condition that gives rise to conflict and guilt. To put it metaphorically (and, therefore, somewhat inaccurately), atoms don't feel guilty about their relationship with other atoms. They tend to lack a sense of irony and humor concerning their strivings. Atoms bounce off one another without much concern or regard for other atoms and without concern or regard for their own mortality.

The polemical focus on empathy, with its implication that one theorist is capable of appreciating a patient's inner state more accurately than other theorists, has had the unfortunate effect of increasing the stridency and the extravagance of the claims on both sides. At the deepest levels of communication, can a therapist really know whether a patient's exigency represents an untamed aggressive drive, a need for self-affirmation, or defensive behavior employed to ward off envious feelings? Each of these explanations is to some extent the product of abstract thinking. A paradigm stands or falls not on the strength of the claims of its proponents but on its usefulness. It is ironic that a debate concerning issues of guilt and narcissism should have evoked accusations and extravagantly self-promoting claims among the proponents of both schools.

Chapter Five

Using Nontechnical Imagery as a Path to Empathy

Empathic responsiveness is enhanced by attention to the patient's emotionally evocative imagery. This task is mediated through many psychological functions—conscious and unconscious, affective and ideational, and adaptive and defensive. Such diverse mental activity as inference, affective resonance, extracting recurrent themes in the patient's free associations by deductive reasoning, distilling meaningful common elements from apparently unrelated themes that occur contiguously on a regular basis, logically relating new themes to what the therapist already knows about the patient, and organizing the data with theoretical formulations make up the therapist's repertory. Sometimes, understanding appears to be immediate; sometimes, it appears to be the outcome of a studied approach to the patient's associations.

That the many functions do not occur in any particular order makes it apparent that theoretical bias may contribute to one's appraisal of the patient at any point along the way. Theory may influence a therapist to emphasize some functions rather than others or direct attention to one set of issues rather than others. In the sections that follow, the use of theory and method will be discussed in order to provide a rationale for focusing attention on the emotionally evocative imagery contained in the patient's narrative.

THEORY AND METHOD

The route to understanding is mediated by particular methods and particular theories. From a historical perspective, it is unclear whether method precedes theory or theory precedes method. Freud and Kohut, having surveyed the territory from distinctive perspectives, provided prospective therapists with guidelines for observing and interacting with patients. They also provided descriptive outlines of what would be discovered if a therapist followed these guidelines. Freud encouraged patients to free-associate without regard for logical or syntactical connections. Physicians were advised to listen with evenly hovering attention to their own inner thoughts and to the patient's material. The information that the therapist recovered was organized using a drive-defense model of the patient. Kohut advised therapists to pay attention to the patient's experience of the therapist. The patient's material was to be organized in terms of the therapist's function as a selfobject for the patient's nuclear self.

Despite their differences, both schools of psychoanalysis counsel the therapist to behave nonjudgmentally. Both schools underpin their method with the claim that a personal analysis provides the therapist with sufficient access to inner conflicts to prevent the inappropriate intrusion of unconscious motivations.

Prospective therapists receive both a method and a map. A given method is understood to produce a given set of orderly relations and constellations. The student receiving the map is not a *tabula rasa*. Students enter a training course with complexly fashioned conscious and unconscious personal values and convictions. Such convictions may include, for example, the belief that a life of useful activity is sufficient to overcome depression or that psychological illness is caused by a neurophysiological deficit. Personal convictions influence a student's choice of theoretical models and the manner in which they are used.

During training in dynamic psychotherapy, the prospective therapist undertakes a dual task. The first is to learn to use a pre-scribed method; the second is to uncover the dim outlines of such mapped-out formulations as an oedipal conflict or a selfobject deficiency. The elation of discovering a meaningful pattern in a patient's narrative (evidence that the therapist is on the right track) can be compared to that of a young medical stu-dent who discovers a meaningful cytological structure under the microscope.

The therapist's use of theoretical knowledge develops from the matrix of the dual task of learning method and theory. It is influenced by such factors as the capacity to tolerate antithetical issues, individual differences, and a state of uncertainty; the methods and theories advocated by supervisors; the outcome of the therapist's own analysis; and the therapist's stage of training.

At times, method and theory can appear to inhibit the thera-pist's native ability to be helpful. At times, the manner in which method and theory are employed reflects a defensive need to maintain a personal value system or to ward off unrecognized conflicts. The propensity to anticipate configurational patterns in a patient's story occasionally induces a therapist to apply meaning or order too hastily. Because therapists devote many years to becoming skilled in the use of a theory, their willingness to objectively examine the methods and assumptions acquired during training may be impeded. Despite many potential pit-falls, the acquisition of knowledge and skill, as well as a personal analysis, is expected to enhance the therapist's appreciation of the presence and influence of blind spots and conflicts. This should increase his capacity to examine with equanimity the the-ories he has learned.

THE INFLUENCE OF IMAGERY

Psychoanalytic theories are not integrated and consistent sys-tems of thought. Because their purpose is to encompass the clin-ical data in a set of orderly relations, they overlook unique attrib-utes of individuals and the subtle differences that result.

A psychological theory is an abstract and general statement describing aspects of thinking, feeling, and behaving. It encompasses only those patterns that lend themselves to generalization. Such concepts as a repressed drive and a selfobject deficiency, for example, do not capture the unique qualities of a patient's narrative (e.g., a patient's complaint that his father belittled him). They also minimize individual differences (e.g., the difference between parental loss as a result of death and parental loss caused by abandonment).

The imagery intrinsic to clinical data is different from the imagery intrinsic to theoretical formulations in form and in the capacity to be emotionally evocative. At one extreme, the personal and familiar imagery of a patient's narrative is the imagery of films, novels, and plays. The scenes consist of individuals interacting in familiar or imaginable settings. At the other extreme, the imagery evoked by a statement of a theoretical concept (which may be formulated at various levels of abstraction) tends to be impersonal. An observer may be moved by a story of a child left behind at a family outing, but not by the imagery of a mirroring need or a repressed drive. The image of two people arguing (especially if they are patient and therapist) is emotionally evocative; the imagery of tension at the junction of two centers of initiative is not.

Holt (1972) described the pervasive duality in psychoanalysis, the two antithetical images of man, as mechanistic on the one hand and humanistic on the other. Rapaport (1959) distinguished the general theory (or metapsychology) of psychoanalysis from its clinical theory. Yankelovich and Barrett (1970) talked about the two worlds, or two truths, of science. The presence of two sets of images is evident in the writings of Freud, Kohut, and the majority of psychoanalytic publications.

Freud's case reports ("Fragment of an Analysis of a Case of Hysteria" [1905], "Analysis of a Phobia in a Five-Year-Old Boy" [1909]) and his works pertaining to art, literature, and history ("The Moses of Michelangelo" [1914b], "Moses and Monotheism" [1939], "Jensen's Gradiva" [1907]) contain predominantly personal and emotionally evocative imagery. His papers on metapsychology, which convey general principles of mental functioning ("Formulations on the Two Principles in Mental Functioning" [1911]) are, on the other hand, characterized by references to nonpersonal forces and to configurations that resemble the structures of neurophysiology and physics.

In Kohut's writings as well, the extremes of imagery are apparent. On the one hand, personal and evocative imagery dominates Kohut's case reports ("The Two Analyses of Mr. Z" [1979]) and his references to literature and art (his discussion of the oedipal myth with an empahsis on the hero's childhood suffering and the story of Ulysses in "Introspection, Empathy, and the Semi-circle of Mental Health" [1982]). On the other hand, Kohut's theoretical constructions contain impersonal configurations that resemble the present-day paradigms of nuclear physics.

Ella Freeman Sharpe (1950a, 1950b) has stated that a well-trained clinician requires a knowledge of both literature and theory. As a clinician, however, she considered a knowledge of literature and a familiarity with a wide array of human activities more useful than a knowledge of theory. She reported instances in which a knowledge of fishing or football would have enhanced her understanding of a patient. In terms of her interest, Sharpe stood opposed to theoreticians such as Hartmann and Rapaport who paid particular attention to Freud's scientifically anchored theories.*

As a theory becomes entrenched and increasingly abstract, clinicians and theoreticians sometimes lose sight of the fact that theoretical formulations only represent a set of orderly relations. As a result, the constructs of a theory may appear to take on the characteristics of *actual* entities and forces. It is in this way that incorrect, mechanistic assumptions may creep into the formulations. The fear of taking on too mechanistic a perspective has prompted some psychoanalysts (e.g., Schafer 1983) to attempt to create new, more personally relevant models, or to use

---

*Whether Freud would have gone as far as Rapaport (1959) did in attempting to clearly delineate the basic assumptions of metapsychology, however, is uncertain.

an intermediate language between the colloquial and the specialized.*

It is difficult to avoid using a dual approach (i.e., technical and humanistic) in dynamic psychotherapy. It is intrinsic to a science to discover useful sets of orderly relations commonly expressed in technical or nonpersonal language. Yet the language and imagery of the clinical setting are necessarily nontechnical and personal. The majority of psychoanalytic publications employ a dual approach encompassing two sets of images. Commonly, they will contain a discussion of theory, clinical illustrations, and a section in which a synthesis of theory and narrative is presented. Because two sets of language are employed, therapy may appear to be depicted on the one hand as a technical endeavor to repair faulty structure and on the other as an artistic endeavor to refashion personal myths.

THE THERAPIST'S USE OF THEORY AND IMAGERY

Although formulations assist therapists in their quest for understanding, a map and the territory it describes are not identical. The therapist's attention is expected to oscillate between the abstract, nonpersonal constructions of theory and the personal, evocative imagery of a patient's narrative. The therapist is engaged in a circular endeavor that entails alternating between different planes of abstraction and different sets of imagery. Theory is used to organize the data, and the patient's narrative is used to help select or validate theory. The therapist's oscillations are influenced by many factors, including a knowledge of method and theory, a facility with patients, and a preference for affectively evocative material as compared with the abstract configurations of theory.

In the early stages of training, a therapist engaged in the necessary task of learning method and theory may pay less attention to the patient's narrative than in the later stages. Fear of

---

*Kernberg (1980, p. 95) claims that Edith Jacobson used an intermediate language in "The Self and the Object World" (1954).

overwhelming puzzlement may cause the therapist to apply the-oretical paradigms overzealously. As method and theory be-come firmly implanted in one's mind, it becomes possible to pay less attention consciously to theoretical formulations. This will allow the therapist to oscillate freely between theory and narra-tive or to listen while holding theoretical formulatons in abey-ance. The therapist can then bear with the patient's narrative for prolonged periods without attempting to impose order or mean-ing. The personal, emotionally evocative imagery of the pa-tient's narrative becomes more important than the nonpersonal imagery of theory. The therapist comes to what might be de-scribed as a theory-distant position.

Negative Capability

A therapist's capacity to bear with the patient's narrative with-out imposing order too quickly requires the ability to tolerate puzzlement. In his advice to physicians to permit themselves to be surprised by the patient's free associations, Freud (1912) pointed out the usefulness of being able to tolerate puzzlement. Bion (1963) conceived of the therapist as serving as a container for the patient's puzzlement. Bennett Simon (1981) has ob-served that empathic understanding (that is, a deep apprecia-tion of a patient's experiential state) often follows a period of misunderstanding or puzzlement. Havens (1982b) and Margulies (1984) consider not knowing and being able to go against the grain of needing to know to be essential attributes of therapists of all schools of psychotherapy.

Speaking of this ability in poets, Keats described it as "nega-tive capability," "that is, when a man is capable of being in uncertainties, Mysteries, doubts, without any irritable reaching after fact and reason" (Bate 1964, p. 56). The emphasis is on *irri-tability*, the closing off of alternatives, rather than the shunning of all fact and reason, as the quotation has sometimes been inter-preted. Keats was concerned with the egotism that in his times permitted the viewer's obtrusive subjectivity to suffuse and ulti-mately to obscure the object of contemplation. His complex, multiple vision made him resist the concept that any one theory, system, or formula could comprehensively explain the world: "The only means of strengthening one's intellect is to make up one's mind about nothing—to let the mind be a thoroughfare for all thoughts" (Bate 1964, p. 56).

Receptivity is clearly closely allied to the quality of negative capability: "Let us not therefore go hurrying about and collecting honey-bee like, buzzing here and there impatiently from a knowledge of what is to be arrived at: but let us open our leaves like a flower and be passive and receptive" (Bate 1964, p. 59). Margulies (1984), taking up the emphasis on passivity, has proposed negative capability as the *precondition* for empathy and the term *positive capability* as the description of empathy itself.

For Margulies, negative capability is descriptive of the possibility of approaching the patient's narrative with a blank slate, or *tabula rasa*, a mind emptied of its contents. The *tabula rasa* concept, however, has been challenged by many investigators. Margulies himself presents the concepts of *tabula rasa* and negative capability as unattainable ideals. But the argument has been forcibly made, by Karl Popper (1968) among others, that perception is always organized. Organization is intrinsic to mental functioning. In the work of Piaget (1954), the concept of the interplay between the assimilation of information and the accommodation of the internal structures of the mind is implicit.

That the mind possessed of negative capability must be actively open, and not merely blank, is clear from a close reading of Keats' letters, the source of his theoretical discussions. To Keats, Shakespeare is the exemplar of the genius of negative capability. His is the mind that can possess external reality without overlooking its essential qualities, without oversimplifying the vision. Simply clearing the mind of previous assumptions or approaching material from a naive vantage point (as Margulies suggests) does not adequately describe negative capability. The mind is not emptied of assumptions; rather, the information and assumptions are held in abeyance, and the investigator avoids applying closure too quickly. It is the presence of a large body of knowledge that creates an opening for new possibilities. Freud's discoveries in psychoanalysis, for example, originated in part from the conscious or unconscious application in a new context of concepts derived from the Jewish interpretative tradition (Bakan 1965).

An essential prerequisite for a state of useful puzzlement is the sense of hopefulness that sooner or later a surprising, unexpected, or unconventional solution will emerge. A therapist's repeatedly interpreting a theme or a pattern despite the interpretation's having been shown to have had no useful effect is often a sign that the therapist has consciously or unconsciously fallen into a state of hopelessness.

Therapeutically useful puzzlement entails a knowledge of method and theory, keen powers of observation, heightened attention to data rather than to theoretical formulations (i.e., a theory-distant position), the capacity to resist needing to know (i.e., the capacity to avoid applying closure too quickly to the data), and a sense of hopefulness. These attributes are embraced by Keats' concept of negative capability.

CASE EXAMPLE

The following clinical example illustrates some of the factors contributing to empathic experiencing:

In the third month of therapy a young male patient with a history of difficulties with women reported the following dream fragment. He was sitting in the apartment of a former girlfriend. The two were arguing. During the argument, the patient noticed that his girlfriend was wearing oversized red leather gloves. As the therapist listened to the material, he felt slightly repulsed. He attributed this feeling to the imagery of the argument and the red gloves the woman was wearing. Almost simultaneously, he heard the patient comment that his former girlfriend had dressed like a prostitute and had a repulsive way of laughing; she sounded like a cackling witch when she laughed.

In supervision the therapist presented his experience as a possible moment of empathic resonance. He remembered that during the therapy session the images of a phallic woman and of Lady Macbeth had come to mind almost simultaneously; the affect and imagery were immediate and striking, imbuing the experience with a sense of authenticity. The therapist also mentioned that he had read Freud's *Interpretation of Dreams* prior to the session. He wondered whether his reading contributed to his attention to symbols. The supervisor suggested that the therapist may have momentarily identified with an object in the patient's inner world. At the end of the supervisory session, the therapist, as an expression of his puzzlement, remembered an incident in a pathology lecture. The lecturer had remarked that in the early days of microscopy, physicians influenced by the current wisdom believed that they were able to discern the dim outlines of a homunculus, a little man, when they examined human sperm under the microscope.

The therapist's putative empathic experience came up for discussion in supervision eight months later. At this juncture in therapy, the theme had emerged of the patient as a woman in man's clothing, a man without a penis. The patient's childhood memories of his mother dressing him in women's underclothes underscored this theme. The theme itself had come to light in the context of a story that the patient had heard at a party. A woman acquaintance related an incident in which she and a girlfriend had been accosted by an exhibitionist. When the man exposed himself to the two women, they were able to hide their surprise and revulsion. Instead, they laughed in his face. The exhibitionist appeared more shocked and dismayed than did his purported victims. Although others at the party were amused by this anecdote, in which the table had apparently been turned, the patient couldn't help feeling sorry for the exhibitionist.

At this point in therapy, the patient's difficulties with women were felt to contain elements of rage toward his mother, a concern that women would emasculate him, and a fear that his repulsive defect (his unmanliness) would be discovered by women.

The therapist's model of the patient had altered over time. The original model was of the patient as a victim of difficult women. This model had been replaced by one in which the patient was perceived as conflicted about women. The conflict was set against a background of maternal deficiency. The therapist and the supervisor agreed that eight months earlier the therapist had correctly sensed the patient's revulsion. The theme that later emerged had in fact been anticipated, albeit approximately, by the therapist's own imagery. The therapist remembered and was fascinated by the fact that eight months earlier in supervision the theme of little men had arisen in a passing remark.*

In the preceding clinical example, it is possible to identify a number of sources that contributed to the therapist's empathic experience: the therapist's awareness that the patient had a history of difficulty with women, a knowledge of Freud's method of dream analysis, and a familiarity with Shakespeare's *Macbeth*. Because neither the image of Lady Macbeth nor that of the phallic woman was derived directly from the patient's own free associations, it is not possible to assess their accuracy with respect to the patient's experiential state. It is reasonable to assume that imagery derived directly from a patient's own free associations about a dream reflects the patient's inner state more accurately than does understanding derived from a book of dream symbols or from the therapist's own imagination.

The interactional nature of mental functioning makes it difficult to know whether the therapist's experience of revulsion resulted from affective resonance with the patient, whether the affect was intrinsic to imagery conjured up by the therapist, or whether the therapist's affective experience of revulsion and his imaginative experience represent two aspects of a single phenomenon (that is, did affect generate imagery, did imagery generate affect, or do affect and imagery represent aspects of a single event?). Although psychoanalysts employ different frameworks to formulate a theory of affect, they agree that affect and ideation intertwine. Each form of cognition interacts with and alters the other.

Both the pervasive presence of dilemma, or antithesis, and

---

*Katan (1950) has discussed in detail the significance of similar imagery.

the influence of theoretical concepts are apparent in the development of the therapist's model of the patient. The therapist's first model of the patient made room for only victimization. The later, more complex model, which was composed of a hierarchy of stories, made room for the patient as victim (regarding his relationship with his mother) as well as agent (regarding his relationships with women). Because the therapist had a rudimentary appreciation of Freud's dream theory, he imbedded his experience in the context of symbolic *elements* (the phallus, the red leather gloves). The therapist's original conviction that the patient was victimized by women may have contributed to the imagery he experienced. The later, more complex model of the patient as agent *and* victim followed from the therapist's attention to the patient's own imagery. The later model, viewed from a classical, conflict-centered perspective, provided some clarification of the therapist's imaginative experience. Had the therapist employed a self psychology framework, which deemphasizes sexual conflicts, the phallic imagery might have been replaced by other imagery. In this case, the therapist would have used affect and imagery to appreciate the patient's sense of self and experience of the therapist. Such a vantage point might have led the therapist to discover, for example, that he was perceived by the patient as someone who failed (as had the mother) to acknowledge the patient's manliness.

The preceding clinical example lends itself to an examination of the difference between empathy and intuition in terms of imagery. Empathy, a function of the experiencing ego, was earlier described as establishing close emotional contact with the patient; intuition, a function of the observing ego, does the same in the realm of ideas. A therapist's sudden and complex appreciation of a patient's emotional state during a reported quarrel with her daughter might be an example of an empathic experience. The sudden recognition that this quarrel resembles arguments with her mother that the patient had previously reported might be an example of an intuitive experience. Although personal imagery is present in the second example, the emphasis is not on the scenario itself or on the affective quality of the patient's experience but on the parallel structure of two sets of relationships. In intuition, the therapist's affective experience is generated by the elation of discovery to a greater extent than in empathy. Because theoretical constructs may have played a significant role in the formation of these experiences, a therapist's sudden experience of the image of a *vagina dentata* (as in a case reported by Beres and Arlow [1974]) or of a phallic woman (as in the preceding clinical vignette) may be both empathic and intuitive. Most sudden realizations contain both empathic and intuitive components.

Because many conscious and unconscious factors contribute to an empathic experience, such an experience is never an exact replica of a patient's inner state. The preceding example demonstrates that a therapist's personal convictions and use of theoretical frameworks organize the material and the manner in which it is understood. A classical therapist will organize and explain a patient's narrative differently than will a self psychologist. As a result, the therapist's imaginative experience may be different. Because organization is intrinsic to mental functioning, the capacity to hold theory at a distance or in abeyance should not be equated with a theory-free state. Nevertheless, the capacity to do so and to recognize that theories provide only a rough scaffold on which to place information will enable a therapist to pay the necessary, prolonged attention to the patient's narrative. It was Gide who said, "Do not know me too quickly."* Out of the crucible of the therapeutic transaction, which is characterized by periods of hopeful puzzlement, misunderstanding, and empathic experiencing, a hierarchy of unanticipated stories will emerge. The use of theoretical formulations provides not an end point but a middle stage of tentative meaning. Among psychoanalysts of all schools, affect and personal imagery are the common denominators of empathic experiencing.

A PARADIGM FOR DYNAMIC PSYCHOTHERAPY

The literary metaphor is a useful one. Balzac said that every life contains a novel. The therapist may be conceived of as the reader or spectator of the patient's novel or drama. Such metaphors are not new in psychoanalysis. Theoretic constructions like "screen

---

*Quoted in the preface of *The Deer Park* (Mailer 1955).

memory" (Freud 1899) and the "representational world" (Sandler and Rosenblatt 1962) are derived from the theater and cinema. This kind of imagery may also have contributed to such concepts as Lichtenberg's "observation platform" (1981). The therapeutic process and empathy itself have been compared to artistic creation (Beres 1957).

In many case reports, the patient's material is alluded to as an unfolding drama. Elements of a patient's narrative are commonly described metaphorically as personal myth.

Every set of comparisons, however, has its own set of limitations. Frye (1963) has pointed out that the entities that are being compared in a metaphor are never quite identical:

> As for metaphor, where you're really saying "this is that" you are turning your back on logic and reason completely because logically two things can never be the same thing and still remain two things. (p. 11)

There is much that the metaphor of the therapist as reader–spectator of the patient's novel or drama fails to capture. For example, the therapist is in fact an agent in the drama, generating material. The story that emerges in the therapeutic transaction is unanticipated by either participant. Finally, dynamic psychotherapy is a serious and often an unpleasant process.

Such a metaphor does, however, highlight a number of features that are essential for empathic understanding. It emphasizes personal, emotionally evocative imagery rather than technical imagery. Because conflict and dilemma are central themes in literature and drama, the metaphor is an appropriate framework for examining the antithetical issues in a patient's narrative. The reader, like the therapist, must bear with hopeful puzzlement. Although readers may be puzzled at first concerning the author's direction or intent, they remain hopeful that sooner or later a sense of order will emerge: The killer will be identified; the hero will resolve his dilemma. Finally, because such a metaphor avoids technical imagery, it removes the discussion of empathy from the prime area of contention in the debate between traditional psychoanalysts and self psychologists. Regardless of one's theoretic orientation, it is the ability to embrace personal rather than nonpersonal imagery in a clinical situation that determines the measure of one's empathy. It is attention to the details of the patient's own imagery that provides an increasingly accurate appreciation of his or her inner state.

To an extent, a literary or theatrical metaphor is appropriate in addressing whether or not an event reported by the patient really happened. Coleridge (1817) advised audiences to suspend their disbelief when the play began. The particulars of a novel or a play cannot be proved or disproved. One doesn't turn to *Hamlet* to learn about the history of Denmark. But if the reader does suspend his disbelief, he will learn from *Hamlet* what happens to a person who gets caught up in a particular parental conflict. A novel doesn't tell you what actually happened, yet it tells you *what happens.*

Therapists must also suspend their disbelief. A patient's memories occupy a similar position with respect to reality as do events in a novel or a play. The therapist's opinion of the historical reality of a reported event is important. Nevertheless, if one is able to suspend one's disbelief, one will be able to appreciate the patient's experiential state. A patient's memories do reflect a psychological reality.

In the chapters that follow, the analogy of the therapist as reader of the patient's novel will be employed to examine the course of psychotherapy. The purpose of this analogy is not to provide a new paradigm that replaces the useful and necessary sets of orderly relations derived from existing theories. The purpose is to present dynamic psychotherapy in a context that deemphasizes the nonpersonal imagery of theory without excluding existing theoretical contributions. It is a flexible metaphor. Both traditional psychoanalysts and self psychologists commonly have recourse to it in clinical reports. Its strength lies in its being sufficiently fanciful and inexact that it will not be mistaken by the reader as anything more than an allusion.

A therapist's growing appreciation of the nature of dynamic psychotherapy can be compared to a reader's comprehension of literature. As Frye (1963) wrote: "All themes and characters and stories . . . belong to one big interlocking family. You can see how true this is if you think of such words as tragedy or comedy or satire or romance: certain typical ways in which stories get told." A reader is always being reminded of another novel he read or a movie he saw. Although such associations are mainly unconscious, they do suggest that "You don't just read one novel or poem after another, but that there's a real subject to be studied, as there is in a science, and that the more you read, the more you learn about literature as a whole." (p. 18)

Part Two

Empathic Understanding
in the Clinical Setting

Chapter Six

Entering the Patient's World

The capacity to imagine oneself in the patient's world and to appreciate the patient's experiential state enhances empathic responsiveness. This begins in the initial phase of therapy, which has been compared to the opening moves of a game of chess (Freud 1913), to the beginning of a journey into an uncharted wilderness (Hollender 1965), and to the start of a mountain climbing expedition with the two participants bound together by a single rope (Basch 1980). Very often the therapist and the patient bring unwarranted assumptions to their first meeting. As with any endeavor in which something new and unpredictable is expected to emerge, they begin with a mixture of hope, anticipation, pleasure, and dread. Along the way, their aims may diverge or their roles may be reversed. Periods of mutual assistance may give way to periods of antagonism or indifference. Although the course of psychotherapy is never as orderly as it may appear to be in a textbook exposition of the subject, it is possible to outline a progression of events and maneuvers that propel therapy forward.

In the preceding chapters, the therapist's stance has been described as an oscillation between the position of close emotional harmony with the patient's inner life and that of objective, intellectual evaluation of the patient's predicament—an oscillation between acting as participant and observer, between listening from within and from without. In the initial stages of therapy, with therapist and patient virtual strangers,t he therapist's position is of necessity that of external observer. In order to begin to take on a more involved role, the therapist is dependent upon gaining entrance to the patient's inner world by means of the story the patient has to tell.

OVERCOMING INTERFERENCES

Overcoming impediments to the narrative is an integral component of eliciting the patient's story. Patterns or affective states that interfere with the patient's talking need to be identified as they arise and communicated to the patient. In the initial stage, because very little is known about the patient, the therapist is limited to such straightforward, uncomplicated statements as, "You seem uncomfortable," "You're silent," or "You appear angry." However, such statements when delivered nonjudgmentally in a tone that also expresses puzzled interest, are usually sufficient to generate a dialogue or to remove an interference. In addition, because the therapist is often not yet a significant character in the patient's world (or the significance of the part one plays is not yet apparent), these statements should minimize the therapist's own contribution to the relationship. A statement such as, "You seem uncomfortable *with me*" brings the therapist into the picture too quickly. In those instances in which the therapist becomes immediately entangled in the patient's world (i.e., a strong and immediate transference reaction), the dialogue generated by the therapist's simply acknowledging the presence of an interference (such as "You seem uncomfortable") will sooner or later give rise to a discussion of the therapist's involvement.

At this stage, a series of interventions should begin with a clearly stated observation. Elaborate interventions are the end result of a complex understanding of the patient and are appropriate only in the late phases of therapy. Particularly in the initial phase of therapy, interventions need to be tempered by the ever-present awareness that the patient perceives the therapist to be both a confidant and an intruder. The explicit or implicit aim of an intervention is to enlist the patient's aid in understanding what is happening in therapy. Presenting patients with a complete interpretation or explanation infantilizes them and at this point will often be based on incorrect assumptions. These points are illustrated in the following case discussions:

An 18-year-old girl suffering from periods of inattentiveness and excessive daydreaming was brought for consultation by her parents. Shortly after entering the therapist's office, she became silent. After a brief waiting period, the therapist remarked on her silence in a puzzled tone. The girl responded by closing her eyes and confessing that she had noticed disturbing patterns of light moving across the ceiling of the office.

In the middle phase of therapy, with a patient considered to be a good candidate for an insight-oriented approach, the therapist might have encouraged the patient to put into words her fantasies with respect to the moving patterns of light. In this instance, however, uncertain about the patient's capacity not to misinterpret perceptions and sensing in her a high level of anxiety, the therapist explained that the patterns were caused by sunlight reflecting off the rooftops of the cars passing by his window. This explanation in fact allayed her anxiety. The patient was able to put aside her immediate concerns and to talk about her problems.

An affable business executive began his initial interview by blandly announcing that he had been fired from his last six positions. His last employer "accused" him of having a "human relations problem." His secretary, however, considered him to be more intelligent and better educated than his colleagues. The patient then proceeded to talk at length about a recent visit to a family doctor who had a loudspeaker in his waiting room. Patients were called into his consulting room by his announcing their names over the loudspeaker. The patient described this procedure as a "typical example of inhuman behavior."

Tuning in to this statement, the therapist asked the patient whether he considered inhuman behavior to be typical of all physicians, including the therapist. The patient responded by berating the therapist for drawing attention to himself rather than focusing on the patient's problems.

In reviewing this session with his supervisor, the therapist recognized that he had brought himself too hastily into the patient's story. His intervention presumed an understanding of the patient without allowing for the latter's participation. A nonjudgmental statement expressing puzzled interest concerning the thrust of the patient's narrative might have been more useful in generating a worthwhile dialogue. Later in therapy, a common theme emerged that brought to light an association between the patient's chief complaint, the story of the loudspeaker, and the patient's attack on the therapist: a need to maintain control of his relationships for fear of being abandoned or ignored.

EXPANDING ON THE PATIENT'S STORIES

In addition to overcoming interferences, the therapist also encourages the patient to recreate as fully as possible significant episodes that surface in the narrative. As in a novel or play, the patient's world is filled with imagery, atmosphere, and a multitude of characters interacting with one another. Patients should be encouraged from the very beginning to give a detailed account of their problems and to anchor them in the evocative personal settings in which the problems surfaced. In doing so, the patient moves the narrative from the general to the particular, from the plural to the singular. In the case, for example, of a patient who complains of recurrent depression (an abstract nonpersonal concept), the therapist's aim should be to elicit the particular setting in which a single recent bout of depression surfaced. In the case of a patient who complains of being fired from several positions, the therapist's aim should be to elicit the events pertaining to a recent dismissal. In a novel, plot and character are introduced not by the use of adjectives or general statements but by the presentation of the main characters as they interact in a single imaginable sequence.*

This approach permits therapists imaginatively to begin to situate themselves inside the patient's world and to sample the patient's state of mind in the context of the concrete, particular setting described. At first, this imaginative step away from the position of external observer is mainly willed and conscious. Furthermore, because one has not yet built up a complex conceptual model of the patient (and therefore, one's empathic understanding of the patient is less comprehensive than it will be later in therapy), one steps into the patient's world not as the patient but as an observer on the scene.** Nevertheless, this step makes it possible for the therapist to experience an emotional state similar to that of the patient. In addition, expanding on their stories makes it possible for patients to reveal and to reexperience more accurately than they would otherwise the emotions associated with the events described. A simple statement from the patient that his father had died six months ago may trigger very little affect in him. A recreation in words of the room, the time, the climate in which the patient learned about or observed his father's death may bring to mind one or two poignant scenes, effectively transforming a bland factual statement into a vivid experience. For example, a patient who claimed to be

---

*Because it refers explicitly to visual imagery and may therefore capture aspects of nonverbal or preverbal behavior more clearly than the metaphor of the novel does, the analogy of a film may be in some senses more apt.

**In the clinical section of this book, the more abstract, less emotionally evocative perspective will continue to be referred to as that of the "external observer." The phrase "observer on the scene" will be used as the new oppositional term. It will replace such terms as "participant," "as the patient," and "placing oneself in the patient's shoes" that were employed in the chapters on theory. The new term has the advantages of capturing the approximateness of the close emotional harmony between therapist and patient (an approximateness that lessens as therapy progresses), of emphasizing the importance of setting, and, as will become apparent in later chapters, of shedding light on transference and countertransference patterns.

depressed because her doctor had put her on a hormone supplement was asked to describe in detail the visit to her doctor. As she described it, she suddenly remembered how defective she felt when she learned about her medical disorder. The point is well made in the poem *The Cool Web* by Robert Graves that discursive language has the capacity to suppress imagery and emotions (quoted in Allison et al. 1983, p. 635).

> . . . We have speech to chill the angry day,
> And speech to dull the rose's cruel scent.
> ....
> There's a cool web of language winds us in
> Retreat from too much joy, or too much fear.

Although the chief complaint often provides the therapist with an initial window into the patient's world, other events may also provide useful windows. Although there is no formula one can use to help select incidents worth expanding on, a rough set of guidelines is provided by the novelist E. M. Forster's statement that if there were no wedding or funeral bells, a writer wouldn't know where to stop (Frye 1963, p. 14). By this he meant that births, deaths, and other periods of transition are the major events in everybody's life. Expanding such events into evocative dramas is invariably useful.

The following examples illustrate the usefulness of imaginatively stepping into the patient's world as an observer on the scene:

> In his initial interview, Mr. Miller, a 65-year-old real estate broker suffering from depression, mentioned several times that his mother had died when he was 12 years old. He needed very little prompting to describe in detail the events pertaining to her death. His mother had died of leukemia in the Depression era. At the time, the family lived over his father's grocery store in a two-bedroom apartment. Mr. Miller's mother was bedridden for several months. During her illness, it was his responsibility to bring her her evening meal. On the evening of her death, he remembered carrying a tray of food into her bedroom and accidentally knocking over a set of

ledger books on her bedside table. He recalled that that evening he was anxious to tell her how much money he had earned that day selling newspapers. Although she was pale and thin and could barely move, when she heard that her son had earned a dollar in tips, she sat up in bed and kissed him. Mr. Miller's father had worked late that night. By the time he came up to see his wife, she was dead. With a mixture of sadness and pride, Mr. Miller stated that he was the last person ever to talk to her.

When the therapist asked about the ledger books on the bedside table, Mr. Miller explained that his mother kept the accounts for the family business and had worked until the day she died. Both parents worked extremely long hours. It still troubled him that the family had been too poor to send her to a proper treatment center.

In this instance, the therapist had been alerted to a significant event by the patient's many references to it. The detailed description of Mr. Miller's last visit with his mother enabled Mr. Miller to reexperience the emotions associated with it and also enabled the therapist to share the patient's perspective. As a result, the therapist was able to understand an important factor contributing to Mr. Miller's recent depression, which coincided with a period of enforced bedrest following a back injury. The physical disability had interfered with his compulsive work habits, habits that were motivated by a need to hold on to his mother's attention and to overcome the poverty to which he attributed her death.

In the following example the therapist used his own imaginative capacity to experientially grasp the patient's emotional state:

On a Monday morning, a resident in psychiatry, returning to the ward on which he worked, was informed by the head nurse that a young girl diagnosed as catatonic had been admitted on the weekend. Since her admission, she had refused to speak or to eat.

The head nurse accompanied the resident to the dining room where he was introduced to the patient who was sitting

motionless at one of the tables. Several orderlies were push-
ing food into her mouth, and a number of patients were
standing by, watching to see the outcome of her ordeal. When
the therapist sat down beside her, he sensed the animosity of
the people around her.

"I wouldn't be surprised," he said to the patient, "if you
told me that you believed the food to be poisoned."

The patient laughed. Speaking for the first time, she said,
"You're crazy, doctor."

That she talked and that she then allowed herself to be fed led
the therapist to believe that his statement had conveyed an
empathic appreciation of her predicament. In this example, the
dining room and the people in it provided the imagery for him.
It was only a small step for the therapist to imagine himself as a
patient in the dining room setting.

In the following example, the therapist was alerted to a pertinent sequence of events by the similarity between the patient's
story and a well-known biblical story.*

Mr. Blackwell, a 60-year-old engineer with a medical history
of several recent fainting spells for which a medical cause had
not been discovered, was referred by his neurologist for a psychiatric assessment. He began the initial interview by stating
that it was unlikely that the fainting spells were caused by
stress. His home life was uneventful, and there were no problems at work. Mr. Blackwell had held his present position for
more than three years. In the past, his usual pattern had been
to take a new job every two years. These job changes were often associated with his moving from one country to another.
At the therapist's request, he described his brief syncopal attacks, which had all occurred in the bathroom while he was
shaving. Asked whether he had ever had similar symptoms in
the past, Mr. Blackwell replied jokingly that he had once felt
faint in Burma during a heat wave but had never fainted.
When the therapist expressed an interest in his exploits in
Burma, Mr. Blackwell volunteered the following story.

---

*In a similar vein, Koff (1957) reported using the imagery of the novel
Robinson Crusoe to appreciate the inner state of an autistic patient.

During World War II, he and his older brother had been stationed in a camp located north of Rangoon as officers in a regiment made up of soldiers who had volunteered to serve in the army to gain their release from prison. During a target practice, his brother was shot and killed. Although some of the men believed that one of the ex-prisoners had murdered him, the brother's death was officially labeled an accident. Shortly after the incident, Mr. Blackwell was transferred to another regiment.

Mr. Blackwell felt that after many years he had been at last able to put the event out of his mind, but he did believe that his father (a former soldier himself) was still writing to the British government demanding that they investigate the murder. The older brother was the father's favorite.

Struck by the similarity between elements in Mr. Blackwell's story (i.e., his wandering and the death of a sibling who was the father's favorite) and the story of Cain and Abel, the therapist decided to focus his attention on the scene in which Mr. Blackwell had received the news of his brother's death. He asked Mr. Blackwell to describe the weather, the setting, and the manner in which the news was conveyed to him. Mr. Blackwell remembered that he hadn't gone to the rifle range that morning because it was so hot that he decided to stay in his tent. A soldier had brought him the news. He remembered a numbness setting in when the soldier identified the killer. It felt as if the soldier expected him to avenge his brother's death, an action he knew he would not be able to carry out. He had been relieved when he was transferred to another unit.

"It's not a pleasant memory," said the patient. He was tearful.

"And you have been wandering from country to country ever since," the therapist said.

Mr. Blackwell immediately recognized the allusion to the story of Cain and Abel. When he remembered that one of the soldiers volunteered to slit the killer's throat, he connected it to his shaving in the bathroom. In addition, he suddenly understood a piece of behavior that had never made sense to him before: Despite his high ranking in the companies that had employed him, out of a vague sense of shame and guilt he had always refused to have a name plate placed on his door.

The patient did not return for a second session, but he did receive follow-up care from his neurologist. Many months later the neurologist informed the psychiatrist that the patient's symptoms had cleared.

Well-known themes often come to light in therapy. Nevertheless, each narrative represents a new novel or drama with its own setting and its own set of characters. Although *Faust* and *Macbeth* may convey to an audience what it feels like to lose one's soul in the process of gaining a kingdom, the casts and the locations of the two plays are utterly different. Patients' expanding on the specific and concrete stories contained in their narratives gives them the opportunity to vividly reexperience their stories. It also enables the therapist, stepping into the narrative as an observer on the scene, to appreciate an aspect of the patient's inner state.

OBSERVING THE FLOW OF THE NARRATIVE

The therapist's usual position, particularly in the initial stage of therapy, is of necessity that of external observer. From this more abstract and less emotionally evocative position, one is able to consider the *relationship* between the many elements in the patient's narrative. One can study its general flow just as playgoers occasionally step back from the scenes that have captured their attention to consider the drama as a whole. The major function is that of pattern matching, looking for themes that bring stories together.

The complexity of the functions associated with the position of external observer stems from the need to take into consideration a wide variety of factors. Sometimes it is useful to inform the patient of a common theme (e.g., "You sound sad" or "Your stories are all about failure"). Sometimes the therapist may arrive inferentially at an approximate appreciation of the patient's experiential state as a whole. For example, if the stories reiterate a theme of being wronged, the therapist may be able to begin to sense how a patient who speaks in this vein feels. At other times, the therapist may discover a paradoxical state, that is, a situation in which something is missing. For example, the patient may talk about being wronged, but the expected sense of sadness or victimization is missing in the therapeutic relationship. The therapist may notice a contiguous relationship between subjects. For example, the patient may talk about sitting on the potty as a child whenever the therapist points out a silence in the sessions. It is important to note that it is from the perspective of external observer that the therapist discovers windows into the patient's world—significant scenarios worth expanding on—that prompt a shift to the role of observer on the scene. The ways in which significant incidents come to light are many. The patient may alert the therapist directly to the significance of a memory. For example, a patient complained of neck pain following a discussion with his wife concerning her wish to have children. The patient himself admitted that his symptom related to his having had to care for his siblings as an adolescent. After exploring the patient's chief complaint with respect to setting, the therapist encouraged him to expand on a troubling incident with his siblings. Indeed, the patient considered them to be a pain in the neck.

Although the relationship between a reported incident and the patient's difficulties may not be immediately apparent, the patient's repeated mention of it may alert the therapist to its significance. Or it may be a chance remark that stands out from the rest of the narrative and directs the therapist to a relevant story, as illustrated in the oblique reference to Burma in the case illustration related earlier. The therapist's identifying a general theme for the patient may also trigger an important memory. For example, when the therapist told her that her stories centered on her own destructiveness, a middle-aged woman suddenly remembered an incident from her childhood in which her mother had placed herself in jeopardy to ensure the patient's safety. As external observer, the therapist monitors the patient's reactions, taking care not to be overly intrusive.

Encouraging the patient to depict in detail an episode or a series of episodes and imaginatively placing oneself in the patient's situation are only occasional endeavors, particularly at this stage in therapy. The patient may not yet be prepared to share or reexperience a painful memory, or to face its implications. Details in these areas will emerge later in therapy when the patient begins to feel at ease. Only then will the focus of the stories become less obscure. The patient who blamed her depression on hormones prescribed by her doctor needed time before she could reveal to herself or to her therapist that she had suffered a blow to her self-esteem.

As has been stated earlier, the therapist oscillates between the positions of external observer and observer on the scene. For example, at first the therapist listened to Mr. Blackwell as external observer. When the patient described the incident of his brother's death, the therapist shifted to the position of observer on the scene. Afterward, shifting back to the perspective of external observer, the therapist was able to discover the overall similarity between Mr. Blackwell's story and the biblical theme.

As therapy progresses beyond these initial stages, the therapist's functions become increasingly complex. The more windows one discovers into the patient's world, the more comprehensive one's empathic appreciation and one's conceptual model of the patient become. With time, the therapist is able to enter the patient's world more as the patient than as observer on the scene. In addition, one's appreciation of the factors contributing to interferences becomes increasingly complex. The function of pattern matching encompasses not only the narrative and the therapeutic relationship but also the therapist's own state of mind. It is from the control-booth perspective of external observer that the therapist decides whether to identify general or paradoxical themes or interferences, or whether to encourage the patient to expand on significant statements.

THE METHOD OF DATA GATHERING

Two methods of data gathering have been generally proposed. The associative method is that of following the narrative and asking the patient to expand on statements or incidents as they appear in the narrative. The medical model approach consists of a prearranged series of questions grouped under such headings as chief complaint, birth history, education, and personal history. Therapists often employ the associative method to start with, switching to the more structured medical model style of questioning if the patient's case turns out to be urgent (e.g., if the patient shows signs of psychosis or organicity).

The associative method of data gathering is preferable to the medical model approach because it gives the patient the freedom to discuss problems without adhering to a specific format. It is important for therapists to introduce the associative method with the clarification that they will pose comments or questions whenever they consider it useful to do so. They should also confirm that all patients present their problems differently; otherwise, the patient may be concerned about straying from an imagined normative path. The therapist needs to monitor the degree to which the absence of an imposed order is disturbing to the patient and to contribute to the dialogue with questions and comments. Toward the end of the initial session, the therapist may want to gently apply the brakes to the narrative, rather than moving into new, potentially disturbing material.

The associative method makes it possible for stories to emerge at relevant points in the narrative. The juxtaposition of stories provides the therapist with clues concerning the relationship between the stories and their relative significance. Furthermore, selecting significant statements and encouraging the patient to expand on them provides the therapist with a richer appreciation of the patient's inner state than does the patient's responding to a prearranged sequence of questions. For example, asking patients to talk about their parents shortly after inquiring about their birth history often gives rise to a lifeless description. On the other hand, asking them to expand on events pertaining to their chief complaint (or other incidents) may provide the therapist with a vivid portrayal of family members in the context of a concrete, specific scenario.

THE ARRANGEMENTS OF THERAPY

In the preceding sections, the initial interview or interviews and the initial phase of psychotherapy were not clearly differentiated. Indeed, the therapist's role and the process itself are not significantly different in the two stages. The division between them is usually established by discussing with the patient the aims and procedures of therapy. Such a discussion often takes place toward the end of the first interview or after several sessions of data gathering.

If a trial of psychotherapy is indicated, the therapist's next step is to outline the aims and procedures of psychotherapy after indicating that it may be helpful. The discussion is commonly introduced with such phrases as "It might be helpful for us to learn more about your problems" or "It might be helpful for us to discover and learn about aspects of yourself that you may not be aware of." The so-called fundamental rule—that is, the instructions to the patient to express freely, without censorship or concern for logic or syntax, thoughts and sensations (including feelings toward the therapist)—should be represented as a liberty (albeit a liberty useful to therapy) rather than as a requirement.

Outlining their contribution to therapy is not significantly different from encouraging patients at the first meeting to talk freely about their problems. Free association does not represent a new form of communication but, rather, an occasional occurrence. Patients need to be informed that as they talk a thought, sensation, or dream that appears to be unrelated to the rest of the narrative or that they may choose not to communicate may come to mind; that such apparently extraneous thoughts are common occurrences in daily life; and that in therapy putting such thoughts into words may facilitate an understanding of their symptoms. The capacity to let oneself free-associate is facilitated, not simply by the therapist's exposition of the fundamental rule but by the patient's growing appreciation of its usefulness. As well, therapists need to monitor their own interventions so as not to inhibit this capacity. Statements such as "I don't understand how topic A leads to topic B," especially if they stem from discomfort with puzzlement, may inhibit patients from talking freely. Although trust develops only with time, the therapist should also inform patients that their disclosures will remain confidential.

It is incorrect for a physician to assume that a patient who has suffered a heart attack is able to assimilate an explanation of the diagnosis and regimen shortly after the event. Similarly, it would be incorrect for the therapist to assume that a single discussion of the goals and procedures of psychotherapy is sufficient to clarify their nature. The patient's appreciation of the therapeutic process may need to be heightened by reiterating its aims and regulations on one or two occasions when a useful discovery comes to light—that is, by illustrating an aim or a procedural principle in the context of what has just happened in the session. For example, when a patient discovers that his behavior toward his son is influenced by a recently uncovered memory of a relationship difficulty with his father, it is important to assess the degree to which the patient appreciates the *general* concept that unconscious memories influence present-day behavior. It is often useful to reiterate this principle in the context of the patient's discovery. As well, pointing out the way in which free-associating contributed to this discovery serves to alter the patient's appreciation of the fundamental rule. Although at first it is considered a liberty, with time the patient comes to understand it as a useful tool of therapy. Indicating to the patient that a story concerning his father and one concerning his son were juxtaposed strengthens the patient's appreciation of the workings of therapy. It is senseless to interpret a dream if the patient believes that dreams are communications from heaven. An appreciation of general psychological concepts, psychological mindedness, develops as therapy progresses.

What is particularly difficult to convey to patients is that bringing previously unrecognized memories to awareness may relieve them of their symptoms. Although therapists do make such claims at the outset, it is often not until patients experience an improved state of mind that they begin to appreciate the nature of the process.

THE THERAPIST'S ATTITUDE

The therapist's attitude toward the patient is an essential component of the forward progress of therapy. In the psychoanalytic literature, such technical terms as *neutrality, the therapeutic alliance,* and *the real relationship* have been used to describe the dispassionate compassion felt to be an essential component of the therapist's repertory. In this chapter the patient's opening narrative has been compared to an unfamiliar novel or drama. It follows that the therapist should approach the patient's story with the same curiosity, fascination, and interest that a reader experiences with a new novel. Just as the reader may lose interest in the novel he is reading, the therapist may lose interest in the patient. Psychologically speaking, the therapist and the patient may not be in the same room. Although unremitting fascination represents an unattainable ideal, an absence of interest should alert therapists to the presence of factors (in themselves and in their patients) that may be interfering with therapy. Interest and fascination motivate therapists to use all their senses to will themselves or to let themselves be drawn into the patient's world.

In the following example, the therapist's permitting himself to be drawn into the patient's world led to the discovery of the interesting and relevant story that lay behind what at first appeared to be a routine complaint:

A resident in psychiatry was called to examine Mr. Whiteside, an elderly male patient on a surgical ward, because the staff felt he was unmanageable. When the resident arrived, one of the nurses informed him that Mr. Whiteside had insisted that he be allowed to use the bathroom. When he was refused permission to do so because of his post-surgical status, he had angrily hurled a bedpan at one of the orderlies. Rather than use a bedpan, he had soiled the bedsheets.

When the psychiatrist entered his room, Mr. Whiteside asked whether he intended to punish him for misbehaving. The resident responded by stating that he was merely interested in hearing what had happened. Mr. Whiteside began to complain of mistreatment at the hands of the hospital staff and to complain about authorities in general, whom he referred to sarcastically as "the smart guys at the top." Placing himself imaginatively in the patient's situation, the psychiatrist experienced a sense of humiliation and helplessness behind the rage. As Mr. Whiteside talked on, the setting of his complaints shifted from the hospital ward to an Air Force base during World War II where he had served in the RAF as a member of a contingent of pilots who had received their initial training in Australia. The authorities failed to realize that pilots trained in Australia had not had sufficient opportunity to fly in inclement conditions. As a result, several Australian pilots sent out on a mission during a storm became confused and crashed.

At the therapist's request, Mr. Whiteside described a mission he had been sent on whose purpose was to intercept enemy bombers. At one point during the flight, he recalled, he momentarily lost his bearings. He had regained control quickly, but he remembered almost wetting his pants. Fortunately, pilots were sent out on missions with a bottle planted between their legs. Mr. Whiteside felt that the authorities didn't want their "precious" planes to be soiled but didn't seem to be perturbed about the loss of a life. When Mr. Whiteside had finished his story, the psychiatrist commented that soiling a plane or a bedsheet was a minor issue compared to the loss of a life. In the end, Mr. Whiteside volunteered to use a bedpan when necessary.

An actor's performance is influenced by the audience's response. Similarly, an interest in patients encourages them to talk. In the preceding clinical example, the therapist felt that his interest in the patient led to a significant disclosure.

SUMMARY

The therapist's major tasks in the initial phase of therapy are to gain access to the patient's world by pointing out patterns in the interaction that reflect an interference and by drawing out the patient's story into dramatic action sequences. In these interactions, therapists need to bear in mind that the patient perceives them both as confidant and intruder. They should phrase their interventions in a manner that encourages the patient to play an active role in the treatment process.

The initial interview (or interviews) and the initial phase of psychotherapy are not clearly distinguishable. A discussion of the aims and procedures of therapy represents an approximate division between the two stages. One of the therapist's tasks is to monitor the patient's psychological mindedness.

As well as imaginatively transporting himself into the patient's world as an observer on the scene, the therapist must also pay attention to the narrative as a whole (including the relationship *between* the patient's stories and thoughts). As observer on the scene, the therapist is able to appreciate (albeit approximately and superficially) aspects of the patient's experiential state with respect to specific incidents. As external observer, the therapist is at times able to experientially understand the patient's state of mind as a whole.

These functions and perspectives represent the major roles the therapist employs not only in the initial phase but throughout therapy. However, as therapy progresses, these tasks become increasingly complex, requiring an integration of an increasing volume of data and attention to the ways in which the therapist becomes entangled as more than a neutral observer in the patient's world.

An increasing number of opportunities to transport oneself into the patient's world and to appreciate imaginatively the patient's experiential state contributes to an increasingly comprehensive empathic appreciation of the patient.

Chapter Seven

Empathy and Levels of Understanding

The more memories one uncovers, the more complex and accurate one's empathic understanding of the patient becomes. Whether recent or from childhood, remembered events constitute the largest part of the patient's narrative. Every act of remembering, however, includes an element of distortion. The question "Did it actually happen that way?" qualifies the therapist's ability to assume an empathic stance. At one level, the therapist needs to recognize that memories do contain distortions. The patient's description of a family argument may bear little resemblance to the patient's parents' (or any other observer's) description of the same scene. At another level, the therapist needs to appreciate that the way in which the patient reports an event does represent a psychological reality (that is, the therapist needs to suspend his disbelief). When a patient reports that his parents were perfect, the therapist needs to empathically appreciate what it feels like to believe (or to need to believe) that one's parents were perfect. For the patient who relates an episode that led him to believe, rightly or wrongly, that his father preferred his older brother to himself, such a belief continues to play a role in his life. Therapists need to incorporate the patient's convictions in their conceptual model of the patient. Whether it is accurate or inaccurate, a set of beliefs, supported by a series of remembered episodes, a constructed narrative, is in itself a motivating force in the patient's life.

As therapy progresses, new data emerges and remembered episodes that were understood in one way are now understood in another. The shift in emphasis may be minimal, or an entirely new theme may be introduced. In the light of such changes a therapist who, for example, during one phase of therapy empathizes with a patient's conviction that his parents were perfect knows that he may need at a later stage to shift scenes and empathize with an altered conviction. The patient's state of mind is influenced not only by remembered episodes but also by episodes that have been actively forgotten or split off (i.e., unconscious or disavowed memories). As new material emerges, the patient's memories and explanations appear to undergo a metamorphosis; the story as well as the meaning of the story shifts.

A simple example of such a metamorphosis was presented in the preceding chapter. As her interview progressed, the middle-aged woman, who had at first attributed her depression to medication, recognized that a diminished sense of self-esteem (precipitated by her receiving an unfavorable medical diagnosis) contributed to her symptoms. In this example, the patient's willingness to examine the onset of her depression in terms of imagery and setting (i.e., in the context of her medical appointment) was sufficient to generate an altered and more comprehensive appreciation of her state of mind.

The manner in which a patient's stories are altered is not a random process. Distortions have a purpose. Although the therapist may at first be unaware of the distortions or of the factors that necessitated them, as therapy progresses such factors become apparent. In the preceding example, further discussions with the patient revealed that she needed to attribute her complaint to an external factor (i.e., she needed to believe that her symptoms were the side effect of the medication her doctor prescribed) to maintain her self-esteem; that she needed to ward off the painful conviction, triggered by her doctor's diagnosis of a medical disorder, that her body was defective; and that the seeds of this conviction had been planted in her childhood. As a rule, a person resorts to distortions (which may be consciously or unconsciously motivated) to maintain self-esteem, to ward off painful emotions or conflicts, or to maintain a belief system with respect to parents or others that bolsters his or her sense of self.* In psychoanalytic theory, mental functions that serve to maintain such distortions are referred to as *mechanisms of defense.*

Because the patient's stories alter over time and new stories emerge in the course of therapy, Freud (1931) compared the therapeutic process to an archaeological expedition. The title of this chapter, "Empathy and Levels of Understanding," acknowledges the usefulness of Freud's comparison. Therapy has also been described variously as a process in which past events are *reconstructed* in the presence of an empathic other; as an experience in which patients, employing more advanced cognitive functions than were available to them as children, reexamine the events of their formative years; and as a transaction in which patients are permitted to grow (i.e., to overcome fixations) under the aegis of an understanding therapist (Basch 1980, 1981). Such descriptions, however, do not sufficiently emphasize that therapy is rooted in the present (Wetzler 1985). An accurate reconstruction of the patient's history represents an unattainable ideal. In therapy, the patient's stories do, however, steadily become less inaccurate. By undoing some of their distortions or defensive maneuvers (i.e., by the therapist and patient working together against forces that oppose the unfolding of new material), therapy moves patients toward an approximate appreciation of their history.

Indeed, therapy needs to be viewed as both a reconstruction of the patient's past and a deconstruction, or analysis, of the patient's patterns, stories, and convictions as they are presently understood.** This alternating perspective leads to a fuller ap-

---

*Sometimes distortions are generated by a wish to maintain a *low* self-esteem.

**The term *deconstruction* is sometimes associated with the work of Jacques Derrida (1977). However, in this chapter it is used in its literal sense (i.e., "to break down" or "to analyze into component parts").

preciation of the manner in which these patterns, stories, and convictions developed. To hold such views simultaneously and evenhandedly, however, is difficult. The notion of objective reality, of what actually happened, is bound to obtrude. It is difficult to hear a story of incarceration at Auschwitz without regarding it as more than a fiction recreated from an irretrievable past. Similarly, it is difficult to hear a patient suddenly rage at his father's occasional unavailability without wondering whether the therapist's recently mentioned vacation plan is the significant issue. The shifting and evolving story demands of therapists a stance that requires them to oscillate between suspending their disbelief and holding on to it, and between viewing the therapeutic process as both a reconstruction of the past and a deconstruction of the present. In addition, one needs to bring all one knows about the patient from one perspective to the other and from one episode to others. This stance partially frees therapists from the constricting notion of objective reality and enhances their appreciation of subjectivity. In a sense, the therapist needs to hold on to a pluralistic view of reality. For example, a reported argument with an employer may refer not only to the patient's relationship with him but also to the therapeutic relationship, as well as to incidents of which the therapist is not yet aware. The ensuing sections of this chapter will examine specifically the manner in which the therapist's appreciation becomes increasingly complex in the context of the patient's evolving (and devolving) narrative.

DECONSTRUCTION AND INTEGRATION

The course of therapy is characterized by periods during which new material emerges and by periods of integrative work. The emergence of new material throws into question a preceding explanation for a symptom, generating puzzlement in the therapist. During periods of integrative work, the new material is incorporated into what is already understood. The fragments are pieced together into a meaningful whole. The therapist must speculate on the relationship between the various fragments.

The questions of the interrelationship between themes must be kept in mind even as the therapist imaginatively enters the patient's world with respect to a given episode. Once again, the therapist must oscillate between positions. This imaginative exercise generates useful questions. Toward the end of a period of integrative work, the patient's understanding becomes consistent at a more complex level. At the same time, new material is generated and the cycle is repeated.

The following two clinical vignettes, in which a segment of narrative is examined with respect to one or two significant episodes in a patient's life, illustrate the manner in which such cycles evolve. In the remainder of this chapter, these two cases will be followed over a brief span of therapy to demonstrate the increasing complexity of the therapist's understanding.

In her initial interview Mrs. Abell, a pleasant, composed young housewife, stated that for more than a week she had awakened in the middle of the night in a state of panic. She attributed these attacks to the stress of caring for a new baby. She had given birth to her first child, a son, six weeks prior to the onset of her symptoms. The child was healthy and normal, and Mrs. Abell indicated that she loved him very much. She described herself as a timid person who avoided unfamiliar situations and yet denied experiencing anxiety or feelings of insecurity about her new duties as a mother. Mrs. Abell's own mother had recently arrived from another city to help out. However, Mrs. Abell believed that she was capable of managing without her mother's assistance. Mrs. Abell's father had died one and a half years earlier; he had suffered from carcinoma of the lung. The patient revealed that she and her mother occasionally discussed Mrs. Abell's husband, a law student, who tended to spend very little time with the baby. Mrs. Abell did not feel that this constituted any problem in the home.

During the interview, the therapist was attuned to a feeling of being kept at a distance by the patient. Attempts to evoke imagery and setting about the panic attacks or an episode in which the patient and her mother were taking care of the child did not provide the therapist with an imaginative point of empathic entry into the patient's world. On the surface Mrs. Abell's explanation for her symptoms (i.e., that they were caused by the stress of caring for a new baby) seemed straightforward and consistent. On the other hand, her composure, her expressed enjoyment of taking care of her son, and her denial of any difficulties in her new role as a mother led the therapist to believe that Mrs. Abell's stated reason for her panic attacks was insufficient to account for the severity of her symptoms.

Toward the middle of the session, the therapist encouraged the patient to once again describe a recent panic attack. He explicitly asked her to imagine herself in her bedroom and to relate her thoughts and sensations as if she just awakened in a state of terror.

"It's just scary," she said, "I'm very frightened. As if I'm about to die."

"What made you think you might die?"

"I don't know," she said.

"What would cause you to die?" the therapist asked.

"I don't know. I guess I couldn't breathe. I think I was afraid of suffocating, as if there was a hole in my chest."

For the first time during the interview, Mrs. Abell lost her composure and began to cry. The therapist waited. When she stopped crying, he asked whether any thoughts came to mind. She answered that she had thought of her father's dying in the hospital. She remembered that her father had had difficulty breathing and that the doctor had inserted a drainage tube into his chest. The therapist encouraged Mrs. Abell to describe in detail the hospital visit with her father. It was this account that at last provided him with the emotionally evocative setting he needed—that is, the opening chapter—to empathically appreciate some aspect of her experiential state.

The therapist might well have used other routes to find a point of entry into the patient's world. For example, following the novelist E. M. Forster's dictum referred to earlier that births and deaths constitute the major turning points in everybody's life, the therapist might have chosen to overlook the patient's chief complaint and instead to address himself immediately to the issue of her father's death. However, the route the therapist followed in Mrs. Abell's case turned out to be useful. New information came to light which signaled that a new, more complex explanation would have to be formulated to understand her symptoms.

As stated earlier, it is clear that a period in therapy during which new material emerges, throwing into question an earlier explanation, generates questions and puzzlement in the therapist. With Mrs. Abell, such questions as "Why did the panic attacks surface at this period in time?" and "How are the stress of caring for a new baby and the sense of loss with respect to her father's death related?" provided the motive force for subsequent integrative work. Such questions generate hypotheses. For example, the therapist wondered whether her husband's perceived lack of interest in the baby reminded Mrs. Abell of her father's absence, whether a wish to display her new baby to her father was evoked, or whether her father's death or the birth of her son left an imagined hole in the patient. The therapist was also struck by the intrinsic relation between the concepts of birth and death.

Discomfort with puzzlement may induce therapists to apply closure to their speculations by finding a ready-made answer from a textbook theory. However, speculative ideas are best included in one's thoughts as questions as one imaginatively enters the patient's world.

Mrs. Abell decided to undertake therapy to learn more about her fearfulness. The therapist thus had an opportunity to bring what he learned about her sense of loss in her father's death into the setting of a subsequent episode. In the third session, Mrs. Abell described a recent episode in which her mother insisted on testing the temperature of the bathwater many times before permitting her to place the baby in the tub. In her excessive concern that the baby be scalded, her mother commented that it was unfortunate that Mr. Abell was absent. Rising to her husband's defense, Mrs. Abell explained that he was obligated to attend lectures.

As he listened, imagining himself in the setting of her home, the therapist was aware of experiencing a fleeting sense of isolation. This prompted him to ask whether the patient had thought about her father while she was bathing the baby. Mrs. Abell replied that bathing her son often brought to mind that she had never permitted herself to wash her father or otherwise care for him during his hospitalization. Only her mother had the right to do such things. It felt as if a lifelong emotional barrier had existed between her father and herself. Had her mother somehow come between them?

In this example, the therapist's empathic appreciation of the patient's sadness about her father's death in the context of an episode in which Mrs. Abell and her mother were bathing the baby gave rise to a useful question that subsequently generated new information.

The following example is taken from a session in the fourth month of therapy:

Mr. Barker, a middle-aged bachelor employed as an accountant, had presented with complaints of low self-esteem, recurring spells of depression lasting two to three hours, and a fear of intimacy with women. The predominant topics in the initial phase of therapy were his compulsion to seek out prostitutes and his concern that women would control or belittle him. Mr. Barker believed his problems stemmed from his mother's beating him as a child. He described her as a cruel and unpredictable woman who on many occasions locked him in a closet. His father, on the other hand, was kind and gentle. The patient's description of being locked in the closet provided the therapist with an early point of empathic entry into Mr. Barker's world, allowing him to organize his questions in the context of this evocative memory.

In the fourth month of therapy, Mr. Barker started a session by stating that on his way to therapy he had noticed an old woman in the lobby of the therapist's office building who had seemed lost. She was standing in the center of the lobby staring awkwardly at passersby as if hoping someone would come to her assistance. Mr. Barker wished he had stopped to help her. The woman reminded him of his mother; it was sad to think that some people were doomed to a life of hardship.

Encouraged by the therapist to talk about his sadness, for the first time Mr. Barker talked about his mother in a compassionate vein. His father's family had never approved of her. His father, siding with his own family in disputes concerning his wife, failed to support her. Mr. Barker shielded her from criticism by never reporting her rages to his father. His mother's excessive demands on him and her brutal behavior stemmed from a sense of unworthiness. She was driven by the need to elevate herself in the family's opinion by raising a son who was well behaved and accomplished.

The emergence of this new material threw into question Mr. Barker's earlier explanation of his difficulty with women (i.e., that it stemmed from his mother's cruelty toward him). It also raised in the therapist's mind such questions as why this information had not come to light earlier in therapy, why up to this point the patient had depicted his parents in black-and-white terms, whether he was concealing acrimonious feelings toward his father, and in what way his compassion for his mother related to his difficulty with women. Rather than formulating an answer to his questions, the therapist undertook the integrative task of bringing together this new information with his imaginative exercise of empathically transporting himself into the patient's world. Mr. Barker once again raised the subject of being locked in a closet as a child. The therapist reentered this setting with new information regarding the complexity of Mr. Barker's emotional state. He asked Mr. Barker whether, during periods of confinement, he had ever thought about his father. Mr. Barker sidestepped the question, instead asserting that he had never directly expressed anger toward his father because his father couldn't tolerate it. His father was a coward. Mr. Barker's feelings about his father carried over into his relationships with men in general. For the first time in therapy, he acknowledged a propensity to feel superior to other men that interfered with his relationships at work. He also admitted that he became enraged when others outdid him.

The preceding examples illustrate that the work of integrating new material into a comprehensive understanding of the patient's experiential state once again triggers the emergence of new data. The cyclic pattern of periods of integrative work and periods in which new material comes to light is propelled forward by speculative questions that result from the juxtaposition of diverse fragments of information and empathically understood experiential states. When one takes into consideration the therapist's oscillations between the positions of external observer and observer on the scene, the cyclic pattern of deconstruction, or analysis, and integrative work becomes more readily depicted as a spiral: With each subsequent imaginative reentry into the patient's world, the therapist attains a more complex and accurate appreciation of the patient's experiential state.

SHIFTS OF SETTING IN THE COURSE OF THERAPY

During the course of therapy, the therapist may discern a second pattern closely related to the cyclic or spiral pattern just described. As therapy progresses, dramatic episodes that were prominent during one phase of therapy often recede into the background. Plots become subplots, and subplots become plots. New episodes, new characters, and new scenarios come to light to replace the old ones. The new episodes often (but not invariably) pertain to a chronologically earlier period in the patient's life. Sometimes an episode that occupied a central position in the patient's narrative in an early phase of therapy recedes and then moves to the forefront again at a later time.

Such shifts were apparent during the course of therapy with both Mrs. Abell and Mr. Barker.

In the first month of therapy, the significant incidents that provided the therapist with an emotionally evocative point of empathic entry into Mrs. Abell's world were, as described earlier, a panic attack, a visit with her dying father, and an episode in which she and her mother bathed the baby. The therapist's interest in Mrs. Abell's difficulties with her father prompted her to describe in detail several aspects of her life as a child: the small suburban bungalow in which she was raised, the peaceful atmosphere that always prevailed in the home. Her parents never argued. Her father spent evenings at home doing carpentry in the basement while her mother did housework in the kitchen. Mrs. Abell was never asked to help; she spent her evenings doing schoolwork in front of the television. Her relatives would often mention that her parents were a perfect couple. She often wondered whether children had a place in a perfect family. An only child, she had often wished for a brother or a sister.

In her tenth session, Mrs. Abell was able to remember an incident that disturbed this peaceful atmosphere. She was eight or nine at the time. She and her father had sat down to supper at the dining room table and were engaged in a discussion concerning a school assignment. As usual, her mother spent most of the meal moving back and forth between the dining room and the kitchen. During the meal her mother made a comment that the patient interpreted as a wilful attempt to disrupt the conversation between herself and her father. Mrs. Abell criticized her mother, but an angry stare from her father stopped her in her tracks. Sobbing, she ran to her bedroom and locked the door. Later, when she returned to the dining room, her parents behaved as if the outburst had never happened. Similar interactions between herself and her parents occurred on many occasions during her adolescence.

In sessions following her description of this incident, the therapist was able to use it (in conjunction with episodes in which Mrs. Abell as a child quietly attended to her schoolwork in front of the television) to examine and to vicariously experience her sense of isolation and anger. It was against the background of this new scenario that the therapist formulated a new set of speculative questions. He wondered about the interdigitation of Mrs. Abell's recent panic attacks and the following factors: her father's death, her mother's recent visit, a concern that her mother would come between herself and her husband (as her mother, in her memory, had come between herself and her father), an awareness that her wish to proudly display her baby (i.e., her "assignment") to father would never be satisfied, a concern that her child would suffer because of her husband's disinterest, and a fear that the presence of a child would be disruptive to the household. There were many possibilities. Although the significant connections between the many possible factors remained unclear, the therapist was confident that new explanations would surface.

The first four months of therapy with Mr. Barker provided the therapist with two emotionally evocative episodes conducive to entrance into the patient's world: that in which Mr. Barker as a child was locked in a closet and his encounters with prostitutes. As therapy progressed, these earlier scenarios receded into the background. Mr. Barker's propensity to regard other men as inferior to himself became the predominant topic in therapy. As well, a new scenario emerged. In the fourth month of therapy, Mr. Barker remembered an incident that occurred when he was 12 years old. He was awakened during the night by a noise from his parents' bedroom. Sitting up in bed, he realized it was his mother crying. He listened for what seemed an interminable period, hoping that the noise would subside. However, the crying continued, and he decided to get out of bed to investigate. He went to his parents' bedroom, and when he knocked on the door, his father told him to come in. In the bedroom he discovered his mother sitting on the edge of the bed, sobbing. His father, who was lying motionless under the covers, gave no indication of reaching out to her. Instead, he explained quietly that Mr. Barker's mother had been awakened by a nightmare. To Mr. Barker's surprise, when his mother noticed him in the room, she immediately stopped crying, as if his mere presence calmed her down. She assured him that she was feeling better and encouraged him to return to bed.

Using this episode as an imaginative point of empathic entry into the patient's world, the therapist was able to sense elements of terror and grandeur in the patient's experiential state. He wondered whether this episode alluded to sexual conflicts and whether Mr. Barker suffered because he was thrust into manhood too quickly without, as a child, receiving adequate parenting. The therapist postulated that a confluence of factors contributed to the patient's presently avoiding relationships with women who were not prostitutes. The factors included a need to recreate a triumphant situation with women, anger directed at women, a need to feel superior to men, a need to ward off a wish to be parented, a need to ward off compassionate feelings toward others, and, emanating from the feeling of having failed his mother and bested his father, a need to make reparations (i.e., to pay for his pleasures). The therapist recognized that the connections were not clearly sketched in, but he was optimistic that these themes would provide him with useful questions in sessions to come.

PERIODS OF INTERFERENCE

Therapy moves forward at an uneven pace. The cyclic or spiral pattern of progress described in the foregoing vignettes is interspersed with periods of interference. Patients may withhold information because to reveal their thoughts would evoke painful emotions. Usually, the propensity to withdraw from the therapist is overcome by the wish to share one's difficulties with another person. Sharing is facilitated when the therapist gives evidence of a capacity to understand.

During periods of interference, the cyclic patterns of deconstruction and integrative work vanish. New episodes fail to emerge. The therapist may notice, for example, that the patient resorts to talking in generalities or presents material in a manner that precludes the therapist's empathically moving into the patient's situation as an observer on the scene. During such periods, the therapist's task is to examine the interferences and nonjudgmentally to point them out to the patient. The therapist's statements should leave open the possibility that an actual or perceived therapeutic failure contributed to the interference. As one learns more about the patient, one is able to present a more detailed and comprehensive description of the interference and the reasons for its appearance. When new information fails to emerge, repressive defenses are felt to be at work. When therapy appears to be impeded with respect to integrative work, splitting mechanisms are felt to be at work. Repressive defenses and splitting mechanisms commonly work together. It is often difficult to attribute an interference to a single set of mechanisms.*

A period of interference became apparent in the seventh month of therapy with Mrs. Abell. It followed a series of sessions during which the dining room episode in which she was thrown into conflict with her mother played a prominent role in her narrative.

For several sessions the therapist was able to imaginatively transport himself into the dining room episode and to vicariously experience a sense of distance and rage. After several such sessions, however, Mrs. Abell's narrative changed abruptly. Her story became difficult to read. For several sessions she complained of forgetfulness and an inability to concentrate. "It's as if I've blanked something out." Her husband had also noticed her absentmindedness and had recently complained about her disinterest in sex. The therapist felt that a barrier had arisen in therapy and wondered whether it reflected an aspect of the patient's relationship with her father. During this period Mrs. Abell's panic attacks, which had remitted shortly after she entered therapy, reappeared.

Mrs. Abell's state of confusion continued for several sessions. It ended in a session in which she reported a panic attack that, unlike her previous attacks, was accompanied by a dream. In the dream a man was standing at her bedside. Mrs. Abell didn't remember the rest of the dream, but she jokingly remarked that it was probably sexual. When the therapist

---

*Periods of interference can be understood from a number of perspectives, all of which are centered in conflict. In this chapter, such periods are discussed in terms of *intrapsychic* conflict. The patient is conceptualized as a self-contained unit; the conflict stems from a tension between wish and defense. In Chapter 8, periods of interference will be examined in terms of the paired relationship of patient and therapist (i.e., in terms of transference and countertransference). In Chapter 9, in order to shed light on some weaknesses of the self psychology model, transference and countertransference with more difficult patients will be discussed. Finally, in Chapter 10, the role of conflict (in the therapist as well as the patient) throughout the course of therapy will be discussed.

raised the possibility that it was difficult for Mrs. Abell to examine sexual issues in therapy, she agreed. The dream had made her remember an aspect of the dining room episode that she had not thought about for many years. It troubled her to raise it in therapy because it depicted her father in a less-than-perfect light. Her father had an offensive habit of scratching his testicles at the dining room table. The habit disturbed her, and she remembered looking away whenever she talked to him. In integrating this new piece of information, the therapist wondered how this memory contributed to her panic attacks and to the emotional barrier she had described as existing between her father and herself.

Periods of interference in Mr. Barker's case were characterized by his becoming angry and unresponsive. Because Mr. Barker's sullen moods appeared to be directed at the therapist, the therapist on several occasions inquired whether his irritation was attributable to an incident in therapy. On one such occasion, Mr. Barker responded by accusing the therapist of infantilizing him. Although the accusation seemed unfounded, the therapist, retracing his steps in a recent episode of interference, recognized that it followed a session in which Mr. Barker had talked about an uncle who was kind to his daughter. Were these periods of interference precipitated by a need to ward off a wish to be cared for? Did the admission of such a wish dampen Mr. Barker's feelings of manliness? Did the discussion of topics that pertained to such a wish evoke feelings of envy in Mr. Barker? Bearing in mind these speculative questions, the therapist examined subsequent periods of interference. He discovered that they seemed to follow sessions in which incidents pertaining to kindly parenting were mentioned. The therapist subsequently pointed out this pattern (but not his speculative thoughts) to Mr. Barker. In addition to overcoming a period of interference, the therapist's statement led Mr. Barker to divulge his distrust of any act of kindness. Although Mr. Barker's admission did not immediately shed light on the therapist's questions, the therapist did recognize that the meaning of Mr. Barker's period of sullenness would become more sharply defined over the course of therapy.

The preceding examples may give the impression that a single intervention or a sudden discovery is sufficient to overcome a period of interference. It must be emphasized that periods of interference punctuate the entire course of therapy and that the therapist's interventions often have only a transitory effect on them.

LEVELS OF COMPLEXITY

Examined in the context of a single episode in the patient's life – the episode in which Mrs. Abell and her mother were bathing the child and the episode in which Mr. Barker as a child was locked in a closet – the preceding clinical examples illustrate the manner in which the therapist's appreciation of the patient's inner state becomes increasingly complex and comprehensive with each subsequent empathic reentry into the patient's world.

At subsequent stages in therapy, with each reentry into the setting in which Mrs. Abell and her mother were bathing the baby, the therapist brought with him his appreciation of such issues as Mrs. Abell's sense of loss with respect to her father, her feeling that her mother came between her father and herself, her concern that the presence of a child might be disruptive to her marriage, her feeling of aloneness with respect to her childhood family, and her description of her father's disturbing habits. As well, the therapist discovered similarities when he compared the scenario in which Mrs. Abell and her mother were bathing the baby with the scenario of the dining room episode. Both touched on the theme of the mother's interfering with Mrs. Abell's wish for attention from a man. In the course of therapy, the apparently simple act of bathing a child was transfigured into a complex psychological event, the patient's understanding of herself was enhanced, and the therapist's questions became increasingly precise. In the initial interview, for example, a question pertaining to the significance of Mrs. Abell's bathing her baby's genitals would not have been considered relevant to the understanding of her symptoms.

In Mr. Barker's case, the therapist's appreciation of his experience of being locked in a closet was augmented at subsequent stages in therapy by an appreciation of such issues as Mr. Barker's mixed feelings regarding his mother, his contempt for his father, his shaky self-esteem, and his drivenness to accomplish. When he compared the episode of being locked in a closet with the bedroom episode in which Mr. Barker's presence calmed his mother, the therapist discovered important similarities and differences between the two settings. Although one episode ended in humiliation and the other in triumph, in both episodes his mother was depicted as powerful and his father as cowardly. The imaginative juxtaposition of the two settings alerted the therapist to issues pertaining to Mr. Barker's fluctuating self-esteem.

A new level of understanding does not invalidate a preceding explanation but augments and embraces it. Mrs. Abell's original explanation that her symptoms were caused by the stress of caring for her new baby and Mr. Barker's explanation that being locked in a closet led to his later difficulties with women do not represent purely defensive rationalizations intended only to lead the therapist astray; they should not be regarded as statements to be discarded once the "real reasons" come to light. Mrs. Abell's caring for her child did contribute to her panic attacks; Mr. Barker's being locked in a closet did contribute to his difficulties with women—but in ways that were exceedingly complex.

In a sense, the patient's explanations at every level of understanding are accurate as well as inaccurate. It is this paradoxical fact that renders the therapist's relationship to the patient's reality exceedingly tricky. At one level, the therapist recognizes that the patient's memories and explanations are inexact. Nevertheless, the road toward greater accuracy is facilitated by the therapist's *attempting* to empathize with the patient in the context of a specific incident or episode by imaginatively embracing the explanation as it stands at the given moment. For example, in the initial interview it was the therapist's attempting yet failing to empathize with Mrs. Abell that alerted him that something was missing in her original explanation of her symptoms. With Mr.

Barker it was the therapist's recognition that his empathic experiences with respect to several episodes in Mr. Barker's life included such feelings as rage, helplessness, and triumph but that a feeling of safety was missing that contributed to his understanding. On the one hand, therapists attempt to empathize with specific incidents in the patient's life; on the other hand, they examine their own empathic experiences for distortions, inaccuracies, and omissions.

THE THERAPIST'S ATTITUDE

In the preceding clinical examples, the many possible connections between the patients' memories, themes, and explanations were sketched in lightly, and the cases were presented in a state of incompleteness (i.e., without a final formulation to explain the presenting complaints) to illustrate the manner in which therapy unfolds. Such questions as "What are the factors contributing to Mrs. Abell's or Mr. Barker's symptoms and conflicts?" fuel the therapist's interest. At each level of understanding, new answers come to light. For example, over the course of therapy the therapist discovered that Mrs. Abell's reported emotional barrier between herself and her father (which contributed to her panic attacks) pertained to a conflict with her mother, to a sense of not belonging in a "perfect" family, to a need to set her father on a pedestal, and to a castration complex. In Mr. Barker's case, over the course of therapy the therapist discovered that Mr. Barker's compulsion to seek out prostitutes related to a fear of being hemmed in by women, a need to ward off compassionate feelings, a need to triumph over others, and a need to ward off a desire to be cared for. A simple explanation for Mrs. Abell's or Mr. Barker's symptoms would be insufficient. Every one of the factors listed contributed to the patients' symptoms. The therapist's task is to remain open to many possibilities and to recognize that every set of answers gives rise to new speculative questions. It is the process of uncovering as many factors as possible, of the therapist's empathizing with as many aspects of the patient as possible, that benefits the patient in the long term.

SUMMARY

Two clinical narratives, in which only a few significant episodes were highlighted, were examined over a brief span of therapy to demonstrate the increasing complexity of the therapist's appreciation of the patient's inner state. The course of therapy is characterized by cycles: The emergence of new material that highlights deficiencies in the patient's earlier stories and explanations is followed by a period of integrative work during which a new level of understanding is attained. At the same time, integrative work facilitates the emergence once again of new material, and the cycle is repeated. During the phase of integrative work, the therapist's task is to convert speculative thoughts (in which theoretical formulations may receive consideration) into useful questions in which diverse pieces of data and experiential states are juxtaposed. The formulation of such questions is facilitated by the therapist's oscillating between the position of external observer and that of observer on the scene. Such questions fuel the continuing dialogue between the patient and the therapist; at each succeeding level of understanding they become more complex.

In addition, as therapy progresses, episodes that occupied a prominent position in the patient's narrative during one phase of therapy are often replaced by episodes pertaining to a chronologically earlier period in the patient's life. The pace of therapy, however, is an uneven one. Periods of progress are interspersed with periods of interference characterized by the cessation of cycles of deconstruction and integrative work, by a blockage in the emergence of new significant episodes, and by the therapist's inability to freely oscillate between the vantage point of external observer and that of observer on the scene. With each subsequent reentry into the patient's world, the therapist's empathic appreciation becomes increasingly complex. As more and more emotionally evocative episodes become accessible, the therapist's overall understanding is enhanced; new explanations augment earlier ones. As reader of the patient's text, the therapist's position is a complicated one; it requires empathizing with the patient and yet looking for discrepancies, suspending one's disbelief and holding on to it, and viewing therapy in terms of a reconstruction of the past and a deconstruction of the present. Clues to this reading are provided by the therapist's monitoring of his own empathic experiences.

Chapter Eight

The Conflictual Therapeutic
Interaction as the Focus of Empathy

Imaginatively placing oneself in the patient's scenario heightens the therapist's appreciation of the patient's inner state. This heightened appreciation is not so intense as to interfere with the therapist's other functions. Indeed, this affective experience (that is, an empathic grasp of the patient's overall condition as well as of the patient's predicament in specific imaginable scenarios) augments the functions of pattern matching, hypothesis building, and identifying general themes, including omissions and distortions, associated with the role of external observer. In Chapters 6 and 7, these many functions were set against a background in which the patient's perception of the therapist as a well-meaning helper prevailed, the patient's capacity for self-awareness required only minimal attention, and the therapist's position as reader/spectator of the patient's novel or drama remained relatively undisturbed.

In this context, it was sufficient to conceptualize periods of interference as stemming from the patient's defensive need to ward off conflictual or painful emotional states. As therapy progresses, however, the therapist may notice significant conflictual elements emerging in the therapeutic relationship itself. From this perspective, the patient's attitude toward the therapist and the therapist's attitude toward the patient (i.e., the interactions to which the therapist contributes directly) become a new source of information concerning the patient's difficulties. In this chapter, periods of interference will be examined in terms of the therapeutic relationship—that is, in terms of transference and countertransference. These terms are defined somewhat differently by the different schools of psychotherapy. The term *transference* refers generally to the patient's approximately recapitulating aspects of significant relationships from childhood in therapy. The term *countertransference* refers generally to the therapist's behavior or emotional state, which bears a relationship to the patient's transference. That therapists bring their own conflicts into the interaction makes the link between the therapist's experiential state and the patient's an approximate one.*

The overriding principle in the various psychoanalytic formulations of transference and countertransference is the concept of transfer or displacement—that is, disturbing patterns or attitudinal states are transferred from the past to the present, from one relationship to another, or from one person to another. The situation in which they ultimately emerge is the therapeutic relationship. Classical theorists emphasize the transfer of sexual or aggressive elements. Self psychologists emphasize the transfer of conflicts pertaining to developmental needs. Object relations theorists emphasize that only aspects of the self are projected onto the other and that only aspects of the other are introjected into the self (i.e., that only an element of an old pattern is recapitulated in therapy), using such terms as *part object relationships* and *self-object units*. The different theories attribute significance

---

*The term *transference neurosis* refers to a specific type of transference phenomenon in which the disturbing pattern is an approximate recapitulation of the patient's oedipal conflicts (which arise at approximately age four). The phase of therapy during which these conflicts emerge is characterized by a remission of symptoms in day-to-day life. The neurosis is instead concentrated in the therapeutic relationship (Nunberg 1955).

to different facets of development. In addition, each school formulates the stages of development differently.

Transference itself is an omnipresent phenomenon in therapy; it does not characterize only periods of interference. The patient's positive regard for the therapist during periods in which therapy is progressing favorably is also an example of transference. Indeed, all relationship patterns—adaptive and defensive, hostile and friendly—have their roots in the individual's past. However, when therapists talk about recognizing or interpreting the transference, they are usually talking about the recapitulation of a *troublesome* childhood relationship that coincides with a period of interference in therapy. Only during periods of interference do transference and countertransference issues stand out. It is only then that they require the therapist's attention.

THE THERAPIST'S SHIFT IN PERSPECTIVE

The emergence of troublesome transference states is an inevitable occurrence in therapy. Therapists are alerted to their presence in a number of ways. They may notice that therapy is faltering—that is, that the cyclic patterns of deconstruction, or analysis, and integrative work have come to a halt. Their capacity to oscillate freely between the positions of observer on the scene and external observer may be impeded. They may discern in themselves a reduced interest in the patient, an inability to pay attention, or dissatisfaction and anger. In addition, they may notice that the patient's attitude toward them is no longer as open or as trusting as it was earlier. The quality of the patient's or the therapist's emotions is less significant (they may be positive or negative, as well as sexual) than that they coincide with a period of interference. For example, a positive attitude toward the therapist may generally contribute to the forward progress of therapy. On the other hand, if such an attitude serves to ward off angry or envious feelings, it represents an interference. With less difficult patients, the features that indicate the nature of the emerging relationship difficulty are usually easily recognizable.

To understand the nature of the transference difficulty, a shift in perspective is required. In Chapter 7, periods of interference were examined in terms of intrapsychic conflict (that is, in terms of wishes and defenses). The patient was conceived of as a self-contained unit. To examine transference, an interactional conceptualization that embraces the paired unit of patient and therapist needs to be employed. The significant story or scenario has moved from the patient's narrative to the therapeutic relationship itself. The latter needs to be examined with the recognition that one is no longer simply the reader/spectator of the patient's novel or drama. It is as if the therapist has unwittingly been drawn as a significant character into the novel or has been pressed into performing in the drama. One's oscillating attention, embracing the dual positions of external observer and observer on the scene, must focus on the session. As observer on the scene, one takes part in the interaction. As external observer, one draws back from the session to examine it as a whole. Although it is natural to feel on the outside of a narrative that does not involve them as participants, it is also natural for therapists to feel on the inside of a relationship that does. The willed component of the imaginative function of entering the patient's scenario consists of shifting from external observer to observer on the scene. With respect to transference, the premeditated component consists of shifting from observer on the scene to external observer. What the therapist looks for is a match (or contradictions) between the patient's reported stories, or memories, and the therapeutic interaction.

DIFFICULTIES IN RECOGNIZING
A DISTURBING TRANSFERENCE STATE

A number of factors may make it difficult to discover a disturbing transference state. Unlike a recalled memory, a transference state is often not accompanied by a dramatic verbal description of what is happening. The therapist is often forced to rely on nonverbal clues. The conceptual shift required places a strain on one's sense of self. Imaginatively entering the patient's scenario entails overcoming a reluctance to share a painful perspective with the patient. Detecting a transference state entails stepping out of oneself and overcoming a reluctance to face up to one's *own* unexpected and painful emotions. Indeed, the initial reaction to a painful emotional state may well be to regard it as antitherapeutic and to deny it. As part of this denial, the first assumption may be that the interference stems from the patient's conflicts, not one's own.

Once they overcome their denial, therapists encounter a second difficulty. Because one's own unconscious conflicts contribute to one's emotional state, it is difficult to establish to what extent this state reflects the patient's difficulties rather than one's own. Indeed, it is this uncertainty that gives rise to the varying definitions of countertransference. The term has been variously defined as (1) the therapist's purely complementary response to the patient's transference, (2) defensive behavior in the therapist generated by the patient's transference, (3) the therapist's emotional state during a period of interference that was generated mainly by the therapist's conflicts, and (4) the therapist's total response to the patient.

In the clinical setting it is difficult to discern the origins of the therapist's emotional state. To a greater or a lesser degree one's own conflicts do contribute to it. Nevertheless, the patient's conflicts and behavior also contribute to it. Transference inevitably evokes countertransference; to some extent, therapists inevitably take on and strive to ward off the roles assigned to them by the patient. In the context of the therapeutic relationship, periods of interference should be designated as disturbing transference–countertransference states. The shift to external observer necessary to detecting such states is facilitated by the therapist's own analysis. At times, examining an interference when the session is over and the therapist's emotions are less intense is also useful.

ANTITHETICAL ISSUES

To discover similarities (and differences) between the therapeutic interaction and the patient's stories, one brings together all that one knows about the patient both as external observer and as observer on the scene. This brings to light potentially significant material and generates hypotheses. An approximate understanding of a disturbing transference–countertransference period evolves from the continuing dialogue between patient and therapist. The therapist poses open-ended questions that are fashioned by hypotheses and by the patient's responses to earlier questions. Each contains a minimum of assumptions. This stepwise procedure provides checks and balances against unwarranted conclusions.

Two antithetical questions need to be borne in mind:

1. Did the patient play a major role in generating the disturbing transference–countertransference period, or did the therapist's conflicts play such a role?
2. Has the therapist taken on the role of a significant person in the patient's world, with the patient responding accordingly, or have their roles been reversed?

For example, the patient may perceive the therapist's behavior as being similar to his father's (and he may induce the therapist to act the part). On the other hand, the patient may assume the role of a critical father, inducing in the therapist the emotions of a helpless child. The answers to these two questions are rarely immediately apparent.

LEVELS OF COMPLEXITY

Each patient tends to employ a more or less characteristic set of defenses and interactional patterns. Hence, for a given patient, periods of interference tend to be similar. For example, in the case of Mrs. Abell (reported in Chapter 7), periods of interference were characterized by the patient's appearing confused and by the therapist's experiencing a sense of isolation. With Mr. Barker, on the other hand, periods of interference were characterized by the patient's expressing sullen anger and by the therapist's experiencing a sense of inadequacy. In each individual case, as therapy progresses, the similarity between one period of interference and another makes it possible to identify such periods more quickly and accurately. At the same time, as more material comes to light, the therapist is alerted to subtle differences between one such period and another. In this way, one's appreciation of the significance of the patient's interactional patterns becomes more comprehensive. These principles are demonstrated in the following discussion of the case of Mrs. Abell:

> Mrs. Abell's sessions lost their momentum following a phase during which the therapist was able to empathize with the patient's rage as a child toward her mother for interrupting a conversation between the patient and her father (i.e., the dining room episode). Guided by Mrs. Abell's associations, the therapist understood the interference as stemming from Mrs. Abell's defensiveness about what turned out to be a sexual conflict (as represented in her originally repressed memory of her father's habit of scratching his testicles).
>
> Whereas this first period was understood as defensiveness, a subsequent period of interference was understood in terms of transference–countertransference. This period, too, was characterized by the therapist's sensing a remoteness between himself and Mrs. Abell. What was different, however, was that Mrs. Abell seemed to have lost her characteristic ability to speak precisely. On earlier occasions she had chided the therapist for his grammatical lapses, jokingly alluding to her mother's poor command of language. This clue prompted the therapist to hypothesize that Mrs. Abell had taken on attributes of her mother, assigning to the therapist the role of the child. Addressing this theme proved to be useful. During subsequent periods of interference, Mrs. Abell's use of language provided the therapist with a quick and helpful guide to their potential significance.
>
> Other periods of interference were understood differently. At times, they represented a recapitulation of Mrs. Abell's guilt-ridden yearning for her father's attention—with the therapist cast in the role of the father. At times, the therapist was assigned the role of the patient's critical mother. On several occasions, the therapist felt that his own conflicts gener-

ated the interference. Each explanation evolved from the dialogue with the patient.

As Mrs. Abell's case illustrates, every new explanation for a period of interference augments the earlier ones. The therapist's enhanced understanding of the patient goes hand in hand with an enhanced understanding of the patient's hierarchy of defenses and interactional patterns.

The following clinical vignettes highlight the appearance of disturbing transference–countertransference periods in therapy:

In the sixth month of therapy, Mr. Charles, a 35-year-old sales and marketing manager of a computer company, began a session with the statement that his co-workers did not appreciate his contribution to the company. He explained that he had held a marketing seminar that day and that not one of the company's directors had bothered to attend it. With this explanation, the momentum of the session faltered. Mr. Charles fell into a silence, and the therapist's mind wandered to issues unrelated to the patient. Realizing that he was inattentive, the therapist stepped back from the session to attempt to examine it as a whole and discovered a congruence between his own behavior and the reported behavior of Mr. Charles' superiors. The therapist also remembered that in the preceding session Mr. Charles brought in a new company brochure that the patient had designed himself. The therapist remembered experiencing an unusual reluctance to express his approval.

To test his assumption, the therapist asked Mr. Charles whether he felt disappointed with the sessions as well.

"Yes, I do," said the patient, "but I don't know why."

"What came to my mind," said the therapist, "was the brochure you brought in last day."

"Yes," said the patient, "I just thought about it, too. You didn't seem to be interested in it."

"Perhaps you felt that I was unappreciative of your efforts."

"I was very surprised by your reaction," said Mr. Charles.

This brief interchange propelled therapy forward. The patient expanded on the troubling events at work. Because it had been discussed in earlier sessions, the therapist expected the topic of Mr. Charles' self-involved parents to come to the fore. To the therapist's surprise, however, Mr. Charles confessed that he had behaved inappropriately during the marketing seminar, exhibiting an inappropriate need to be the center of attention. At the end of the session, the therapist was puzzled by the direction the narrative had taken.

Reviewing his notes at the end of the day, the therapist discovered that he had forgotten an event that had transpired *two* sessions earlier. On that day, after his session had ended, Mr. Charles had returned to the therapist's office and despite evidence that another session was in progress, had barged into the office to ask whether he had left his umbrella behind. Retrospectively, the therapist realized that Mr. Charles had reenacted in therapy behavior reminiscent of his mother's behavior. During the patient's teenage years, Mr. Charles' mother had often barged into his bedroom unannounced. The therapist wondered whether his disinterest in the patient's brochure had represented a reaction to the patient's interrupting him.

Mr. Charles' case illustrates how difficult it is to attribute a period of interference to the patient or to the therapist. It highlights the importance of a self-interrogative, nonjudgmental approach. Although the therapist believed that he himself had instigated the interference, he introduced his assumptions in a tentative fashion. His understanding of the transference-countertransference state was accomplished in a stepwise progression that extended beyond the time frame of the session.

Mrs. Duncan, a 33-year-old married woman with two children, experienced incapacitating episodes of envy and guilt. Despite her symptoms she managed to raise a family and to work as a journalist. Mrs. Duncan attributed her symptoms to a lifelong disappointment in her mother. In the eleventh month of therapy, the patient's narrative centered on the death of her maternal grandmother. The grandmother, a widow who had lived with the patient's family, had died when the patient was three. Mrs. Duncan's memories of her grandmother were vague. Subsequent to her grandmother's death, however, her mother informed her that she had, as a child, demanded a great deal of attention from her grandmother. The grandmother's death coincided with the birth of a sibling. Mrs. Duncan's clearest memories at age three were that her mother had become depressed and sharply critical of the children. Mrs. Duncan's father, an engineer, took no notice of the difficulties in the home. It felt as if the responsibility of managing the household had fallen to the children.

As the therapist listened, it struck him that Mrs. Duncan felt accused of contributing to her grandmother's death. At the end of the session, he communicated his thoughts to the patient.

Mrs. Duncan arrived at her next session depressed and disappointed in herself. That morning she had fought with her 6-year-old son because he had refused to wear the clothes she had picked out for him. She shouldn't have shouted at him. "It's a replay of the arguments between my mother and myself," she said. "My mother was always imposing her will on me." After a pause, she went on to talk about spending afternoons with her mother, looking out the window of her mother's bedroom. "We would look out the window together," she said. "She would talk about the neighbors. All she ever talked about was people suffering or dying. My mother was fascinated by morbid events. Even when we weren't fighting, it felt as if she was imposing something on me. I never liked the way she depicted the world. I remember making up my mind never to accept her version of things."

Mrs. Duncan fell into a silence. The therapist sensed an irritation in himself stemming from the patient's ignoring his interpretation of the preceding session. He remembered delivering it with an air of certainty—and it did have a morbid quality—and wondered whether he had inadvertently reenacted the role of Mrs. Duncan's mother. To test his assumption, he asked her whether she had any thoughts about the preceding session.

"I don't remember it," she said. "There was something about it I didn't like."

The therapist reminded her of his intervention. It was then

that Mrs. Duncan remembered that the therapist's statement had upset her.

"Perhaps you were feeling that I was trying to make you accept a view of yourself that was morbid?"

"Yes," said the patient, "you sounded very much like my mother."

As with any piece of integrative work, therapy was propelled forward and new material emerged. For the first time Mrs. Duncan revealed that as a child she was fearful that her mother would someday kill her.

In Mrs. Duncan's case, the therapist's countertransference was revealed in his interpretation. To what extent the therapist's behavior was evoked by Mrs. Duncan's transference or derived from his own conflicts—for example, a narcissistic need to impress the patient with his perspicacity—is uncertain. Mrs. Duncan's contribution to the dialogue (i.e., her failure to mention the therapist's intervention) facilitated an understanding of her experiential state.

Mr. Forman, a married, 27-year-old school teacher, presented initially with symptoms of inertia, obsessional ideation, and an inability to make decisions. In the first year of therapy, his narrative was dominated by his complaints concerning his father. Mr. Forman felt that his father never acknowledged his successes in school or in sports. Mr. Forman's father was a stockbroker who was often absent from the home during the patient's childhood. The father's major contact with his son as a child entailed assigning him chores. Mr. Forman remembered as a teenager repeatedly forgetting to mow the lawn, despite his father's daily reminders. He was well intentioned but had a forgetful nature. Unlike his mother, Mr. Forman's father was intolerant of his forgetfulness.

In the first year of therapy, Mr. Forman exhibited occasional lapses of memory. Several times he arrived late for an appointment claiming, for example, that he had absentmindedly walked past the therapist's office building. Understanding such lapses as at times a wish to recapitulate his mother's indulgence and at times an attempt to evoke in the therapist the feelings of an unnoticed child was sufficient to overcome them. In the twelfth month of therapy, Mr. Forman's lateness became a regular pattern. At month end, he repeatedly failed to pay the therapist's bill. At the same time, Mr. Forman's complaints concerning his father's inconsiderateness became more insistent. Therapy appeared to lose its momentum. Sensing his own growing irritation with Mr. Forman's forgetfulness, the therapist, imaginatively stepping back from the sessions, recognized that at this juncture he identified with Mr. Forman's father. Up to now, the therapist had sympathized with the patient's predicament. In the light of the therapeutic interaction, Mr. Forman's description of himself as purely the victim of his father's inconsiderateness suddenly seemed one-sided.

During a session in which Mr. Forman complained bitterly that his father had neglected to visit him and his wife in their new home, the therapist, curious to learn more about the interaction, asked whether he had extended an invitation to his father.

Mr. Forman responded angrily, "Of course I have," he said, "more than once. We've lived in the new house for three months."

The therapist encouraged him to describe a recent conversation in which he had invited his father to visit.

"Well," he said, "I usually phone them. I talk to my mother. Dad's at work when I call."

"When do you call?" asked the therapist.

"Tuesday at noon. My mother and I set that time aside to talk on the phone. It's convenient for both of us."

"Oh," said the therapist, "do you ever call in the evenings?"

"No," said Mr. Forman, "they're usually tired. . . . Oh, I see what you're getting at. I guess I really can't expect my father to be at home at noon. Is that what you mean?"

"Yes," said the therapist, "but perhaps you could describe a conversation with your mother."

"I really do invite them over."

"And how does your mother respond?"

"She usually says they don't like to go out in the evenings. Dad's too tired when he gets home from work. Instead, Mom offers to come over on the weekend when Dad's away at the farm. She always comes over alone. Dad likes to go to the farm on the weekend."

After a silence Mr. Forman said, "I'm thinking about my mother. She always gave me the message that Dad wasn't interested in me — and I guess I went along with it. I didn't mention it before, but Dad gave me a check to help pay for the house."

As a result of this interchange, therapy was propelled forward. The mother's contribution to the difficulties between the patient and his father became the new focus of attention.

Both Mrs. Duncan's and Mr. Forman's cases illustrate that it is necessary to consciously and deliberately distance or remove oneself from the interaction (i.e., to move toward the position of external observer) in order to discover its significance. The case of Mr. Forman also illustrates the manner in which countertransference may be used to discover a discrepancy in the patient's narrative.

SUMMARY

In this chapter, periods of interference were examined in terms of the conflictual therapeutic relationship—that is, in terms of transference and countertransference. Transference refers to the patient's approximately recapitulating an aspect of a childhood relationship in therapy. Countertransference refers to the therapist's experiencing thoughts and emotions that bear an approximate relationship to the patient's transference. Transference and countertransference are ubiquitous elements in therapy that require attention only when they interfere with forward progress. A disturbing transference state is always accompanied by a disturbing countertransference state because to a degree therapists actually take on the roles assigned to them. It requires all their skills to step back and to examine what is happening.

A therapist in such a case must recognize that the patient's story includes the interaction between patient and therapist; despite himself, the therapist has become a significant player in the patient's narrative. The therapist needs to examine the sessions both as observer on the scene and as external observer. The willed component of the therapist's oscillating perspective is the imaginative act of stepping back from the session to examine it as a whole. This exercise entails overcoming a resistance to experiencing painful and unexpected emotions.

The therapist's speculations must include two antithetical questions:

1. Has the period of interference been generated mainly by the patient's difficulties and conficts or mainly by the therapist's difficulties and conflicts?
2. Is the patient assuming the role of the child and assigning the role of parent (or significant other) to the therapist, or have the role assignments been reversed?

A correct understanding of a transference-countertransference period evolves from the ongoing dialogue between the therapist and the patient.

Disturbing transference–countertransference periods are an inevitable occurrence in therapy. Recognizing their significance is essential for an understanding of the patient. With each subsequent examination of a disturbing transference–countertransference period, the therapist's appreciation of the patient (in terms of the patient's hierarchy of defenses and interactional patterns) becomes increasingly complex.

Chapter Nine

Empathizing with Deficiency in the Context of Conflict

More than one point of view is necessary for a complex empathic understanding of patients. Self psychologists deemphasize conflict and affective wishes, postulating that the patient's difficulties stem from an *actual* early childhood deficit in parenting. They set themselves in opposition both to the classical concept of an inborn drive model and to the classical model of conflict. They believe transference–countertransference disturbances should be understood mainly in terms of the therapist/parent's failure to meet the patient/child's needs. They furthermore claim that issues of self and self-development take precedence over affective wishes. Their view of transference and counter-transference, they believe, fosters acceptance of the patient's behavior, whereas the drive model fosters disapproval.

The self psychology model was developed from the clinical study of difficult narcissistic patients. Some therapists, hoping to bridge the gap between classical psychoanalysis and self psychology, have recommended using the classical theory with less difficult patients and self psychology with more difficult patients (Kohut 1971, Eagle and Wolitzky 1982). This chapter will explore the opposing models and, in particular, the issues of deficiency versus conflict in the context of a number of clinical examples of more difficult paients.

THE DIFFICULT PATIENT

The therapist confirms the patient's reality and also presses beyond it to attain deeper understanding. Total and unflinching attention to the task at hand, however, is an unattainable ideal. Lapses are unavoidable. In addition to such conspicuous interruptions as, for example, the therapist's need to cancel one or several appointments, the therapist's mind will often wander to personal matters during the session itself. In the face of such all-too-human lapses, less difficult patients exhibit a resilience. Their capacity for oscillating self-awareness (that is, the ability to experience and to reflect) remains relatively unimpaired (Bach 1984). Indeed, this capacity, the counterpart of the therapist's oscillating attention, grows as therapy progresses. Such a state of affairs might be labeled *good enough* therapy. For the most part, it permits the therapist to conceive of the patient's difficulties as stemming from the patient as a self-contained unit. When periods of interference do surface, requiring a shift in focus to the paired unit of patient and therapist, the pertinent transference–countertransference elements are usually not difficult to discern.

With many patients, however, periods of extensive interference represent not the exception but the norm. The therapist experiences prolonged periods of dissatisfaction or discomfort. Difficulties surface in a variety of ways. Patients may exhibit sudden shifts of emotion; with apparently little provocation, they may express rage or imbue the therapist with the trappings of omniscience. On the other hand, the therapist may feel bored. Instead of expressing distress in image-laden language, patients may resort to language that is literal, utilitarian, and concerned with the minutiae of external events (Taylor 1984). They may have difficulty identifying emotions or may express distress in such somatic symptoms as anorexia or physical pain.

The therapist may feel ignored or ill-treated or may experience prolonged periods of puzzlement, disturbing emotions, or troubling visceral sensations. The ability to examine the patient's narrative with equanimity may be impeded. The narrative may be difficult to read, as if there were pages missing from the text. There may be little or no opportunity to empathize with the patient. It may appear as if the patient has a wish not to be understood.

The patient may act as if aspects of self are not clearly distinguishable from those of the therapist. For example, patients may imbue the therapist with moods or traits that are congruent with their own. If they are depressed or physically ill, they may assume that the therapist is depressed or physically ill. The usual distinction between fantasy and reality may have vanished. Patients may behave as if the therapist were some other person without sufficiently grasping the "as if" quality of their behavior. Under such circumstances, the patient and the therapist may not feel at ease with or kindly disposed toward each other.

Clearly, the difficulties mentioned in the preceding paragraphs embrace a heterogeneous group of patients. Although a patient who presents with difficulties in one area of functioning is likely to have difficulty in other areas, patients vary in their presentation. For example, some withdraw, whereas others are highly emotional.

The reasons for categorizing patients according to the ways in which they engage in relationships (as opposed to their symptomatology) are several. Once therapy begins, it is not uncommon for symptoms to remit or for the patient to lose interest in them. Instead, patients will often turn their attention to significant incidents in their histories that pertain to relationship difficulties. Such difficulties appear to be more fundamental than symptoms. At the same time, the nature of the patient's relationship difficulties often is not at first apparent. As the transference unfolds, patients who originally presented with different symptoms (e.g., one who is tied to a compulsive ritual and another who has suffered from a panic attack) may reveal similar relationship difficulties. On the other hand, patients who originally presented with similar symptoms may reveal different relationship difficulties.

The regular recurrence of such patterns has led some therapists to postulate that a classification of psychopathology based on the ways in which patients relate (i.e., based on the nature of the transference) would provide a more useful and holistic nosology than would one based on discrete symptoms (Scott 1962, Langs 1978–1979). Although the notion that it should be possible to outline a hierarchy of disorders ranging from least to most problematical is central to this thesis, at present there is no consensus concerning the criteria for such a classification. Nevertheless, therapists do agree that some cases are more difficult than others and that a clearer understanding of the factors that generate difficulties in therapy would assist in the creation of such a classification. For the purpose of this discussion (particularly in the absence of an agreed-upon classification), it is sufficient to categorize patients as less difficult and more difficult.

THE THERAPIST'S SHIFT IN PERSPECTIVE

In the following clinical example, a period of interference surfaced at the outset of psychotherapy:

> In her initial interview, Ms. Levitt, a divorced 35-year-old legal editor, asserted that her relationships with men always ended badly. She was torn between two countervailing explanations: first, that she tended to fall in love with self-serving men, and second, that she became unbearably possessive in relationships. As long as she avoided involvements, she functioned well. In a relationship, however, her career and her self-esteem suffered. The man became the center of her life. In her first interview, the therapist learned that her father had abandoned the family when she was 2 years old, that she admired her mother for single-handedly raising two children, and that an idealized older brother had died in his twenties as a result of a hunting accident. At the end of the interview, while putting on her coat, Ms. Levitt remembered that she had neglected to mention her bouts of anxiety.

"I should have mentioned it earlier," she said, "but I guess it slipped my mind. Could you give me a prescription for tranquillizers?"

The therapist explained that he preferred to hold off prescribing medication until he knew more about her. "Let's talk about your nervousness next day," he said.

Ms. Levitt became indignant. "I knew you'd refuse." she said and walked out of the office in a huff.

Ms. Levitt did return. The interaction that marked the end of the first interview, however, set the tone of subsequent sessions. Ms. Levitt considered the therapist to be withholding and self-involved. Her belief that he treated her unfairly seemed unshakable.

Although there are differences in emphasis, some of the principles self psychologists employ in dealing with patients such as Ms. Levitt are no different from the principles propounded by traditional therapists. For example, self psychologists recommend paying attention to the unstated rhythms of therapy (i.e., to process rather than to content). In addition, they emphasize that therapists should frame their interventions to include their own actual or perceived lapses. They recognize, as do traditional therapists, that the wishes expressed by the patient are the wishes of the child in the adult. Hence, the wishes may appear to be inordinate or unrealistic. With Ms. Levitt, instead of immediately pointing out, for example, that her excessive demands were a recapitulation of her conflictual relationships with men, an experienced therapist would bear with her to learn more about her sense of victimization. In addition, perspicacious therapists, no matter what school they adhered to, would have noticed that her outburst coincided with the session's ending. Every session ends; for Ms. Levitt, however, this may have represented an unforgivable failure on the therapist's part.*

The world of the child in the adult may be governed by premises that are unconventional by the usual standards of adulthood. To extend their understanding of the therapeutic relationship, therapists sometimes need to recognize that the world in

---

*That the therapist should bear with the patient's stories of victimization *but should also move beyond them* will be considered in later sections of this chapter.

which they and the patient are caught up is an unconventional one. In this world, the boundaries between one person and another may be hazy. At times, the body of one person is imagined to merge with that of another (Silverman and Lachmann 1985). A person may experience a feeling of discontinuity over time, changing, for example, from a celebrated hero on one occasion to a condemned criminal on another. Individuals may consider themselves to be a loose connection of disparate parts. A frown may have the shattering effect of a deadly weapon. As object relations theorists point out, individuals may project aspects of themselves into others, divide themselve into good and bad parts, or absorb the attributes of others (Kernberg 1974).

The principles involved in examining a disturbing transference–countertransference period are no different from those described in Chapter 8. The scenario of note is the session itself; the willed component of the therapist's oscillating pattern is the imaginative act of stepping back from the session. What needs to be added in the cases of some patients is an awareness that the narrative or novel seems to belong to the world of science fiction. The therapist's task is to discover the premises governing the patient's world and to study their effect on the patient. Terence's assertion, "I am a man; nothing human is alien to me," needs to be augmented with the statement, "I was a child; nothing childlike is alien to me."

In the following case examples, the therapist discovered unconventional premises that were especially demanding. Paying attention to his own perceived or actual lapses made it possible for him to understand the patient's behavior.

Mr. Garth, a 19-year-old accountancy student who lived with his parents, was referred for assessment by his family doctor. He had experienced recurrent episodes of chest pain and shortness of breath. Discussion of these symptoms revealed that they were triggered by such events as an upcoming examination, an argument with his parents, or a breakup with his girlfriend. Mr. Garth admitted he was easily frustrated. For example, he would break into tears if the solution to a problem eluded him. His father, an accountant, encouraged his academic pursuits. With women, Mr. Garth experienced extremes of emotion. A slight kindness evoked a state of elation; a rejection mortified him. As a result, his relationships with women were stormy. He described his mother as a chronic worrier. Sensing her nervousness to be infectious, he avoided her company. Mr. Garth did recognize that he sometimes "acted like a baby." In the throes of a quandary, however, his feelings overwhelmed him.

Psychotherapy with Mr. Garth was arduous from the start. His manner of speaking was tedious. Often he took no notice of the therapist's presence. When demands surfaced, they often centered on physical symptoms. Mr. Garth expected the therapist to do something quickly to relieve him of his symptoms. His narrative did not readily lend itself to a psychological understanding of his behavior. As a result of these difficulties, the therapist often found himself withdrawing emotionally from the interaction. When he did offer a tentative intervention, it appeared to be ineffective. After two months of once-weekly sessions, the therapist instituted a trial of medication, prescribing an antidepressant for the patient.

Two days later he received a phone call from Mr. Garth's mother. Her son had awakened that morning complaining of a dry mouth. Mr. Garth had informed her (as the therapist had informed him) that the symptom was simply a side effect of the antidepressant. Nevertheless, she couldn't help wondering whether the medication was harmful.

The therapist reassured her that the symptom was harmless. After he hung up the phone, it struck him that although he had not talked to her before, Mrs. Garth had clearly neglected to express any interest in her son's psychological well-being. All her concerns were instead centered on an isolated physical symptom.

Talking with Mr. Garth's mother made the therapist wonder whether the feelings Mr. Garth evoked in him approximated what it felt like for Mr. Garth to be constantly assailed by his mother's anxiety. Perhaps Mr. Garth communicated his distress in solely physical terms because these were the only terms to which his mother responded. By prescribing medication, the therapist had inadvertently recapitulated her role. He was focusing on physical symptoms, and thus an early troubling relationship was being repeated in therapy.

At this juncture, the therapist understood Mr. Garth's behavior in terms of victimization. Although recognizing the tentativeness of his formulation, he postulated that Mr. Garth's outbursts were grounded in his feeling of having received insufficient attention from his mother. Although he did not immediately discontinue the medication, he was alerted to the potential significance of the disruptions he experienced.

Guided by these thoughts, the therapist was able to discern the following pattern. Mr. Garth resorted to somatic complaints *after* the therapist withdrew his attention from the session. Demanding an immediate solution to such problems as an argument with his girlfriend or difficulty with a school assignment prompted the withdrawal. The therapist postulated that these demands were generated by a feeling of deprivation. The therapist's not responding gave rise to somatic complaints.

In the interventions that followed, the therapist made sure he mentioned his own lack of response to the patient's current dilemma. For example: "When I didn't give you my opinion as to whether or not the girl you met in the theater was attracted to you, you began to complain of chest pain." To tentatively acknowledge Mr. Garth's feelings of victimization, the therapist added such comments as, "I wonder if my not offering a solution leads you to believe that I'm capable of dealing only with physical symptoms." Sometimes Mr. Garth's narrative would move to the topic of his mother's preoccupation with physical symptoms. To enhance his appreciation, the therapist occasionally used a referent from his own childhood. When he was five, he had suffered an episode of delirium brought on by a high fever. The episode had coincided with a period of turmoil in his family. Although he didn't mention the episode to Mr. Garth, he felt it provided him with an approximate appreciation of Mr. Garth's inner state.

Mrs. Quinn, a 33-year-old teacher, had separated from her husband one month prior to undertaking psychotherapy. Her husband had left her because of her inexplicable outbursts of anger, outbursts that predated the marriage. Even as a child

Mrs. Quinn had exhibited fits of temper. When she was an infant, she had been placed in a foster home for several months. She believed that the placement was necessitated by her parents' constant fighting. Her father eventually left the family when she was eight. Mrs. Quinn regretted never seeing him again. She and a younger brother were brought up by her mother, a well-educated woman who worked for an insurance company. However, the mother drank excessively, and Mrs. Quinn considered her emotionally needy. In addition to these outbursts of anger, Mrs. Quinn listed other problems. She was obese and attributed her obesity to compulsive eating habits. She felt that because of her need to please, particularly at work, people often took advantage of her. Finally, she considered herself unduly competitive with men.

The first two sessions were uneventful. Mrs. Quinn expanded on her history, describing in detail her relationships at work and with her family. In her third session, however, she noticed that a chair in the office had been replaced. She asked the therapist whether he had had it removed.

"Yes, you may have noticed that it was broken."

Visibly upset by the therapist's reply, Mrs. Quinn stood up and moved to a far corner of the office, staring at the therapist diffidently. Although the therapist encouraged her to voice her concerns, she refused to speak. Was she concerned that the therapist would discard her the moment he discovered her flaws? He postulated that she experienced a fear of abandonment.

Subsequent events also pointed to such a fear. For example, Mrs. Quinn often ended her sessions several minutes before her time was up because she couldn't bear to hear the therapist announce that the session was over. Prior to one of the therapist's vacation breaks, she took an overdose of medication she had secretly acquired. Fortunately, she phoned the therapist immediately and agreed to be taken by ambulance to a hospital. On other occasions, she had requested a personal item (the therapist's pen, for example) to keep while he was away. When he returned, she was often disappointed and angry that he didn't praise her sufficiently for having weathered his absence.

Her manner in the office was lively and charming, but her questions often encroached on the therapist's privacy. He often felt drowsy during her sessions. Two dream fragments she reported contributed to an understanding of her behavior. In one, she was in a hospital bed, being fed through an intravenous tube. In the second, she was sitting in the therapist's office. Her body remained in the chair while her spirit rose, preparing to depart. Her body attempted to commit suicide. However, the therapist ignored her.

From Mrs. Quinn's associations to her dreams, the therapist learned that she considered every separation to be permanent. In addition, separations were disruptive to her sense of *physical* well-being. "Whenever you go away," she said, "it feels like you're taking a piece of me with you." The imagery of the therapist as a lifeline and as an extension of her body contributed to his understanding of Mrs. Quinn's inner state.

Mr. Harris, a 26-year-old stereo wholesaler whose business required him to travel, undertook therapy to overcome a phobia of journeying beyond the outskirts of the city he lived in. Traveling evoked a fear of becoming ill. At a distance from his home or business, he felt frail. In their proximity, he felt powerful. Although Mr. Harris was successful at his business, it soon came to light that he believed himself to be capable of even greater success. What stood in his way were small-minded people who envied him, shackling him with unnecessary rules and regulations. Included in the category of small-minded people were Mr. Harris's own parents. His mother had suffered a depressive illness when he was very young. He felt as if he had spent his entire childhood cheering her up. On the other hand, talking with his mother was exhilarating. She thought the world of him. They were always on the same wavelength. Mr. Harris's father was an ordinary working stiff lacking in intelligence who didn't appreciate art or literature the way he and his mother did.

Mr. Harris's alternating view of himself, sometimes as frail, sometimes as impressively powerful, manifested itself early in therapy. The therapist was perceived as demeaning of his frailty or envious of his success. Despite interventions linking his oscillating view of the therapist with alterations in his own self-esteem, the transference quickly lost its "as if" quality. Mr. Harris considered his perceptions to be true.

As therapy progressed, the therapist discovered that his minor behavioral fluctuations had a profound effect on Mr. Harris. A failure to praise him evoked feelings of frailty; a warm greeting evoked feelings of omnipotence. Examining Mr. Harris's fluctuating self-esteem in the context of his own behavior led the therapist to an altered appreciation of Mr. Harris's childhood. For example, Mr. Harris remembered that his mother's adulation was inconsistent, governed by her own, not the patient's, needs. Although Mr. Harris resented laboring for her attention, he still felt omnipotent in her presence. He also remembered that his father had a habit of excluding himself from family discussions, handing over his son's problems to his wife.

DIFFERENCES BETWEEN
TRADITIONAL THERAPY AND SELF PSYCHOLOGY

The case discussions of Mr. Garth, Mrs. Quinn, and Mr. Harris illustrate that therapists do need to tie in their own actual or perceived lapses with the patient's unconventional stories of victimization. However, other stories, ones of agency, also often appear. In the following continuation of the foregoing case reports, we will look more closely at the relevance of the conflict model:

The therapist instituted twice-weekly sessions with Mr. Garth. Although he appreciated that it was possible to explain Mr. Garth's demandingness and his tendency to somatize as stemming from an attachment to his mother and a rejection of his father, the narrative did not lend itself to an exploration of these issues. Whether or not, for example, his childlike behavior stemmed from a regressive avoidance of sexual issues remained uncertain. Influenced by the telephone conversation with Mr. Garth's mother, the therapist continued to frame the patient's narrative in a story of victimization. He also provided a model of affect for the patient. For example, when Mr. Garth complained of chest pain following an argument with his mother, the therapist stated that under similar circumstances he himself might have experienced anger rather than chest pain.

Mr. Garth terminated therapy after six months. From follow-up visits the therapist learned that Mr. Garth did complete his accountancy course and that he did marry. His work record, however, was spotty. After failing at several jobs, he took a position in his father's firm. It is possible that therapy contributed to a slightly enhanced psychological sense of self or that it generated a slight shift with respect to unconscious conflicts. However, his follow-up visits, prompted by marital or work-related crises, revealed no significant improvement in his behavior.

Empathizing with Mrs. Quinn's sense of deficiency and linking her difficulties with her mother's neediness and her father's abandoning her was useful. The following vignettes indicate, however, the presence of stories of agency:

Following the therapist's canceling a session, Mrs. Quinn arrived in an anxious state. "I didn't know how long I could hold out," she said. Her narrative at first centered on the therapist's function as a lifeline and then shifted to her relationships at work, particularly with the head of her department. "He's always asking me to do this or that. I fight with him a lot, but I don't mind fighting with him. He gives me hell when I step out of line. He'll let me scream and yell, but he won't let himself be stepped on".

"And in here?" asked the therapist.

"I'm not sure. Sometimes I feel you let me get away with too much. You don't show your anger. I think you simply withdraw. I know it's my own fault."

The narrative then turned to Mrs. Quinn's mother. "I used to steal money from her purse. She knew about it, but she didn't punish me. I guess she felt sorry for me because I didn't have a father."

On a second occasion, prior to the therapist's leaving for vacation, Mrs. Quinn began a session by mentioning how lost

she would feel during his absence. "At least I'll have something to keep me busy," she said. "It's my niece's first birthday next weekend. I've been asked to bake something for it.
My brother wants to make it a grand occasion. There'll be lots
of out-of-town guests . . . just imagine, the universe will be
stopping simply because it's my niece's birthday." She went
on to talk about a recent visit with her mother. "I don't know
what got into her. She was so talkative, yacking all the time.
She followed me around the house, even came into the wash-
room. I felt like scraping her off me. . . . You feel that way
with me, don't you? I'm always talking, always asking you
questions. You probably wouldn't need a vacation if I didn't
bother you all the time. I used to think that my dad left because my mother wouldn't stop pestering him for attention.
He used to lose his temper a lot. He never spent much time
with me, but I really liked him. I feel empty when I think
about his leaving."

Mrs. Quinn's associations clearly indicated an awareness
that she was sometimes the agent and sometimes the victim of
her predicament. Her associations also hinted at such issues
as guilt feelings and penis envy. Her preference for her father
rather than her mother, her feeling that a piece of her was lost
when the therapist went away, her need to hold on to his pen
during his absence, and her purported competitive behavior
with respect to men all pointed to sexual conflicts.

Such conflicts did in fact emerge. In one session, Mrs.
Quinn reported losing her temper with a male colleague at
work. "It just came out of the blue," she said. "I really like the
guy. I hope I didn't hurt his feelings." Her wide-eyed profes-
sion of innocence caused the therapist to notice the youthful
pinafore she was wearing. To most sessions Mrs. Quinn wore
jeans. When he mentioned this to her, she asserted that she
always wore a skirt when her period was due. "Haven't you
figured that out yet?" she asked. "I always got bitchy with my
husband at this time of month." She then talked about another facet of her mother, not the helpless alcoholic who had
required attention but the domineering woman who had re-
jected men after she'd used them. As a child, the patient had
stolen money not only from her mother's purse but also from

the coat pockets of her mother's boyfriends. Her teenage relationships with men had been stormy and brief. She had discarded her boyfriends after they'd fallen in love with her. "Sometimes I worry that I'll turn out like my mother."

In the third year of therapy, Mr. Harris's narrative shifted from his mother's fluctuating attention to his father's unavailability. Mr. Harris also perceived the therapist as uncaring and as someone incapable of experiencing deep emotions. Shallowness of emotions was a masculine trait; only women experienced deeply. Mr. Harris himself was superior to other men because he was capable of experiencing deeper emotions than they were. Unfortunately, this capacity also generated feelings of unmanliness. He was doomed by his special gifts to remain an outsider among men.

At this juncture in therapy, Mr. Harris reported a dream in which a wrestler was walking toward him. At a distance the wrestler looked powerful, but as he drew closer, he seemed to grow smaller. The setting of the dream then shifted. Mr. Harris found himself standing in his warehouse, arguing with an employee. Mr. Harris then admitted that he had masturbated the night before the session, a fact he hadn't intended to mention because he was convinced the therapist disapproved of masturbation. As was often the case, Mr. Harris turned his statement concerning the therapist into a criticism of therapists in general. Their disapproving of masturbation revealed how conventional they were and that they were incapable of experiencing deep or unconventional feelings.

"You seem to have turned me into an insignificant person," said the therapist.

"I don't like to talk about sexual feelings when I think of you as somebody important."

"When you speak of deep feelings, you seem to mean feelings you have when you masturbate."

"Yes," he replied, "I masturbate a lot. I always did. I knew about sex when I was four or five, long before any of my friends did. It made me feel different, superior. I used to talk about my feelings with my mother, who would laugh and call me naughty. She considered me precocious, well ahead of my years."

"And your father?" asked the therapist.

"I never talked to him about sex. He wouldn't have understood . . . well, maybe I thought he'd disapprove."

At this juncture, Mr. Harris recognized that the theme of his father's unavailability camouflaged his having pushed him away. Demeaning his father had served to overcome the guilt engendered by incestuous sexual feelings for his mother. "My father may have been kinder to me than I remember," said the patient. "My mother says so. He did bring me presents when I was young. It's all so hazy. I wish I could remember more about my childhood."

Mr. Garth did not benefit significantly from therapy. It is possible that the therapist fell into the error of understanding his narrative only in terms of deficiency or that Mr. Garth resisted facing up to his conflicts. By introducing a model for affect, the therapist clearly moved away from a purely analytic approach. Mr. Garth's decision to terminate therapy may have been generated by this move.

Mrs. Quinn and Mr. Harris did benefit from therapy. Their capacity to examine their stories from several perspectives (i.e., in terms of agency and victimization) made it possible for them to appreciate the conflictual nature of their difficulties. Mrs. Quinn's relationships became less stormy as she developed a more stable sense of self. Mr. Harris's fear of traveling lessened as his self-regard became less extreme.

Although therapist and patient strive to discover what *actually* happened in the patient's past, their only sources of information are narrative and behavior as they are revealed in the therapeutic interaction. The narrative is made up of a multiplicity of stories, some leading in one direction, some in another. The patient's yearnings are cloaked in stories of responsibility, guilt, and deficiency.

In the clinical setting, the differences between self psychology and the conflict-centered theories tend to stand out less. In this setting, the imagery is always personal and evocative as it is in novels and plays. The patient is not conceived of as a disembodied drive or need but as a person with strivings. Mrs. Quinn's attachment wish and Mr. Harris's sexual wish are inseparable from their personal biographies. The part is always considered within the whole and the whole in the context of its parts.

Is a sexual drive significantly different from a need for self-affirmation? Mrs. Quinn's attachment wishes occupied center stage during one phase of therapy. Later they gave way to a new story that emphasized competitive strivings with men. Mr. Harris's narrative focused on grandiosity during one phase of therapy and on incestuous wishes during another. The desire for love, merger, and unwavering attention is universal. Every patient wants to be the object of the therapist/parent's desire. Sometimes yearnings are cloaked in one set of stories, sometimes in another. Sexual feelings and grandiose wishes, those timeless mythic yearnings, arise from a common matrix. It is impossible to associate them with one period of development as opposed to another. To assume that one form of desire is more fundamental than another, that at one stage in life the patient experienced a genetically programmed incestuous *drive*, or that actual *deficits* occurred is to slide from the level of story to the level of personal conviction. Therapists who make such assumptions are merely couching their convictions (or their countertransference) in neuropsychological metaphors.* By simply following the narrative, without insisting that Mrs. Quinn's wish for attachment or Mr. Harris's grandiose strivings must stem either from an inborn *drive* or a fundamental *need*, the therapist discovered a conflict model of the patient containing two sets of stories.

Ideally, the therapist should maintain a neutral position in which responsibility for an interference is attributed neither to

---

*Self psychology sets itself in opposition to both a conflict theory and a drive theory. The terms *conflict theory* and *drive theory* are not synonymous. A drive theory embodies the notion of mechanistic forces. Interestingly, self psychology introduces the notion of *unmet needs*, a concept that is hardly less mechanistic than that of *drives*. The conflict theory proposed here refers to conflicts pertaining to wishes. The term *wish* is used to circumvent the question of whether the patient's behavior is rooted in an actual deficit that requires fulfillment or an actual drive that requires taming.

the patient in the form of a *drive* nor to the therapist/parent in the form of an unmet *need*. In practice, such neutrality is impossible. Therapists are troubled by the same conflicts they uncover in their patients. The therapist's judgment will err at times in one direction, at times in another. (Mr. Garth's case in which the patient's story was understood only in terms of victimization is likely an example of such an error in judgment.) Nevertheless, being open to both points of view (i.e., to agency and to victimization) will make the therapist more effective.

At their best, therapists neither gratify nor tame patients but enhance understanding. Understanding frees patients from the grip of their stories. Because one can ultimately discover stories of both agency and victimization in the patient's narrative, it is unlikely that less difficult patients would benefit most from one point of view or theoretical framework and more difficult patients from another. It may indeed be that with difficult patients the therapist needs to empathize with stories of victimization for prolonged periods of time before stories of agency surface. The outcome of the cases presented in this chapter suggests that therapy works best when patients are able to consider their difficulties from more than one perspective, from the conflictual perspectives of both victimization and agency.

SUMMARY

The notion of less difficult versus more difficult patients was introduced in this chapter not to expand on issues of classification but to serve as a vehicle for examining the opposing models of transference and countertransference.

Although with more difficult patients, the oscillating pattern necessary for understanding is no different from the one described in Chapter 8 and is fraught with similar countertransference resistances, the demands on the therapist are greater. The more difficult patient's world may be appropriately compared to the world of a science fiction novel. The therapist's function is to discover the unconventional premises that govern it. In these cases, in which lapses that might otherwise be ignored may have a cataclysmic effect, therapists must take particular care in including their own lapses in their interventions.

In the clinical setting, some of the differences between self psychology and the conflict-centered theories quickly become less important. The patient's difficulties clearly must be examined both in terms of the patient as a whole and in terms of conflictual wishes, both in terms of agency and of victimization. To postulate a *drive* or a *need* and to claim that one is more fundamental than the other is to introduce unwarranted assumptions. In the therapist's task of both sharing the patient's perspective and pressing beyond the edge of awareness, more than one point of view is clearly necessary to attain a complex understanding of the patient's conflicts.

Chapter Ten

Inexactness and Empathy

Empathy is enhanced by using multiple perspectives, by appreciating what patients are experiencing and what they are disregarding, by focusing on the patient as a whole person and on conflictual elements. As observer on the scene, one shares the patient's perspective. As external observer, one examines the narrative as a whole. Periods of interference are examined in terms of defensive behavior and in terms of transference-countertransference patterns, in terms of the patient's difficulties and in terms of the therapist's. In a similar vein, the narrative is considered from the perspectives of both agency and victimization. This general empathic capacity to use multiple perspectives is further enhanced by the therapist's growing appreciation of inexactness.

In defining them, the various functions, phases of therapy, and perspectives have been neatly pigeonholed. In the initial stage of learning therapeutic practice, it simplifies matters to adhere to discrete definitions. A grasp of vocabulary and grammar and a familiarity with literature is necessary before the reader of a novel can turn his attention to the broader issue of the aims and usefulness of literature in general. As therapists become experienced and more proficient at their work, the scope of their inquiry also expands. They begin to appreciate some of the ways in which their view is obscured and some of the ways in which the concepts they employ in their work are inaccurate. The so-called fundamental rule, through which the therapist encourages the patient to say what comes to mind without regard for logical or syntactical connections, is itself a complex and inexact set of regulations. It is presented as a liberty, with the hope that it will become an aim. Yet, it is an unattainable ideal, a task at which the patient will inevitably fail. Therapists want it to become an inclination but not an obligation. At the same time, they must pay attention to the patient's disinclination to free-associate.

The following clinically oriented sections focus on inexactness as it applies to the therapist's alternating positions (external observer versus observer on the scene) and to phases of therapy (periods of interference versus periods of progress). In addition, the manner in which the therapist alters the field of observation will be illustrated. In the course of these discussions, the coalescence of factors that occasionally gives rise to a momentary close match between the patient's difficulties or conflicts and those of the therapist will be described.

THE THERAPIST'S PERSPECTIVES

The following case discussions illustrate the inexact and interdependent nature of the dual positions of external observer and observer on the scene:

> Mr. Sands, a middle–aged reporter for a newspaper, talks in a session about being turned down for promotion. This morning he received the news of this decision from his senior editor. Although Mr. Sands talks as if the therapist were familiar with the events leading up to the incident, the therapist doesn't remember hearing about a possible promotion. The patient claims he "deserved it." His words are ambiguous:

Did he deserve the promotion, or to be turned down for it? The narrative then turns to a recent series of articles Mr. Sands has written on starvation in Africa for which he received a letter of praise from the head office. The narrative again takes a turn, this time to his plans about adopting a child. Six months ago, his wife's only pregnancy ended in miscarriage. Recently, Mr. Sands has heard of a young woman who is pregnant. To hold on to her government benefits, she will be obliged to give up the child. Yesterday, Mr. Sands contacted a lawyer to inquire about adoption proceedings. He wants to adopt for his wife's sake.

After a pause, Mr. Sands returns to the missed promotion. He was not selected for the post because he couldn't impress his superiors. He admonishes himself for expressing his ideas in the pedantic manner of an academic. His life is a story of "almosts." He almost completed his Ph.D. in history; he was almost hired as a lecturer at a university; today he almost received a promotion. He always falls betwixt and between, neither an academic nor a journalist. Last night he had dreamt of placing a hot pan on the kitchen counter, which left a burn mark on the counter top. He tried to remove the mark but couldn't expunge it. In the dream his wife was furious with him. He pauses. Returning to the subject of work, he says he considers himself someone who needs to hold on to failure. Is he fated to fail? Does failure define him?

The therapist waits for a suitable moment to ask a question and then asks Mr. Sands to expand on the meeting with his editor. Mr. Sands describes in detail being called in to the administrative office and receiving the disappointing news. The promotion, a position he coveted, would have moved him to the foreign affairs desk. His editor, a gentlemanly father figure, offered him a cup of coffee before breakng the news to him and assured him that a special niche would be carved out for him. A consolation prize.

As he listens, the therapist imaginatively transports himself into the setting Mr. Sands has just described. To augment his empathic appreciation of Mr. Sands's sense of failure, he attempts to recall an incident in his own life comparable to the patient's predicament. At the moment, however, it is difficult to recall such an incident. Finally, his thoughts settle on an episode from his adolescence of being fired from a hardware store. The incident, however, was not one of being turned down for promotion, nor did it jeopardize his own ambition of someday becoming a doctor. Working in the store was a temporary job, not a stepping-stone toward a medical career. The dismissal could not possibly have had the same effect on the therapist as not receiving the promotion had on Mr. Sands. Still, he was mortified at the time.

As observer on the scene, the therapist's appreciation of the patient's inner state is derived from imagery pieced together from the patient's description of an incident at work and from imagery stemming from an incident in the therapist's past. But how accurate, how exact, is this appreciation? The boss the therapist remembers is not the patient's boss. The circumstances and significance of the episode the therapist remembers are different from those of the incident reported by the patient. Clearly, the therapist's empathic appreciation is inexact.

As external observer, the therapist looks for connections. A missed promotion. Starving children. A woman for whom money (i.e., government benefits) is more important than a child. An impulse to rescue a child by adoption from a disinterested woman for the sake of another woman. A dream in which a woman criticizes him for carelessness. In addition, the therapist remembers Mr. Sands's description of his mother in previous sessions, her disdain for weak men and her conviction that all the men in her family were cursed with weak genes (genes passed on to the patient?). On one occasion, Mr. Sands reported an incident of his mother's berating his father, a successful academic, for not being successful at business as well as at scholarship. It has not escaped the therapist's attention that, as an academic, Mr. Sands's father occupies one of those stools which the patient falls betwixt and between. Nor has the therapist failed to notice the pattern in the sessions. When he leaves a session in which he believes his performance was below par, Mr. Sands is critical of himself.

Although his narrative is replete with associations, at the moment Mr. Sands does not notice them. They are not at the center of his consciousness. The therapist, however, does notice them and is aware of dim connections between the patient's difficulties at work, his early history, and his behavior in therapy. They point to patterns worth bringing to the patient's attention. As external observer, the therapist is in this instance slightly ahead of the patient. Nevertheless, he has only an indefinite sense of the direction the narrative will take. The exact nature of the themes that will emerge is uncertain.

In addition, the functions associated with the dual positions of external observer and observer on the scene are not independent of each other. The therapist's awareness of the recurring themes of failure and rejection in the narrative as a whole prompted him to regard the scenario of the missed promotion as being more significant than other scenarios (more significant, for example, than the scenario in which the patient discussed adoption proceedings with his lawyer). Similarly, the scenario the therapist selected from the patient's narrative as a window to his world colored his understanding of these themes in the narrative as a whole.

In today's session Mrs. Warner is silent and rigid. She is often silent and rigid. Today as she talks she looks away from the therapist. Her words are barely audible. Her husband is inattentive. Yesterday, he went off to play tennis shortly after supper, leaving Mrs. Warner to cope with their two young children. As a lawyer, he often works late. Mrs. Warner rarely has time for herself. She pauses and then castigates herself for voicing such petty complaints. Another pause. She has been bleeding for several days, though her period is not due for two weeks. Perhaps too hastily, the therapist asks whether she has contacted her doctor. She replies that she hasn't done so. Her words fade into silence. At the end of the session she scurries out of the office as if she were escaping from a torture chamber.

In the following session she reports having telephoned her doctor. "I've arranged to see him later today," she says. "I guess I should have called him right away." She also reports a dream in which she is awakened from her sleep by a noise. Creeping downstairs from her bedroom, she encounters a strange man with a knife who must have slipped in through the back door. The moment she sees him she wakes up. The dream terrified her. She relates it to her fear of medical doctors. The fear is not a fear of needles or surgery but one of being "mishandled."

It is unusual for Mrs. Warner to report a dream. The therapist considers it a gift for having paid attention to her medical complaint. He imaginatively pictures himself in the setting of the dream and in a doctor's office. Although his fear of strangers with knives may be similar to Mrs. Warner's, it is unlikely that their fears are identical. The doctor's office in which the therapist imaginatively situates himself is his own doctor's office. Recently, he consulted his internist for an abdominal complaint. The fear that this visit evoked, however, was not one of being mishandled but of the doctor's discovering a life-threatening condition. Clearly, as an observer on the scene, the therapist's appreciation of Mrs. Warner's subjective state is limited.

As external observer, the therapist makes connections. For example, he remembers her reporting a similar dream on another occasion. At that time, too, the dream report came close on the heels of an intervention intended to be helpful. Mrs. Warner's reactions to interventions and her defensiveness in general have not escaped the therapist's notice. He suspects she experiences interventions of any kind as dangerous intrusions. Such a notion may be at the periphery of her consciousness. At the moment, however, the significance of her behavior has eluded her. As external observer, the therapist is slightly ahead of Mrs. Warner. He has a sense of the direction the narrative will take but not of the specific themes that will emerge.

In addition, the therapist's attributing significance to some episodes as opposed to others (i.e., his selecting the setting of the dream and the visit to her doctor as significant, as opposed to, for example, an episode of her interacting with her husband) is influenced by his awareness of the recurring theme of fearfulness. Similarly, the scenarios that the therapist selected from her narrative to gain access to her world colored his objective appreciation of the narrative as a whole.

Clearly, subjectivity alters the therapist's appreciation of the patient's inner state. In the preceding examples, the therapist worked to enhance his appreciation by deliberately comparing a scenario in the patient's world with one in his own. Even without such a conscious comparison, his subjectivity (that is, his conscious and unconscious memories) would intrude on, provide reference points for, and limit his appreciation of the patient's inner state. For example, it is unlikely that the therapist was able to bypass his own subjectivity to appreciate accurately the experience of menstrual bleeding or the invasive feeling associated with a gynecological procedure. The preceding examples merely highlight the reality that, even in the role of observer on the scene, the therapist is not a *tabula rasa*.

In addition, although an objective appreciation of the narrative as a whole may place the therapist slightly ahead of the patient, it provides only an indefinite sense of the direction the narrative will take. As the ensuing discussions illustrate, the ultimate direction a narrative takes is unpredictable. The preceding case discussions also illustrate the interdependent nature of the two positions of external observer and observer on the scene. What the therapist learned about these patients from one perspective influenced and altered what he learned about them from the other.

PERIODS OF INTERFERENCE AND PERIODS OF PROGRESS

Therapy moves forward more slowly at some stages than at others. The following continuations of the discussions of the preceding cases illustrate, however, that periods of interference and periods of progress are often not clearly distinguishable from each other and that periods of interference are not clearly attributable to one participant or the other.

Repeatedly posing the question of whether or not he is fated to fail, Mr. Sands is clearly not in a mood to reflect. For example, relevant events from his early history are absent from the narrative. The therapist comments that at the moment Mr. Sands is able to contemplate only one explanation for his not having received a promotion. This raises Mr. Sands's spirits. "Of course," he says, "I should have thought of that. It could be office politics or seniority or some other factor I haven't considered." His relief, however, is short-lived. "I'm just looking for an excuse," he says, returning to the theme of inadequacy. The journalist who did receive the promotion deserved it. When he leaves the session, Mr. Sands is dejected.

The moment Mr. Sands has left, several thoughts spring to the therapist's mind. Today Mr. Sands was supposed to discuss altering the timetable of his appointments to increase the frequency of his sessions. Mr. Sands, however, forgot to mention it. Mr. Sands's mother used to withhold his allowance or deny him such pleasures as attending a film or a concert if he exhibited weakness or failure. The therapist postulates that Mr. Sands is experiencing a troublesome transference state. Punishing himself as his mother once punished him, he has denied himself the right to increase the frequency of the sessions. The possible presence of a troublesome countertransference state is indicated by the therapist's also having forgotten this matter. His failure to mention the extra session is tantamount to withholding it. He has unwittingly taken on the role of Mr. Sands's punitive mother.

Another thought had also slipped the therapist's mind. Only six months earlier he himself had been turned down for promotion at the hospital he attended. The details of this incident were similar to those described by the patient. The hospital incident did not spring to mind during the session. The therapist had instead reached far into his past for an incident that was considerably different from the patient's recent setback. Clearly, the therapist was conflicted (as was the patient) about pursuing the subject of failure. To the extent that it was intended to quickly lift Mr. Sands's mood, the therapist's intervention encouraging him to consider other reasons for his setback was likely generated by the desire to avoid examining this troublesome subject. A conflict or difficulty in the patient had touched off a conflict or difficulty in the therapist.

Nevertheless, therapy was propelled forward. In the next

session, Mr. Sands remembered his omission. He recognized the significance of his failure to mention the new arrangements for therapy. He also reported a dream of stealing a sports car and was able to connect his omission and the events of the dream with his mother's interest in flashy, successful men. Finally, new material emerged. Mr. Sands related the story, told him by his mother, of his family's escape from Nazi-occupied Prague. His grandfather, the only member of the family who was of Jewish origin, had been paralyzed by the arrival of the Nazis, but Mr. Sands's grandmother, taking the family in hand, obtained travel documents and planned the route of exit. A successful businessman prior to the war, his grandfather ended his days in North America as an unemployed idler.

In this session, issues that had previously occupied the periphery of Mr. Sands's consciousness moved to the center. New issues emerged at the periphery, issues of annihilation and race. The therapist wondered whether Mr. Sands's mother equated weak-willed genes with Jewish genes. The new issues would undoubtedly touch off new conflicts in the therapist (as well as in the patient), giving rise to a new period of interference. As did the conflicts pertaining to failure, the new conflicts would create a dilemma for the therapist. Once again he would be torn between the inclination to pursue understanding and the inclination to avoid it.

Mrs. Warner's dream of the stranger with the knife prompted her to talk briefly of being mistreated by doctors. This was followed by silence. The therapist asked her to tell more, encouraging her to add details to her dream. His urgings, however, were unsuccessful in eliciting new material. In the ensuing silence, his mind wandered, and he pictured himself taking his young son to a hockey game. At the entrance to the arena, he encountered Mrs. Warner. When the therapist drew back from this pleasant fantasy, he recognized that he had momentarily fled from the session and that his pressuring Mrs. Warner to expand on her dream was grounded in irritability. Had he tried to escape from her projections? In his fantasy, he was convincing her of his competence as a parent. Had he sensed in her behavior an accusation that his parenting skills were deficient? His pressuring her to expand on her dream and the hasty intervention that had prompted her to contact her doctor also may have stemmed from a desire to ward off examining conflict in himself. Clearly, a period of interference had surfaced.

Nevertheless, therapy was propelled forward. In her next session, Mrs. Warner was able to use this material to examine her relationship with her father. The manner in which this came about, however, will be discussed later in this chapter.

A patient's maintaining an unalterable point of view or pressuring the therapist for answers may stem from an inclination to avoid self-inquiry. A therapist's accepting explanations as they stand or pressuring the patient to analyze the narrative may also stem from such an inclination. Conflicts and difficulties in the patient always touch off conflicts and difficulties in the therapist. Mr. Sands's conflicts concerning failure and Mrs. Warner's conflicts pertaining to parenting touched off conflicts in the therapist. The cases reported illustrate how difficult it is to ascertain whether a period of interference is generated mainly by the patient's conflicts or mainly by the therapist's.

In addition, as Mr. Sands's case illustrates, periods of interference are not significantly different from periods of progress. Indeed, progress entails advancing from one period of interference to the next. As stated before, a friendly atmosphere should not be equated with progress. At times, the patient needs to be angry, critical, or silent. An intervention that reduces a patient's anger may spring from the therapist's intolerance of such behavior. At times, the therapist needs to press beyond the edges of a friendly tête-á-tête to uncover hidden rancor. Understanding the significance of a period of interference, rather than defusing it, is indispensable to therapy. In the process, the patient's sphere of self-awareness is expanded.

Therapy progresses when the inclination to pursue self-inquiry outweighs the inclination not to pursue it and falters when the situation is reversed (Gardner 1983). The ubiquitous presence of conflict (in the therapist as well as in the patient) makes it necessary to recognize its contribution at every stage of therapy. The therapist's conflicts and difficulties determine the degree to which the therapeutic process is promoted or retarded, the degree to which the therapist imaginatively moves into a scenario in the patient's world, and the manner in which recurring themes in the narrative as a whole are selected. Conflict is an unavoidable component of the therapist's subjectivity.

MULTIPLE VISION

In searching for connections, therapists examine the part within the whole and the whole in the context of its parts. Wondering about the patient, they wonder about themselves. They encourage the patient to wonder. They look for themes at the periphery of the patient's consciousness and at the periphery of their own. At its best, therapy is an expanding spiral of mutual self-inquiry (Gardner 1983).

As one becomes proficient at moving from one function to another and from one position to another, the various mental activities often move to the back of one's consciousness. Deliberate actions such as imaginatively transporting oneself into the patient's scenario or comparing the patient's predicament with one from one's own experience are augmented by evenly hovering attention. The therapist may engage in such activities without knowing it.

Occasionally, therapists may experience a brief period of multiple vision. At such moments, both present-day episodes and issues from the past are included in the scope of their vision. They are able simultaneously to grasp an aspect of the patient's experiential state and an aspect of their own from the dual positions of external observer and observer on the scene. Individually, each perspective is inexact and limited. However, the ability to oscillate freely from one to the other or to experience them simultaneously makes it possible for the therapist to appreciate aspects of the patient's subjectivity from an objective perspective. During such moments, therapists may discover a close match between the patient's conflicts or difficulties and their

own. Proficiency, however, is only one of several essential pre-
conditions. The therapist and the patient need to have learned
something about each other. Their inclination (as well as their
courage) to pursue self-inquiry needs to outweigh their inclination to avoid it. The participants need to press forward with their
own self-inquiry rather than impelling it in the other. They need
to be comfortable with each other but not too comfortable. It
should not be imagined that such moments are free of tension.
There is always some difference, a degree of misunderstanding,
between them.

Moments when therapists recognize a close match between
the patient's conflicts and their own are often characterized by
personal evocative imagery. The patient's imagery and affect
closely resemble the therapist's. As with dreams and poetry, the
imagery is compact and powerfully allusive. It is as if the patient's narrative has shifted momentarily from prose to poetry.

This shift is succinctly illustrated by the following literary example (Frye 1963, p. 27). The English poet, W. B. Yeats, revised
an early poem in the following manner. The original read as
follows:

And then you came with those red mournful lips,
And with you came the whole of the world's tears,
And all the trouble of her labouring ships,
And all the trouble of her myriad years.

In the final edition of this poetry, the lines read:

A girl arose that had red mournful lips
And seemed the greatness of the world in tears,
Doomed like Odysseus and the labouring ships
And proud as Priam murdered with his peers.

Yeats believed the second version was more poetic (that is, less
prose-like) than the first because the language was more specific, precise, and allusive. For example, the second version contains specific references to the stories of Odysseus and Priam.
During a period of close match between the patient's and the

therapist's conflicts, the language of the narrative can be said to gain the richness of poetry.

Mr. Sands's session did not give rise to the imagery described in the foregoing paragraph. With Mrs. Warner, however, a moment of close match between the patient's and the therapist's conflicts did emerge. The following discussion illustrates how, by pursuing his own associations, the therapist discovered imagery congruent with Mrs. Warner's:

> During the session, the therapist had postulated that the fantasy of meeting Mrs. Warner while taking his son to a hockey game stemmed from a desire to reassure himself that his parenting skills were satisfactory—that is, from a desire to ward off conflict. When the session was over, the fantasy returned. Its persistence puzzled him. Reexamining it, he discovered an inconsistency. The setting depicted was not the wintry day one associates with hockey but a hot summer's day. The therapist turned his attention to the large park next to the arena. A light breeze. Open stretches of green in which children were playing. Off in the distance the screen door of the public building in the center of the park was swinging back and forth. Was there really such a door on the building in the park? Focusing on the door, he remembered Mrs. Warner's dream. The stranger with the knife had entered through the back door of the house. The therapist envisioned it as a flimsy screen door and wondered whether Mrs. Warner also pictured it this way. Screen doors. Screen memories. Arcadian doors and dangerous doors. Wondering about doors, his mind traced its way to a similar door in his childhood.
>
> When he was seven, he and his mother had spent a summer at a cottage on a farm. Although the cottage had a screen door, it wasn't an ominous door. No stranger with a knife burst in through it. The memories with which it was imbued were idyllic. It was through this door that he had raced to meet his friends. His father stepped through it when he arrived for the weekend. All week he would anticipate the arrival of his father who, in those days, was an endless source of wisdom and pleasure. Since then many incidents had come between them that were painful to think about.

That summer the therapist had read Stevenson's *Treasure Island*. His father had bought it for him. It was his father who had introduced him to literature. Sitting on a rock beside the cottage, he read *Treasure Island*. Since he had not yet learned to read well, many passages were beyond his comprehension. Nevertheless, he had enjoyed the book. He remembered hobbling along on the rock pretending to be Long John Silver, who of the many characters in the novel had intrigued him the most. A wonderful, terrible man. A man whom one sets up on a pedestal but who ultimately disappoints. A great man who uses a child for his own ends. Wonderful fathers and terrible fathers. The image of Long John Silver had stayed with him.

Many years later, reading another of Stevenson's novels, he met Long John Silver again, this time in the guise of Dr. Jekyll and Mr. Hyde. Good men and evil men. Good fathers and evil fathers. At this time, the therapist was torn between love and hate for his father. Yearning and anger, reasonable and unreasonable motives had merged. The factors contributing to the uneasy truce that existed between them were difficult to determine. Fathers and fatherhood. Returning to the present, the therapist wondered whether his fear of the oncoming struggle with his own son interfered with his functions as a parent. Did he worry too much that his son's first idol would some day be shown to have feet of clay? How ironic that a novel bought for him by his father should open his eyes to the painful struggle with fathers.

Mrs. Warner's behavior had generated a simple scenario. In one direction stood an arena, obstructing the view, facilitating disavowal. In the other direction was a park, opening the way to a string of associations.

In the session following, Mrs. Warner described her visit to her doctor. The appointment had gone well. Despite the doctor's considerateness, however, she couldn't completely subdue her distrustfulness. Fondness for men was a dangerous feeling because men were not attuned to a woman's needs. Her husband had a pattern of occasionally treating her kindly, but this behavior didn't fool her. His needs always came first. After a pause, she talked about her childhood in Nova Scotia.

Her father, a longshoreman, worked at a seaport many miles from home and was often absent for weeks at a time. During his absences, Mrs. Warner looked forward to his return. His visits, however, were always a disappointment. He showed little interest in her and quarrelled incessantly with her mother. When he was home, he spent most of his evenings at a local tavern. When he returned to work, she and her mother were relieved. Yet during his absences her hopeful fantasies returned. She pictured him fondly embracing her the next time he visited.*

"I used to think of him as a swashbuckler," she said. "It was many years before I stopped thinking of him that way." Her words prompted her to remember the dream of the stranger with the knife. "Swashbucklers carry knives," she said. Heroes and cutthroats. Fathers we love and hate. Fathers we disappoint and who disappoint us. Cycles of yearning and disillusionment. Sifting through associations, patient and therapist had uncovered similar imagery and conflicts.

THE FIELD OF OBSERVATION

In the preceding case, the patient and therapist experiencing similar conflicts and imagery was not accidental. Their conflicts and imagery evolved from a common source. The touchstone was the therapeutic relationship. The yearnings and conflicts that relationships trigger give rise to a common body of symbols, images, and myths. The patient's conflicts and imagery were similar to and different from the therapist's to the extent that all human beings are similar to and different from each other.

The stories it is possible to glean from a patient's narrative are as numerous as the symbols, images, and myths through which human experience is manifested. In Mrs. Warner's case, the mythical world of romance on the high seas provided the com-

---

*Encoded in Mrs. Warner's narrative were her perceptions of the therapist as well. These perceptions were a blend of accurate observation, transference, and projections of aspects of herself.

mon symbolic referents by means of which the patient's and the therapist's subjectivities came into close contact. Even within this particular world the possibilities had not been exhausted. The significance of the image of Long John Silver, for example, was not fully explored. The therapist recognized that lurking in the background were the outlines of darker plots, of bloody violence, of encounters with swashbuckling mothers.

To assert that each participant examined and reexamined the therapeutic relationship (in the context of children and fathers) until an aspect of commonality emerged would be too static a description of the events that transpired. Each participant acted upon and altered the other. For example, the therapist's prior knowledge of Mrs. Warner's father's occupation likely played a role in bringing to mind Stevenson's *Treasure Island*. The therapist's interventions likely played a role in fashioning the manner in which Mrs. Warner's conflicts emerged. For example, his recommendation that she should contact her doctor, triggered by both a wish to be helpful and a wish that she seek help elsewhere, set in motion the cycle of yearning and disillusionment that Mrs. Warner reported in the context of her father's absences. Clearly, the therapist's presence altered the field of observation.

SUMMARY

With experience, therapists begin to appreciate some of the ways in which their work and the concepts they use are inexact. As observer on the scene, one's vision is limited and skewed by one's own subjectivity. Although the position of external observer may place the therapist slightly ahead of the patient, it provides only an indirect sense of the ultimate direction the narrative will take. In addition, the functions associated with these vantage points are interdependent.

Furthermore, periods of interference are not significantly different from periods of progress. Indeed, progress entails moving forward from one period of interference to the next. Conflict, particularly conflict over pursuing understanding as opposed to not pursuing it, is present in every phase of therapy. It is an inevitable aspect of the therapist's (as well as the patient's) subjectivity.

Occasionally, therapists experience multiple vision in which aspects of the patient's difficulties and aspects of their own, elements of present-day patterns, and elements from the past are all included in the scope of their perceptions. Despite the ubiquitous presence of inexactness and conflict, the ability to oscillate freely between the dual positions makes it possible for the therapist to appreciate aspects of the patient's subjectivity from an objective perspective. At points where the patient's conflicts closely match those of the therapist, the patient's imagery will often resemble the therapist's. Although they are not tension-free, such moments are characterized by both participants pressing forward with their own self-inquiry. At such moments, it becomes clear how the observer alters the field of observation.

Chapter Eleven

Empathic Interventions

In this chapter, those qualities of an intervention that propel therapy forward and promote empathy and understanding will be discussed. The concept of forward motion, or progress, may imply a desired and foreseeable endpoint, a known final page to the novel. In therapy, however, to set one's sights on one path as opposed to another (that is, to follow a course of action that leads to one set of explanatory stories instead of another set) is a misapplication of this concept. To leave room for unexpected turns, therapists need to press forward without pressing in one direction more than in another. In this context, the fundamental tasks are to keep things happening, to keep patients talking, and to help them discover significant themes and behavioral patterns.

Discomfort is the major factor that compels patients to undertake therapy. In the sessions, the major factor that keeps things happening is the relationship itself. The coming together of two human beings sets in motion (in the therapist and in the patient) yearnings and conflicts as well as measures to ward them off. One way in which therapists contribute to the process is by permitting themselves occasionally and partially to be drawn into the relationship. If they adopt an uninvolved stance—that is, if they consider themselves to be nothing more than a mirror—they will inhibit the process. If they allow themselves to be drawn completely into the relationship, therapy will become a repetition of the patient's long-standing troublesome patterns. At times, therapists imaginatively place themselves in the patient's scenario. At other times, they are drawn in unwittingly. Occasionally, they use the patient to reenact a scenario from their own lives. From time to time, they need to step back and to conceptualize what is happening.

The patterns, stories, and convictions that emerge need to be discussed. Although facial gestures and postural shifts are important forms of communication, language is the major communicative instrument. Yearnings, conflicts, and behavioral patterns are most clearly conveyed and reflected upon through the medium of language, which facilitates shared contemplation and gives rise to new stories, patterns, and explanations.

Interventions take many forms. They are often a combination of spontaneity and careful construction. Observation and speculative thinking prepare the ground for them. A discrepancy, a word, or a gesture that stands out in the narrative or a pattern that surfaces over the course of several sessions starts the therapist thinking. Some interventions take the form of questions (e.g., requesting information). Others are clarifications (e.g., explaining that it is the patient, not the therapist, who is feeling sad or angry). Some may focus on unconscious themes; others may prepare the way for interventions that follow. Occasionally, the therapist may find it useful to summarize significant points expressed by the patient. Interventions may call attention to the relationship, to the patient's narrative, or to the ongoing communicative process itself (Leavy 1973).

THE STRUCTURE OF
INTERVENTIONS: QUESTIONS AND ANSWERS

Many patients begin psychotherapy with the notion that the therapist is a knowledgeable teacher (i.e., someone who will impart self-understanding by giving advice or by answering questions). To an extent, therapists do provide answers. For example, they may point out that today the patient is talking mainly about failure, that the patient's self-critical behavior at work bears a resemblance to his behavior at home, or that the emotional barrier characterizing the therapeutic relationship is similar to one that characterized the patient's relationship with his father. Therapists answer some questions but not others. Often they answer questions that patients don't know they are asking.

In themselves, answers bring closure to a subject. Since Plato's time, teachers have recognized that simply providing information is not conducive to learning.* Indeed, in many instances it is the teacher, not the student, who asks the questions. Asking questions opens the way to new possibilities. The riddling or ironical quality of the questions Greek philosophers often posed broke down the students' repressions and helped them discover what they knew.** The therapist also asks questions. Asking patients to expand on an episode, to put their sadness into words, or to continue talking about a dream helps them discover what they know about themselves.

Indeed, every intervention is both an answer and a question. When one points out that today the patient is talking mainly about failure, that his self-critical behavior at work is no different from his behavior at home, or that the emotional barrier that the patient experiences in therapy resembles a barrier he described as existing between himself and his father, one is also asking the patient whether he considers these issues to be significant. When therapists ask their patients to expand on an episode, to put their sadness into words, or to continue talking about a dream, they are also telling the patient that they consider this episode, emotional state, or dream to be significant.

Furthermore, because the patient's stories arise in the context of the therapeutic relationship and directly or indirectly allude to it, these answers and questions need to be directed to the thera-

---

*The teacher's function of lifting the student's repressions is discussed in the introduction to *The Great Code* (Frye 1982).

**More accurately, questions help students discover what they didn't know they knew.

pist as well as to the patient. When one mentions the presence of the theme of failure or points to similarities between the patient's patterns at work, at home, and in the session, one also needs to consider similar themes in oneself. When one asks the patient to expand on an episode, to put his sadness into words, or to continue talking about a dream, one needs to present similar tasks to oneself.

ENHANCING THE PATIENT'S SELF-UNDERSTANDING

The ultimate aim of an intervention is to help the patient discover significant new themes and associations. In the process, new data emerge. In essence, what the therapist who has this aim in mind is saying to the patient is, "Let's consider together, that is, let's compare and contrast, what you are saying about your wife in the light of what you said about your mother," or "Let's consider what you do with your boss in the light of what you do with other men," or "Let's compare and contrast how you felt about yourself yesterday with how you feel about yourself today."

On the one hand, an intervention interrupts the flow of the narrative. For example, hearing the therapist compare a pattern at work with one at home makes it difficult for the patient to blithely continue talking about these patterns without examining them in a new light. On the other hand, by encouraging the patient to consider new themes or connections, an intervention moves the narrative forward.

One of the important ways in which an intervention enhances understanding is by bringing together significant themes in the narrative with patterns that emerge in the therapeutic relationship. At times—for example, when the patient is talking about seductive behavior with his mother without noticing a similar pattern developing in therapy—the therapist needs to bring attention to the interaction. At times—for example, when the patient is caught in the throes of a therapeutic relationship so intense that he has stopped talking—the therapist needs to bring attention to a comparable pattern outside of therapy. Sometimes therapists need to move the discussion toward the topic of the relationship; sometimes they need to move it away from the relationship. Their aim is to sustain the narrative and to occasionally tie it in with what is happening in therapy.

THE QUALITIES OF AN INTERVENTION: SIMPLICITY, ALLUSIVENESS, AND INDIRECTNESS

The therapist strives to communicate concepts and connections in a way that brings out the patient's own stories and imagery. An intervention should be emotionally evocative; it should strike a chord in the patient. Interventions that are lengthy or complex bring attention to language and to theoretical abstractions. The most effective interventions are those that are simply worded. For the same reason, interventions should be allusive, employing whenever possible the patient's own words and imagery.

Because they work at the edge of awareness, therapists are always making detours. Straightforwardly asking a patient why he is angry or late gives rise only to conscious explanations. In order to go deeper, therapists need to approach such subjects indirectly. They need to examine the patient's anger or lateness in the context of the narrative. By learning about the patient's difficulties at work, they discover the significance of the patient's behavior in the sessions. By observing the patient in the sessions, they learn about patterns at work. Furthermore, interventions should not be put forward imperiously. Unequivocal answers cast the therapist in the role of the imparter of knowledge and the patient in the role of the uninformed student. Exhortative questions cast the therapist in the role of the intrusive interrogator and the patient in the role of the pressured respondent. Forcible statements generate an unnecessarily adversarial stance that interferes with the relationship. The following clinical examples demonstrate how the therapist (without being cryptic or oracular) uses simply worded allusive phrases to make connections between one story or piece of behavior and another.

A young lawyer found it difficult to talk about a recent promotion at work. The therapist remembered that the patient's parents were indifferent to his excellent school marks. In order to connect these events, the therapist said, "It seems difficult to bring *home* good news to me."

A young secretary reported that she had spent the evening at a trendy nightclub. "You've probably never heard of it," she said to the therapist, "I don't imagine you get out much." The therapist remembered that the patient's mother, a fashion model, often referred to the patient as a "drag." In order to connect her relationship with her mother to her attitude in therapy, the therapist said, "I guess you consider me to be a drag."

In the case (discussed in Chapter 6) in which the therapist recognized a similarity between the patient's story and the biblical story of Cain, the therapist did not directly confront the patient with the possibility that his symptoms stemmed from pleasure and guilt over his brother's death. (His brother had died during World War II on a target range in Burma.) Instead, he alluded to it with the statement, "And you have been wandering ever since."

In these examples, the therapist used simply worded allusive interventions to bring attention to significant links between one theme or aspect of behavior and another.

INEXACTNESS, SUBJECTIVITY, AND CONFLICT

Interventions are not simply a repetition of what the patient already knows. Therapists also press forward in new directions and in doing so often reveal their own preferences and conflicts. The degree to which therapists need to be viewed as interrogators or imparters of knowledge, the degree to which they need to be talked about or not talked about, and the degree to which they need to impose their own views on the patient color the form and the content of their interventions. Pressing forward entails risk taking. Although therapists aim for exactness, their interventions invariably fall short of it. Consequently, they should put forward their ideas tentatively (e.g., "You *look* sad" rather than "You *are* sad"). To an extent, inexactness may be detrimental to therapy. Nevertheless, to the extent that it reveals therapists to be human, it also fuels the relationship.*

THE DIALOGUE

Interventions build on each other. They are not self-contained units that can be considered separately from the responses that follow them or from the dialogue as a whole. Sometimes, as the following case illustrates, an intervention simply prepares the way for later interventions:

In a session the patient, a young businesswoman, vacillated over her wedding plans. Should she marry before becoming pregnant, or should she delay making wedding arrangements until she was pregnant? The patient and her boyfriend had discussed her dilemma on many occasions. The therapist suspected that the patient's uncertainty stemmed from difficulties with her father, difficulties centering on a wish for unconditional attention and a feeling of defectiveness. To test his hypothesis, the therapist asked the patient to describe what her feelings would be like in the setting of the wedding hall.

"What would it be like if you were pregnant?" he asked.

"I think I'd feel embarrassed," she said. "People would think that my boyfriend was marrying me because he was forced into it, not because he loved me."

"And if you were not pregnant?" the therapist asked.

"I'd be worried about disappointing him," said the patient. "I often worry that I won't be able to have children."

These answers supported the therapist's hypothesis. As a

---

*Indeed, inexactness conveys the truth that our understanding is limited.

next step, the therapist said, "A need to be loved without any strings attached and a concern that there is something physically wrong with you." These phrases had been used in previous discussions of the patient's relationship with her father.

"I thought I was finished with those feelings," said the patient. "I didn't think that my father was still in the background. But you're right. I dreamed about him last night."

In this example, by encouraging the patient to expand on her feelings in the context of the setting and by providing a bridge between events with simply worded phrases, the therapist helped her understand her indecisiveness in a new light. If her response to his initial intervention had failed to support his hypothesis, the therapist would have been forced to retrace his steps and to alter it. Therapy often moves forward in a maze-like fashion. Therapists often come up against a barrier (generated both by themselves and by the patient) that forces them to turn back and to set out in a new direction.

It is only indirectly and retrospectively that the therapist discovers whether or not an intervention or a series of interventions touched on a significant theme. The patient's first response to an intervention—for example, simple agreement or disagreement—is often not sufficient to support or disprove its usefulness. Patients may agree or comply out of a need to maintain the therapist in the role of the imparter of knowledge. They may disagree out of a need to maintain the therapist in the role of the intrusive interrogator. In addition, the patient's first response may be difficult to interpret. A patient's responding with silence may signify amazement at the therapist's perspicacity. However, silence may also represent disagreement. The patient may resist expanding on an episode on one occasion, yet discuss it at a later time in a way that confirms its significance. In order to evaluate the usefulness of an intervention, the therapist needs to examine its overall effect on the course of therapy. Indeed, one needs to consider both conscious and unconscious responses. For example, the patient may agree with an intervention. At the same time, his associations may lead him to talk about surgeons who cut patients open. Clearly, the patient's conscious and unconscious responses to an intervention may be antithetical. In the long term, useful interventions lead to an improvement in the patient's symptoms. In the short term, they generate new levels of understanding. In the process, new data comes to the surface.

The patient's response to an intervention also provides therapists with feedback concerning their own subjectivity and conflicts. Directly or indirectly, they may discover that their statements were moralistic or patronizing, or that their words revealed an element of impatience.

Timing

At times, it is useful to step back and to talk about the patient's patterns. At times, it is useful to bear with them (although this too may necessitate an acknowledgment that the therapist appreciates what the patient is experiencing). Because interventions vary in their function and because much depends on what is happening in therapy, it is possible to discuss the timing of an intervention only in general terms. Interventions are useful when the patient has stopped talking for a prolonged period or has fallen into a persistent repetitive pattern, when new material has ceased to appear, or when the therapist discovers a potentially significant theme that the patient has overlooked. The patient should be given the opportunity of talking and of considering the significance of what is happening before the therapist intervenes. It is mainly through the patient's narrative that the patient and the therapist discover (directly or indirectly) the significance of what is happening.

Therapists are often instructed not to make an interpretation until the patient is ready for it. A more practical directive is one that advises the therapist to press forward in new directions in small increments only. Therapy advances at a slow rate. Once an intervention has been made, paying close attention to the patient's response, particularly to the way in which the intervention failed to propel therapy forward, should take precedence over any other considerations. These general guidelines mitigate against the danger of poor timing.

THE PERFECT INTERVENTION

The perfect intervention (a mythical concept because it represents an unattainable ideal) should be both a tentative question and a tentative answer directed both to the patient and to the therapist. The manner in which it is presented should avoid casting the therapist in the role of the imparter of knowledge or of the intrusive interrogator. The patient should be able to talk without losing sight of the narrative's content—that is, without overlooking the significance of reported events in the light of what is happening in therapy. Wording should be simple and allusive, employing the patient's own words and imagery. On the one hand, it should communicate the degree to which the therapist understands the patient (i.e., the therapist's appreciation of the patient's inner state); on the other hand, it should press forward in search of new connections.

The concept of the perfect intervention breaks down when one realizes that inexactness and subjectivity are unavoidable, that it is impossible to consider every factor entailed in the creation of an intervention, that one can assess its usefulness only in light of the patient's response to it, and that different functions need to be instituted at different moments in therapy. Occasionally, the patient's behavior (e.g., a suicidal threat) forces the therapist to step out of the contemplative role and to take action, or a crisis arises (e.g., the death of the patient's parent) that necessitates an altered approach. Therapy doesn't move forward at a steady, inexorable rate.

Nevertheless, as therapists become increasingly proficient at their work, they are able to encompass a greater number of factors in their scope. As a body, their interventions move toward the ideal; they take on those qualities that promote empathy. For example, hearing a patient say, "I never fainted before, not even in Burma," an inexperienced therapist might say, "Your mentioning Burma is probably significant" or "Tell me what happened in Burma." An experienced therapist might simply repeat the word *Burma* in a quizzical tone, wondering in what way the word is significant to the patient and to himself, giving the patient the choice of expanding on his statement or of not expanding on it and paying attention to the way in which the patient responds. Clearly, interventions that are exhortative or intrusive and that contain technical imagery (e.g., "You have *repressed* something") or that stem from an irritability with puzzlement interfere with an empathic relationship.

To capture the qualities of a useful intervention, the analogy of the therapist as a reader of the patient's novel needs to be replaced by one in which the therapist is depicted as an editor and the patient's narrative as a novel in progress. In this analogy, interventions constitute editorial comments. The therapist/editor's task is to recommend expanding one episode rather than another, to provide assistance during periods of writer's block, to tentatively suggest new directions in which to take the narrative, and to inform the patient/writer that earlier chapters need to be rewritten in the light of what has emerged in later chapters. All the while, the therapist/editor, taking care not to impose personal preferences on the developing novel, remains respectful of the patient/novelist's creative abilities.*

CLINICAL ILLUSTRATIONS

The following clinical vignettes illustrate some of the ways in which interventions facilitate empathy and understanding:

In the sixth month of therapy, Miss King, a 45-year-old secretary, began a session by announcing that she had planned a trip around the world and would be away for the next four weeks. The news took the therapist by surprise. He recalled, however, Miss King's having mentioned previously that during her childhood her parents often took lengthy vacations. Miss King's father worked for an airline. The therapist wondered whether her parents also announced their plans at the very last moment. He waited and listened. Miss King moved on to talk about office politics, a subject that appeared to have

---

*Roustang (1980) has employed a similar metaphor to describe the therapeutic process.

no bearing on the topic of the upcoming vacation. The last four or five sessions had been characterized by Miss King's flitting from one mundane topic to another. If anything was to be accomplished, the therapist would have to press forward against opposition.

In his first intervention, he mentioned only a fragment of what he was thinking. "What came to mind as you were talking," he said, "was that your parents also took vacations."

"You must have been dwelling on it for some time," she said. "I've been talking about work for the last ten minutes. To tell the truth, when I made my plans, I didn't give any thought to the possibility that they might upset your schedule."

The therapist had indeed dwelled on Miss King's vacation, and his intervention did reveal his irritation. The thoughtless way in which she had planned her trip was only one example of what he felt to be an increasingly irresponsible attitude toward therapy. She didn't seem to be working at it.

His intervention, however, did prompt her to talk about her parents' vacations. She spontaneously mentioned that her parents often neglected to inform her of their plans until they were on the verge of leaving. "Sometimes I didn't know they were leaving until my grandmother arrived with her overnight bag," she said. "I don't think they meant to do me any harm. They probably felt that telling me at the last minute would lessen the blow."

Using one of Miss King's own phrases to bring her attention to the therapeutic interaction, the therapist pointed out, "It seems that I'm learning about your trip when you're on the verge of leaving."

"My first thought," she said, "is that perhaps I didn't want to upset you. But I don't think that's right." At this juncture the narrative took an unexpected turn. "It's not that," she said. "It wasn't that they didn't tell me about their vacation plans until the very last minute. It's that mother looked so pleased to be leaving. Mother always complained about doing housework. Having a home and a family seemed to be an encroachment on her freedom. I don't think she ever missed me.

What bothered me was to see her looking so happy to get away. . . . That's how I've been feeling about my job recently. I'm getting irritated with the politics at work. I'm looking forward to getting away."

The therapist, bringing her back to the therapeutic relationship, put into words what he had sensed in the last few sessions. "Perhaps therapy has been feeling like housework."

"You're right," said Miss King. "I think I've been trying to get away from here as well."

"And giving me a taste of what it's like to be with your mother?"

At this juncture new data emerged. Miss King talked about the time her mother had walked out of the home. Later that day her mother called home to tell her husband that she wasn't coming back. "Dad pleaded with her to come back. I remember standing beside him and saying, 'We don't need her.' I was ten or eleven at the time. When mother returned later that day, I was terribly embarrassed by what I'd said. Fortunately, neither of them ever mentioned the incident again."

In this example the therapist could have guessed at the outset that Miss King's decision to take a vacation was a form of acting out, that it entailed a wish to get away from therapy. He could have confronted her immediately with the significance of her behavior. However, such a confrontation would have cast him in an adversarial role. By taking a detour through her past, he helped the patient discover the significance of her behavior in a more subtle and complex fashion than a direct confrontation would have accomplished. In the process new data emerged.

Mrs. Radclyffe spent the first two years of therapy complaining of her husband's insensitivity. Her husband, a busy dentist, maintained close ties with his parents but took no notice that they treated his wife with disdain, disparaging her European background. Because her own family was distant, Mrs. Radclyffe felt isolated in Canada. She warded off this feeling by keeping busy, immersing herself in housework, and

organizing dance and fitness classes. Her therapy was characterized by long periods of silence. She was distrustful of the
therapist's motives and never talked about sexual issues. Very
occasionally, she had admitted to fantasies of running off to a
South Sea island with a movie star.

Toward the end of her second year of therapy, Mrs.
Radclyffe reported that her daughter was having difficulty at
school. As a result, she was obliged to meet with her daughter's male teacher, meetings she resented. The teacher was a
judgmental man who put Ms. Radclyffe on the defensive. It
reminded her of disdainful obstetricians who were insensitive
to the feelings of women. She herself would go only to a female obstetrician. The general drift of the material led the
therapist to speculate that the theme of men holding an
unflattering opinion of women was emerging.

"There is something about men judging or assessing
women that troubles you," he said.

His statement was followed by a silence. When she resumed talking, Mrs. Radclyffe acted as if she hadn't heard the
therapist's statement.

"My words seem to have vanished," said the therapist.

"I heard you," said Mrs. Radclyffe curtly. This time her silence persisted until the session ended.

In the following session, Mrs. Radclyffe reported two incidents from her teenage years. She remembered on one occasion parading around the house in panties and a bra. Her
mother had criticized her for behaving inappropriately. Mrs.
Radclyffe didn't remember whether or not her father was
home at the time. The second incident entailed a visit from the
local minister in which he had pinched her bottom while they
were sitting in the living room. She had been mortified, but
her mother had simply laughed. Later she learned that her
younger sister tolerated the minister's behavior and as a result
received small gifts whenever he visited. She felt isolated.
There was no one with whom she could discuss her outrage.

Having recounted these episodes, Mrs. Radclyffe became
silent. The therapist attempted to understand her silence in
the context of the episodes she had reported. Perhaps opening up in therapy was analogous to parading around in pan-

ties and a bra. Was she concerned that the therapist would take liberties with her?

"You started talking, but then you stopped," he said. His aim was to encourage the patient to consider the significance of her behavior in the light of the stories she had reported.

"Yes," said Mrs. Radclyffe. "Yesterday I felt you were pressuring me to open up. You were right to do so. After all, there's no point in coming to therapy if I don't say anything. Today I made up my mind to force myself to talk."

"It's an effort," said the therapist.

"It is, but I do have to start trusting you sometime."

"Trusting that I won't take liberties with you?" the therapist asked.

"I suppose so," said the patient. "I've never considered it in that light before. . . . It's true that I've always considered men to be an enigma. I don't know what they want from women or what women want from men. I know it sounds naive to say that. I'm not sure whether I'm talking about sex or something else. . . . Last night I remembered another incident from my childhood, but I couldn't bring myself to mention it today. When I was twelve, I danced in a school play. My parents didn't come to see me. Afterward, I decided not to wash off my makeup, wanting my parents to see what I looked like in the play. When I walked in the door, my father called me a whore. I still remember how ashamed I felt."

"My being a man must make it difficult for you in here," said the therapist.

"Yes, it does," she said. "I feel you look at me the way my father did. The funny thing is that I chose to see a male therapist. I could have picked a woman, but I decided I'd rather talk to a man."

Mrs. Radclyffe's case demonstrates how the narrative often moves forward haltingly, twisting and winding, only to return to a point not far removed from the therapist's original speculations. The therapist revealed his own subjectivity and conflicts in his irritable intervention, stating that Mrs. Radclyffe ignored him. In the dialogue following, elements of her own conflictual story surfaced.

SUMMARY

The therapist's fundamental tasks are to keep patients talking and to help them discover significant themes and connections in their narrative and behavior. Language is the major communicative instrument through which the therapist engages the patient in the process of shared contemplation.

Interventions take many forms and serve many functions. At their best, they are both tentative answers and tentative questions directed to the patient and to the therapist. When they are simply worded and allusive, employing whenever possible the patient's own words and imagery, they are most likely to strike a chord in the patient. To avoid putting themselves in an unnecessarily adversarial position, therapists should frame their interventions so that they are neither unequivocal answers nor imperious questions. In addition, the therapist needs to take detours, to examine recent events in order to discover the significance of what purportedly happened many years earlier, and to examine remote events in order to discover the significance of what is presently happening in therapy. At times, the discussion should be directed toward the therapeutic relationship; at other times, away from it.

Interventions are not self-contained units; they constitute part of the ongoing dialogue. Their usefulness can be assessed only in the light of the patient's response to them. Interventions communicate the degree to which the therapist understands the patient. When they press forward in new directions, they also reveal the therapist's own conflicts. Therapy will often move forward in a maze-like fashion; sometimes a barrier is encountered that makes it necessary to retrace one's steps and to set out in a new direction. In the process, new significant data emerge.

The therapist's interventions can be compared to editorial comments; they should facilitate the emergence of the patient's novel-in-progress without restraining the patient/author's creative genius.

Chapter Twelve

The Emergence
of Empathic Understanding

To consider the memories that the patient uncovers in therapy to be historically accurate would be incorrect. At most, they are figures or shadows of the truth, mirroring the past and alluding to the ongoing relationship. The patient's narrative is in many ways the story of the two participants interacting. It recounts how they reach out, avoid reaching out, symbolically meet each other's needs, and disappoint each other. The two participants strive to understand each other, but they sometimes deceive themselves into missing the point. As was demonstrated in the preceding clinical chapters, interpersonal and intra-psychic conflict (in both therapist and patient) characterizes the course of therapy. Out of this conflictual dynamic, empathic understanding emerges. As patients learn more about their stories and convictions, they develop a comprehensive and integrated sense of self.

The preceding clinical chapters were devoted to reexamining the principles outlined in the section on theory in the context of the clinical setting. This chapter is devoted to an examination of the intricate and at times paradoxical relationship between theory and empathy as it is experienced in the therapist's work. The following case presentations prepare the way for this discussion:

Mr. Clark, a 40-year-old accountant, was referred for psychotherapy shortly after his release from a psychiatric inpatient unit. He had been hospitalized for fourteen days following a suicidal gesture. In the hospital, he was agitated, depressed, and delusional. Although the doctor on the unit questioned his readiness to be discharged, Mr. Clark, with his wife's support, pressed for his immediate release. The doctor encouraged him to continue taking the same antidepressant and antipsychotic medication he had received in the hospital.

Mr. Clark arrived for his first appointment in an agitated state. He was a tall, angular man with an intense, forceful manner. During the interview, he refused to sit down. Instead, like a caged animal, he paced back and forth, occasionally stopping to stare out the window. He made it clear at the outset that the doctors had been wrong to "set him free" and that therapy was unlikely to help him. At the moment, he was a good-for-nothing. Simply making the trip to the therapist's office had been an ordeal for him. "People on the street stared at me," he said. "Any right-thinking policeman would have locked me up for vagrancy."

Following his discharge from the hospital, Mr. Clark incarcerated himself in his bedroom at home. Only his wife and his two sons were permitted to visit or to talk with him. He held off returning to work, claiming that his mind had stopped functioning. Even the simple task of opening his mail filled him with trepidation.

Whenever the therapist's questions touched on the topic of his illness, Mr. Clark brushed them aside. The therapist was unable to elicit the factors that had predisposed him to his breakdown or that had triggered it, or to learn whether similar breakdowns had occurred in the past. Mr. Clark denied ever wanting or attempting to kill himself. Because his narrative lacked eventful scenarios, it was impossible to understand his circumstances in terms of agency or of victimization. It was as if his life had come to a standstill, fixed in a self-portrait of ineptitude.

Nevertheless, the therapist did notice several hopeful signs. Mr. Clark arrived for his appointment by himself. His speech was coherent. Although the emotions he experienced were painful and extreme, he communicated his distress in a lucid and intelligible manner, and from this the therapist was able to grasp how he felt. Furthermore, at the end of the interview, Mr. Clark agreed to return for further appointments.

Mr. Clark's agitated state remained unchanged for the next five sessions. He arrived in a furtive mood, sorry, surprised, and relieved that the police hadn't apprehended him. During the session, he paced back and forth. When he left, he braced himself for the inevitability of being arrested and imprisoned.

Although his "inability to function" (Mr. Clark's urgent definition of himself) was the main subject of his discourse, he also talked about his father. Mr. Clark and his father both worked for the same multinational corporation. Up until two months ago, his father had been the chairman of the company's board of directors. He had retired from this post at the age of 75. Despite his age, however, he remained active in the company's affairs, traveling around the globe, visiting the company's branch offices, and speaking at luncheons. In his third session, Mr. Clark showed the therapist two articles he had clipped from the newspapers describing his father's accomplishments. "Look at these reports," he said to the therapist. "Do you think I'll ever be as successful as my father?"

For five sessions the therapist listened and puzzled over the material. He listened to Mr. Clark's complaints that he was useless, that his mind wandered, that he deserved to be put away, that his legs ached whenever he climbed the stairs, and that he often fell asleep reading the newspaper. As he listened and wondered, it suddenly dawned on the therapist that the complaints expressed were those of an ailing septuagenarian. This discovery led the therapist to consider whether Mr. Clark's father was truly as active as Mr. Clark described him or whether the patient had taken on some of the dysfunctional attributes he had observed in his father. Had

Mr. Clark identified with his father as an ailing old man to ward off guilt-provoking conflictual feelings toward him? Was the static or timeless quality the therapist experienced in the sessions related to Mr. Clark's concern that his father was dying? The therapist postulated that role reversal between Mr. Clark and his father accounted for the patient's symptoms.

The therapist also noticed something else. The way Mr. Clark paced back and forth made the therapist think of an energetic young man rebelling against the limitations of space and time, perhaps also rebelling against the need to remain loyal to a failing father. Was it possible that the inordinate symptoms Mr. Clark experienced were an expression of the age-old conflict between fathers and sons?

In the middle of the sixth session, the therapist introduced his observations with the statement, "You seem fit and energetic. However, your words make me think that you're feeling like a very old man."

"You're right," said Mr. Clark. However, instead of stopping to consider the therapist's statement, he continued to pace back and forth, condemning himself as he paced.

The therapist went a step further. "I wonder if you've noticed some of the failings you attribute to yourself in your father?" he said. "It seems as if you've traded places with him."

This time Mr. Clark stopped pacing. He looked bewildered.

"Are you troubled by what I said?"

"I think so," said Mr. Clark. However, instead of expanding on his statement, he stared out the window. When he left, he apologized for his silence. The subdued way in which Mr. Clark left the office made the therapist wonder whether he had presented his ideas too forcibly.

To the therapist's surprise, Mr. Clark arrived for his next appointment in a considerably altered state. The agitation had vanished. There was no mention of the hazards of walking through the street. Instead of pacing back and forth, Mr. Clark sat down in the chair next to the therapist's desk.

"It's amazing," he said. "I feel a lot better than I did. Most of my fears seem to have disappeared. Believe it or not, yesterday I went back to work. . . . I talked with my wife about stopping my medication, but she said I should discuss it with you."

"I'm curious to know what happened," said the therapist.

"I'm not sure," said the patient. "Do you think it's what you said about my father? I thought about it after our session. He *is* getting older. He doesn't walk as quickly as he used to. Sometimes, when I talk to him, he doesn't listen. I think he gets confused."

"The way you felt confused?"

"Yes," said the patient. "After our last session, I remembered something. A month ago I overheard two secretaries at work talking. One of them said my father isn't half the man he used to be. It made me sad to hear her say that."

Mr. Clark also remembered a dream about his father. In it, he and his father were attending a company banquet. His father was one of the scheduled speakers. When it was his father's turn to speak, Mr. Clark took the microphone from him and delivered a eulogy on fathers.

"I mentioned the dream to my wife," he said. "She thinks my admiration for my father is unrealistic."

"It might be worth talking about," said the therapist.

"Oh," said the patient, reacting with surprise to the therapist's suggestion, "I was expecting you to say we could stop therapy. In fact, I was hoping this would be our last session."

"Is there some urgency to stop?"

"Well, not exactly," said the patient. "It's just that I feel so much better now. I've wasted too much time being depressed. It's time to forget about it and to get on with my life. . . . I guess I'm like my father. His favorite expression was, 'Actions speak louder than words.' "

Mr. Clark showed no curiosity to delve into the factors leading up to his depression. Despite the therapist's recommendation that it would be helpful to look at what had happened over the last several weeks in greater detail, Mr. Clark persisted in wanting to end therapy. In the final minutes of the session, the therapist discussed a schedule for the gradual withdrawal of the medication Mr. Clark was taking and arranged for follow-up appointments. Reluctantly, Mr. Clark agreed to return for two appointments; they were scheduled at monthly intervals.

Mr. Clark's two follow-up visits were brief. He showed no evidence of agitation or delusional behavior and reported that he was functioning well at home and at work. Convinced that he was cured, he considered it pointless to talk at length about his illness.

The therapist was pleased with the marked improvement Mr. Clark exhibited. His identification with his father as a man of action was clearly more adaptive than his identification with an ailing old man. Nevertheless, the therapist was also disappointed. The many stories and conflicts that lay behind Mr. Clark's original symptoms remained untouched. For example, the therapist had noticed that during the sessions Mr. Clark didn't mention his mother and that he appeared to be inordinately reliant on his wife. The therapist postulated that Mr. Clark's abrupt termination of therapy reflected a continuing conflict with men. He had left therapy with the same sense of urgency that he had left the psychiatric hospital.

Mr. Andrews, a 32-year-old architect, undertook psychotherapy mainly at his wife's insistence.* He did admit to occasional outbursts of excessive rage over objectively trivial issues. The young therapist who discussed Mr. Andrews's case with her supervisor described him as aloof and noncommunicative. Mr. Andrews regarded others as inferior to himself.

Early in supervision, the therapist indicated that Mr. Andrews also regarded her with disdain and that he withheld significant information from her. She postulated that his difficulties stemmed from an exquisite sensitivity to narcissistic injury and that as a child he had failed to receive the attention necessary for the development of a firm, cohesive self. Although the articles on self psychology she had recently read had contributed significantly to her formulation, she did recognize the speculativeness of her hypothesis. Her ability to

*This case was reported in an article published in the *American Journal of Psychotherapy* (Berger 1984).

tolerate puzzlement, a state of mind encouraged by her supervisor, permitted her to let go of theory and to try to move empathically into the patient's novel. In supervision, the analogy of the therapist as the reader/editor of the patient's novel was used extensively.

A period ensued that was characterized by Mr. Andrews's complaining bitterly about his father's insensitivity toward him. During this period, Mr. Andrews was reluctant to talk about his home life or personal issues, focusing instead on incidents at work. The therapist moved into his world, imaginatively sharing the distress he experienced. After several sessions of doing so, however, she felt that therapy had ground to a halt.

In supervision, she questioned the usefulness of continuing to bear with Mr. Andrews's contempt for his father. Her supervisor suggested that the way Mr. Andrews expressed his contempt—in general terms rather than expanding on significant incidents—made it difficult for her to empathize with him. The attributes of a fictional character are most clearly conveyed to the reader, not by adjectival phrases, but by the author's letting the reader observe the protagonist interact with others in a specific setting. Up to now, Mr. Andrews's description of his father had been limited to adjectives such as "controlling," "ungiving," and "disinterested," and to blanket statements such as "He always complained about my going out to have a good time." Encouraging Mr. Andrews to expand on significant episodes would bring his father to life and would also have the secondary benefit of permitting him to remember his experiences more accurately than before and to experience more fully the emotions associated with them. To an extent, the therapist empathized with Mr. Andrews as a child misunderstood by his father. At this juncture, however, the father, himself a significant character in the novel, was nothing more than a pasteboard figure.

In the sessions that followed this discussion, the therapist asked Mr. Andrews to expand on incidents that illustrated the difficulties he had experienced with his father. To her surprise, he ignored her requests. Using the excuse that his memory was faulty, he would change the subject or continue to talk in generalities. This and other patterns (such as his habitually coming late for appointments) led the therapist to recognize that things were happening in therapy of which she was unaware. In addition, her own interest was waning. Her puzzlement and discomfort induced her to consider presenting Mr. Andrews's case to a psychiatric conference. She raised this possibility with him, explaining that it entailed being interviewed in the presence of other therapists. Mr. Andrews balked at the suggestion, responding with hurt and disappointment.

When the therapist reported these incidents to her supervisor, he remarked that, as in a novel, the course of events in therapy could be understood from several perspectives. On the one hand, the narrative contained the story of the patient as a child misunderstood by his father. On the other hand, it was possible that a second, less-available story was being played out in the therapeutic interaction itself.

In the sessions, the therapist focused her attention on the therapeutic relationship. However, when she pointed out to Mr. Andrews that his lateness revealed a dissatisfaction with therapy, he denied it. In his opinion, therapy was progressing favorably; his lateness was simply caused by difficulties at work.

At this juncture, the therapist and the supervisor discussed the vicissitudes of the therapist's role in the paired relationship. She had entered the patient's novel as a shadowy stalker without traits, intending only to be helpful. Yet, over time, despite herself, she became imbued with a story. She was reacting to, interacting with, or being acted upon by the patient. The supervisor advised her to consider herself a new, significant character in the novel. New clues to the hidden story might be discovered by examining her own emotional state. Because this would entail searching out painful, less-available aspects of herself, it was not proposed as an easy task.

The therapist volunteered that she had recently felt helpless in the patient's presence. She understood the principles of transference and countertransference and also understood that one person's experiential state (e.g., sadness) could be transferred to another person. However, she questioned the degree to which her sense of helplessness reflected Mr. Andrews's experiential state. Could it not equally stem from her own difficulties as a beginning therapist? To what extent was her own novel contributing to her feelings?

Theory was also discussed at this juncture. Although theory provides therapists with useful bearings, it is sometimes used defensively to avoid interacting with the patient or struggling to understand what is happening in therapy. The therapist admitted that her decision to present Mr. Andrews to a conference likely stemmed from such a motive. After some deliberation, she decided to cancel the conference.

When in the following session she informed Mr. Andrews of her decision, he was relieved. In addition, as she listened with evenly hovering attention, she discovered a new feeling in herself, the feeling of being ignored. Indeed, it had been present from the outset of therapy. Without guilt or blame, she informed Mr. Andrews of this feeling. He acknowledged its significance and added that he often felt ignored by his mother. Up to now Mr. Andrews's mother had played only a minor role in the narrative. At this point, however, she became a significant character. Mr. Andrews talked at length about her scorn for his father. She had paid attention to the patient himself as a child only when she could hold him up as an object to be admired by others. One set of events in particular stood out in his memory. When he was very young, his mother had denied him a pacifier. His grandmother had given him one, but this indulgence had to be kept secret from his mother. These disclosures evoked sadness in Mr. Andrews and provided the therapist with an emotionally evocative appreciation of his feelings.

The steps leading up to this period of empathic understanding were discussed in supervision. The course of events was understood retrospectively in the following way. At first, unbeknown to the therapist, Mr. Andrews had cast her in his mother's role. To win his mother/therapist's favor, he denigrated his father and talked mainly about work (i.e., accomplishments). The discomfort the therapist had experienced stemmed from being cast in a role she couldn't fathom and from his anger toward her. The therapist had assumed aspects of his mother in two ways: Her interest in Mr. Andrews waned over the course of therapy, and her decision to hold him up to a group of psychiatrists recapitulated his mother's practice of holding him up as an object to be admired by others. In addition, by ignoring the therapist, Mr. Andrews communicated to her how it felt to be ignored by his mother.

The process of extricating herself from the novel started when the therapist focused her attention on the relationship and on her own involvement in it. By canceling Mr. Andrews's interview and by voicing her feeling of being ignored, she had stepped out of the story contained in the relationship (i.e., she had moved from observer on the scene to external observer). Now, she and Mr. Andrews were able to examine side by side the significance of what had happened between them and to tie it in with his memories. Her intervention also expressed her understanding of how Mr. Andrews had felt as a child. In the process, new material emerged that pertained to his mother, not, as the therapist had expected, to his father.

This period of empathic understanding lasted four or five sessions. As therapy continued, the therapist found herself once again embroiled in the relationship in a manner that puzzled her.

THEORY AND THE CLINICAL SETTING

With Mr. Clark, the therapist discovered a conflict between son and father.* With Mr. Andrews, the therapist found herself cast in the role of withholding mother. In these case examples, dis-

---

*More accurately, the conflict the therapist discovered was an intrapsychic one—that is, a conflict *within* Mr. Clark played out in a drama between a father and a son. Furthermore, describing himself as incompetent had a transference meaning for him. It is likely that by denigrating himself in the therapist's presence, yet rebelling against engaging in a more extensive course of therapy, Mr. Clark played out his intrapsychic conflict in the therapeutic relationship. Although phrases such as "a conflict between son and father" and "a struggle between a son and his withholding mother" do not capture the many nuances intended, they are used in clinical discussions such as this one as a matter of convenience.

covery and the puzzlement and embroilment that precede it were seen to be essential components of the therapeutic process. That therapists have theories at their disposal to provide them with instructions and to predict the themes they will uncover would seem inconsistent with the notion of therapy as a voyage of discovery. After all, how is it possible to set out on a voyage of discovery with a comprehensive guidebook in one's back pocket?

To an extent, the sense of adventure is accounted for by individual differences among patients and by the incompleteness of the psychodynamic theories. For example, to the extent that all individuals are unique, the obsessive-compulsive patients Freud has described are different from those the therapist will encounter. In addition, the therapist will inevitably discover new areas uncharted by theory. However, the major factor that accounts for the pivotal position of surprise and discovery is that the therapist's work entails not simply observing but experiencing. It is uniquely human to be able to experience memories and fantasies and to share such experiences with another person through the use of symbols and language. Patients use the therapeutic relationship to relive their stories of loving, hating, winning, and losing. As participants in the therapeutic relationship (by not only actively projecting themselves into the patient's scenario but also permitting themselves to be drawn into it), therapists take part in the drama. In addition, the conflicts the patient experiences touch off similar ones in the therapist. The puzzlement that precedes discovery is not simply the end result of the inexactness of theory. Sharing the patient's perspective entails sharing puzzlement as well. Therapists are destined to lose their way—that is, to become embroiled in the patient's difficulties. They are fated to miss the significance of what is happening just as the patient is fated to do so. With Mr. Clark, the therapist needed to lose his way before he could discover that the conflict between the patient and his father was tied in to issues of dying and immortality. The therapist who treated Mr. Clark will no doubt reexperience and rediscover this theme with many other patients just as the therapist who treated Mr. Andrews will no doubt have to struggle again and again to extricate herself from the story of a son's conflictual relationship with his mother.

Experiencing (albeit partially and vicariously) goes hand in hand with misunderstanding. One of the therapist's tasks is to persistently work against the forces that cause us to relive our stories instead of remembering them.

Theories are retrospective accounts of how pioneers in the field such as Freud, Klein, and Kohut overcame their puzzlement following a period of experiencing. The therapist is fated to retrace the steps of the original workers. The purpose of theory is to provide therapists not with shortcuts that circumvent experiencing but with principles to help them extricate themselves from a puzzled state. A knowledge of the principles of identification, role reversal, and countertransference helped guide the therapists who treated Mr. Clark and Mr. Andrews out of their bewilderment. Theories can be seen as incomplete guidebooks to territories similar to but not identical with the territory the reader/traveler is exploring. They inform us that we will inevitably become disoriented—otherwise the journey is meaningless. At the same time, they provide us with guidelines to help us recover our way.

THE EMPATHIC PROCESS

The cases presented in the preceding clinical chapters illustrate that the many functions and perspectives the therapist employs should all be considered aspects of that complex capacity labeled *empathy*. Empathic understanding entails both emotional and intellectual factors. Indeed, the two forms of ideation interdigitate. At times, the therapist needs to pay attention to emotions. With Mr. Andrews, the therapist experienced the feeling of being ignored in the therapeutic relationship. She also experienced this feeling side by side with the patient when he reported a similar incident with his mother. At times, intellectual ideation, including theoretical knowledge, contributes to empathy. For example, it is often helpful to recognize more or less intellectually that the therapist's canceling an appointment accounts for a patient's anger. With Mr. Clark and Mr. Andrews, the therapists employed such theoretical principles as role reversal,

identification, and countertransference to help them understand the patient. Many of the principles propounded by the
psychodynamic theories are simply formal explications of the
ways in which we think, feel, and interact.

Emotional and intellectual cognition are components of every
one of the therapist's positions. As observer on the scene, the
therapist who treated Mr. Andrews used both forms of cognition to appreciate the patient's experience of being ignored by
his mother. As external observer, therapists listen objectively to
the patient's narrative. However, they also strive to comprehend the emotional factors that impel patients to say the things
they are saying. For example, by listening objectively to Mr.
Clark's narrative, the therapist discovered that his relationship
with his father constituted a significant dynamic. By placing
himself in the patient's shoes, by striving to understand what it
felt like to be saying the things Mr. Clark said in the therapist's
presence, the therapist appreciated the dynamic more fully. He
was able to sense the ongoing struggle between an energetic
young man and an ailing father. With Mr. Andrews, the therapist was alerted to her countertransference by noticing more or
less intellectually the sparseness of her notes. Her appreciation
of the countertransference was enhanced when she discovered
her own feeling of being ignored.

Empathic understanding is an interpersonal process. It requires an empathizer and someone with whom to empathize. At
times, it entails empathizing with the patient's wish not to be
understood. However, it is also an intrapsychic process that requires introspection. Understanding what it means to be human
is integral to empathy. In Mr. Clark's case, the therapist needed
to understand what it felt like to be thwarted by time. Although
self-referents are necessary, at times it is also necessary to use
referents acquired from one's observations of others and from
literature and art. The therapist likely employed such referents
to capture, in Mr. Clark's case, the state of mind of an aging father. In Mr. Andrews's case, the therapist likely employed such
referents to comprehend the theme of the young man striving
for the sole possession of his mother. The compassion that empathy embraces is compassion for the human dilemma: Being
mortal we strive for immortality; being imperfect we strive for

perfection in ourselves and in our relationships. Elements of the human dilemma lie hidden at the heart of all our conflicts.

The many functions and positions that contribute to empathic understanding do not occur in any particular order. It is likely that the more functions therapists use and the more routes they follow, the more comprehensive their appreciation of the patient's experiential state will be. Measures one considers defensive as well as measures one considers therapeutically adaptive contribute to the process. For example, the therapist's defensive behavior in Mr. Andrews's case (i.e., her decision to present him to a psychiatric conference) in the end helped her understand what was happening in therapy.

The preceding clinical chapters have emphasized that emotional involvement with the patient, heightened by the use of evocative personal imagery, enhances the therapist's empathic understanding of the patient. Envisioning Mr. Clark's conflict in terms of the images of an energetic young man and an ailing father enhanced the therapist's emotional appreciation of what the patient was experiencing. The therapist's original formulation regarding Mr. Andrews was not far removed from her later understanding. Yet it was different. Her later understanding was enhanced by the countertransference she had experienced. Before pressing forward in new directions, it is useful to look at the edge of awareness from within the patient's frame of reference as well as from without. This exercise entails searching for painful emotions in oneself, often placing a strain on the therapist's sense of self.

Empathic understanding is approximate and incomplete. With Mr. Clark and Mr. Andrews, the therapist appreciated only an element of each patient's conflicts. At the same time, each moment of understanding contributes to the next. With Mr. Andrews it is likely that the therapist will incorporate the state she experienced as she develops her model of the patient and as her empathic understanding becomes increasingly complex and comprehensive.

Empathic understanding is part of all human relationships. Therapists are individuals who are specially trained not in the application of theoretical knowledge but in the use of empathy. Their interventions, aimed at engaging the patient in shared contemplation, are guided by empathy. At times, the therapist intervenes forcibly (as he did with Mr. Clark); at times, tentatively (as the therapist did with Mr. Andrews). Stepping back from the relationship—that is, stepping out of the patient's novel—is necessary before the patient and the therapist can engage in the shared contemplation that propels therapy forward.

SUMMARY

Every one of the therapist's functions and perspectives contributes to an empathic understanding of the patient, which is the end result of both conscious and unconscious factors, both emotional and intellectual ideation, and both defensive and adaptive measures. Theory contributes to empathy by guiding the therapist out of puzzlement.

The painstaking process leading up to empathic understanding, to which puzzlement is integral, is often a prolonged one. Although empathic understanding is approximate and incomplete, it is likely that the more routes one follows, the more comprehensive the understanding will be. Limited as they may be, each moment of empathic understanding contributes to the therapist's developing model of the patient.

The preceding clinical chapters emphasized the usefulness of employing evocative personal imagery to enhance one's empathic entry into the patient's world. The strain on therapists caused by the necessity of examining painful emotions in themselves should not be discounted. It is also important to recognize that therapists must step back from the patient's novel before they can engage the patient in shared contemplation.

Chapter Thirteen

Empathy as a Curative Factor

Therapists dispute the degree to which empathy contributes to cure. In order to expand on this subject, it is necessary to reexamine the points concerning curative factors raised in the section on theory in light of the description of therapy presented in this section. In psychotherapy, cure is generally defined as the patient's achieving a relatively enduring, adaptive alteration in symptoms, behavior, or experiential state. The terms used by psychoanalysts to signify long-lasting changes – structural change, cohesive self, an increase in ego strength, and a reduction in the rigidity of the ego's defenses, to list only a few – may give the impression that our understanding of the changes associated with improvement is grounded in rigorously developed constructions. In fact, we know very little about the difference between short-lived improvement and enduring change, or about the factors that contribute to cure. At most, the terms we use allude to *presumed* alterations in psychological organization and to *presumably* curative factors. Nevertheless, the contributions that have been brought to bear on these issues by many experienced clinicians make it possible to examine this subject with a degree of credibility.

Curative factors are commonly separated into two groups: those factors pertaining to interpretation and insight and those pertaining to the patient–therapist relationship. A common debate among therapists centers on the relative importance of these two groups of factors. In this chapter, this debate will be used as a backdrop for the discussion of empathy as a curative factor. Only a selective review of pertinent publications will be presented.

HISTORICAL BACKGROUND

Disagreement concerning the concept of cure first surfaced in the Freud–Ferenczi controversy (Balint 1968). Stressing the curative powers of therapeutic interpretation and the patient's ensuing insight, Freud advocated an attitude of neutrality. Ferenczi, concerned that the neutrality Freud advocated generated an overly adversarial ambience, recommended a more active involvement with the patient. This debate has continued in psychoanalytic circles. For traditional Freudians (e.g., Bibring and Rangell), the patient's insight remains the critical curative factor. For the heirs of Ferenczi (Klein, Balint, and the English object relations school), patient–therapist relationship factors have assumed increasing importance (Eagle and Wolitzky 1982). From a different perspective, the new school of self psychology also stresses the importance of relationship factors. Indeed, in North America, self psychologists have become the most outspoken critics of the effect Freud's emphasis on neutrality and interpretation has had on the practice of psychotherapy.

As a result of these historical factors, the two sides of this sometimes confusing debate are distinguishable along several axes. For example, therapists who consider relationship factors to be of paramount curative importance commonly (but not always) focus their attention on pre-oedipal as opposed to oedipal issues or on self theory as opposed to drive theory. They also often use the analogy of the child–mother relationship to describe the patient–therapist relationship. Finally, the patients they describe appear to be more disturbed than the patients described by other therapists. Therapists who emphasize the curative effect of insight often stress neutrality, drive theory, and oedipal conflicts.

A brief review of insight and of relationship factors will be presented prior to further discussion of their role in the clinical setting and the problematical concept of cure.

INSIGHT AND WORKING THROUGH

Stated somewhat simplistically for the purpose of exposition, cure in the traditional psychodynamic model of therapy is associated with patients' gradually acquiring insight into the sources of their symptoms, emotions, or behavioral patterns. Insight is the consequence of properly timed, effectively presented interpretations (Scharfman and Blacker 1981). Although the definition of the term *insight* emphasizes intellectual understanding, emotional ideation also contributes to the process. On the one hand, patients experience an emotional state or a behavioral pattern; on the other hand, they reflect on its significance. In Sterba's view (1934), the patient's oscillation between experiencing and reflecting requires a dissociation of the ego (i.e., a capacity both to experience and to reflect on one's experiences).

A single episode of understanding, however, is clearly insufficient to alter the patient's experiential state or behavioral patterns. For the patient to change, the cycles of experiencing and understanding need to be repeated in the context of many different settings and stories. For example, a patient needs to discover over and over again that a conflict with his father plays a role in his behavior toward his son, toward male colleagues at work, and toward strangers who behave imperiously. Each discovery, each repetition, adds a slightly new dimension of understanding to the pattern or experience under examination. In the process of making these discoveries, the patient also experiences and contemplates the significance of the same pattern over and over again in the therapeutic relationship. Freud (1914a) labeled this repetitive process *working through*. Its purpose is to counter and wear away at the patient's resistances, the most significant of which is the propensity to recapitulate old patterns (i.e., the repetition compulsion).

Fenichel (1941) compared working through to mourning. In mourning the loss of a friend, one needs to experience the loss in every situation that reminds one of the friend—that is, one needs to come to terms with the loss in many different settings and contexts. The friend is represented in a number of memory complexes, and detachment needs to take place separately in each of them. Fenichel believed that giving up old unconscious patterns was a similar process.

The work of transferring what one learns in therapy to other settings and relationships is also considered part of the working-through process. In the view of traditional psychoanalysts (e.g., Greenson 1965b), the therapist's major contribution to the process is to repeatedly interpret—that is, to repeatedly point out the unconscious pattern and the patient's resistance to recognizing it. In the case of Mr. Harris reported in Chapter 9, for example, the therapist had to repeatedly point out that the patient invariably demeaned the therapist whenever he felt guilty about his actions before Mr. Harris was able to recognize the significance of this pattern. Although Mr. Harris's recognition of it may have seemed an instantaneous response to a single interpretation, much preparatory work preceded the moment of insight. Furthermore, further discussions were necessary before his day-to-day patterns and his self-esteem difficulties were significantly altered.

RELATIONSHIP FACTORS

Some therapists, in contrast to the emphasis on insight in the traditional model of therapy, have emphasized the critical contribution of relationship factors, especially the therapist's attitude toward the patient. This view proposes that certain therapist attributes to some extent facilitate the process by which the patient's self-understanding is enhanced.* Weiss and col-

---

*The arguments favoring relationship factors put forward in this chapter are an accumulation from different schools and practitioners. In comparison, therapists who stress the importance of interpretation and insight constitute a more unified and cohesive group.

leagues (1977, 1980), who support this view, present evidence that under "conditions of safety" (i.e., when the patient feels secure that the therapist is trustworthy) new material emerges spontaneously. Under such conditions, patients develop insight without the therapist's making interpretations.

Volkan (1982), whose studies focus on patients with serious ego defects, proposes that for more seriously disturbed patients identification with the representation of the therapist is a primary curative factor. These patients project aspects of archaic self- and object-representations onto the therapist. The introjection by the patient of aspects of the therapist, especially an attitude of positive, nonjudgmental regard, helps to decontaminate the patient's archaic representations. As with interpretations, the projective-introjective process contributes to the patient's ability to organize material that was previously less organized and to comprehend at a more sophisticated level of psychological organization material that was previously not understandable.

Self psychologists claim that a good therapeutic experience provides patients at least partially with the understanding or empathy they failed to receive in childhood. Their emphasis on relationship factors reflects the opinion that a good experience is as useful as patients' discovering the sources of their difficulties. Some therapists who hold similar views assert that in addition to a nonjudgmental attitude such characteristics as compassion, warmth, and a positive regard for the patient contribute to cure.

This point of view is consistent with the findings of psychotherapy outcome studies conducted by nonpsychoanalytic researchers (Truax et al. 1966). They report that the ratings of such therapist characteristics as warmth and acceptance (as measured by observers from tapes of sessions) correlate highly with patient ratings of the worthwhileness, or goodness, of therapy. These findings are unaffected by the therapist's theoretical preference. That patients respond favorably to therapy no matter what theory the therapist employs (Marmor 1982) has led some clinicians to postulate that the accuracy of a theoretical model is less important than that it provide patients with a coherent, integrated framework with which to organize their self-concept (and therapists with a framework with which to organize *their* model of the patient).

Contributors to this subject often spell out the therapeutic attitude they consider most beneficial for the patient. However, there is no clear *general* consensus concerning the most effective attitude. Therapists who emphasize the usefulness of insight recommend neutrality. Therapists who emphasize relationship factors recommend warmth, acceptance, and positive nonjudgmental regard.

Kohut and Wolf (1982) recommend empathic understanding as the therapeutic attitude most beneficial to the patient. However, they use the term in a way that is at odds with its use by traditional psychoanalysts.* For the latter, *empathic understanding* denotes experientially knowing the patient's inner state. For Kohut and Wolf, it further denotes an attitude toward the knowing, a specific form of compassion consistent with the self psychology formulation of the patient as the victim of insufficient care. Furthermore, it takes on explanatory powers: A lack of empathic understanding during childhood contributed to the patient's difficulties. In the view of these authors, the useful effect of an interpretation is not simply that patients learn something new about themselves but that they furthermore experience a feeling of being understood, a feeling absent in their childhood. As a curative factor, the degree to which an interpretation promotes such a feeling is felt to take precedence over its accuracy. Although he insists that a milk-giving, hand-holding interaction is not therapeutic, Tuttman (1982) agrees with Kohut and Wolf in his view that with more disturbed patients the treatment setting should parallel the mother–child facilitating environment.

Weiss and coauthors (1977, 1980) present evidence that patients want to master (i.e., to understand) their libidinal wishes rather than to gratify them. Indeed, patients perceive the possibility of gratification as a threat. These authors demonstrate that "conditions of safety" prevail when patients discover that their anger or criticism will not destroy the therapist or that the therapist will not be seduced or drawn in by the patient's wishes or demands.

---

*Kohut and Wolf's use of the phrase *empathic understanding* is also at odds with the manner in which it is used in the clinical section of this book.

In Kernberg's view (1982), severely disturbed borderline patients exhibit contradictory emotional states because of a dissociation of good and bad self-object representations. He argues against the idea that difficult patients require a warm, accepting therapist. Such an attitude, he feels, perpetuates maladaptive splitting mechanisms and permits the patient to avoid facing up to bad self-object representations. Kernberg uses the term "object constancy" to describe the therapeutic attitude that facilitates the integration of good and bad.

Running through the debate concerning the proper therapeutic attitude is the complex issue of regression. To what extent should the patient be permitted to regress to developmentally earlier or, by adult standards, to less adaptive modes of functioning? To the extent that therapy facilitates the approximate recapitulation of childhood relationships, every therapeutic relationship is regressive. Indeed, this is true of every interpersonal relationship. Therapists such as Kohut, Wolf, and Tuttman, who compare the therapeutic relationship to that of a child and its mother, appear to be less concerned with the regressve potential of therapy than are therapists such as Kernberg. The issue of regression is in itself intertwined with the question of whether the therapist's theoretical framework emphasizes victimization or conflict. In this context, the notion of victimization is roughly equated with the view of the patient as a child, and the notion of conflict is roughly equated with the view that the patient is both a child and a responsible adult.

THE ACCURACY OF AN INTERVENTION

Several points raised in the debate concerning curative factors touch on the complex issue of the accuracy of an interpretation. Many psychoanalysts argue that because historical truth is inaccessible, it is analytically sufficient to uncover in an interpretation only the narrative truth (Wetzler 1985, Michels 1985). Does this mean that any convenient fiction will suffice to explain an event? In this context, it is important to distinguish the therapist's *imposing* a story or explanation on patients as opposed to helping them uncover their *own* significant stories. It seems logical to assume that for a story to be significant to the patient, it needs to be influenced and constrained by actual historical circumstances.* As a by-product of therapy, it is likely that the patient's recollections will become increasingly complex and less inaccurate. Although there is disagreement concerning the degree to which a correct interpretation is able to capture historical truth, most therapists would agree that, as a minimal measure of accuracy, an interpretation should allude to stories or convictions significant to the patient's present experiential state (Wallerstein 1985).

That patients have been shown to improve (on patient rating scales employed by both patients and therapists) no matter what theoretical framework the therapist uses does not discount the usefulness of accurate insight. The issues raised by this finding are complex. For example, apparently disparate theories may not be significantly disparate. Different schools of psychotherapy may in fact use different technical terms to develop similar themes; the various theories may focus on different aspects of the same larger themes. After all, in human development there are only a limited number of significantly different overriding motifs. Furthermore, a theoretical framework provides not an end point but merely an avenue of approach to the patient's experiential state. To argue that the accuracy of an interpretation is inconsequential because patients are helped by therapists who use different avenues of approach in their quest to uncover significant stories is specious.

The question of whether an intervention is useful because it expands self-understanding or because it provides the patient with a feeling of being understood needs to be examined from several perspectives. At one level, it is clear that the degree to which the patient feels understood must bear some relationship

---

*A story may be significant because it mirrors a significant personal myth or fantasy. For example, a young boy who is unable to tolerate being excluded from his parents' bedroom may create the story (and conviction) that his father is impotent. This story may represent a highly selective portrait of his father. Nevertheless, in the broadest sense—even as a negation—this story too is grounded in experience.

to the accuracy of an intervention. Surely no therapist would recommend a fictitious interpretation simply because it will make the patient feel better. However, at another level this question touches on the therapist's precarious position of, on the one hand, bearing with the patient's predicament (i.e., moving as observer on the scene into the patient's scenario) while, on the other hand, pressing beyond it to new levels of understanding (i.e., examining the narrative as a whole as external observer and withdrawing from the transference–countertransference state of the therapeutic relationship to examine its significance).

For example, an unsuccessful businessman may state in a session that he wants to overcome a feeling of defectiveness. However, the therapist may sense that the patient is conflicted about this wish. In addition to wishing to overcome this feeling, the patient may be communicating that he has a wish to hold on to it out of loyalty to an idealized father (or the representation of an idealized father).* At this juncture in therapy, the patient's and the therapist's understanding may be at odds with each other. Presumably, interventions aimed at expanding self-awareness might lead to the patient's temporarily feeling misunderstood. However, if the therapist's aim is *only* to provide the patient with a feeling of being understood, he may collude with the patient in overlooking unconscious or warded-off contents. By looking for themes beyond the patient's immediate awareness, the therapist will ultimately provide understanding (and a feeling of being understood) at a more complex level of comprehension.

INSIGHT VERSUS RELATIONSHIP
FACTORS IN THE CLINICAL SETTING

To the extent that the debate concerning curative factors addresses itself only to the relative importance of insight as opposed to relationship factors and does not extend into other areas (e.g., into that area, to be discussed later, that pits "sooth-

---

*The case of Mr. Clark (reported in Chapter 12) demonstrated such a conflict.

ers" against "interpreters"), it does not present any difficulties for the therapist. No dynamic psychotherapist would dismiss either of the two groups of category as insignificant to the outcome of therapy. A close reading of Weiss and coauthors (1977, 1980) and of Volkan, writers who emphasize relationship factors, reveals that they also consider interpretation and insight important. For example, "conditions of safety" are the outcome of the patient's consciously and unconsciously testing to see if the therapist will be seduced by the patient's libidinal demands and the therapist's successfully passing the test. Clearly, such an interaction entails interpretations. Furthermore, Weiss and colleagues consider it necessary for new material to emerge in order for therapy to progress. Similarly, the therapist with whom the patient identifies in order to decontaminate archaic imagoes is clearly not a speechless being. That Volkan's conceptualization of decontamination entails the patient's replacing archaic imagoes with a coherent new set of "meaning schemes" suggests that insight plays a role in his model of therapy. In a similar vein, those authors who emphasize interpretation and insight also consider relationship factors, especially transference and countertransference states, important.

To distinguish the words of interpretation from the music of the relationship may have heuristic value. However, in the clinical setting, the two go hand in hand. Interpretations are not disembodied phenomena. The words therapists use, their tone of voice and manner of presentation are all components of their attitude toward the patient. In that they reveal the therapist's subjectivity and conflicts, interpretations (as well as silences) are a constituent component of the relationship. Similarly, the therapist's attitude toward the patient influences the effectiveness of interpretations. Each set of factors is shaped by and in turn influences the other.

Some therapists believe that transference–countertransference patterns should be the major focus of an interpretation (Langs 1982). Others (e.g., Bemporad [1982] in his work with depressed patients) recommend focusing interventions on extratherapeutic patterns. However, that to a greater or lesser extent every interpretation directly or indirectly reflects on the therapeutic interaction brings the two categories of factors closer together.

It also needs to be emphasized that the course of therapy is not a monolithic one. At times, new material emerges spontaneously under conditions of safety. At times, new material emerges as a result of the patient's fear of rejection.* At yet other times, the therapist needs to press forward with speculative constructions in order to generate new material. Similarly, although identification, projection, and introjection may sometimes facilitate the decontamination of archaic imagoes, at other times interpretations are necessary to facilitate this process.

THE THERAPIST'S ATTITUDE
IN THE CLINICAL SETTING

The spectrum of recommended therapeutic attitudes ranges from neutrality on the one hand to warm acceptance or positive nonjudgmental regard on the other. To what extent the poles of this spectrum of emotions represent significantly different or mutually exclusive attitudes is by no means clear. For example, in what way is an attitude that provides the patient with a "constant object" (Kernberg's view) distinguishable from an attitude of neutrality or one that parallels the mother–child facilitating environment (Tuttman's recommendation)? Furthermore, the terms used to describe the therapist's attitude take on different meanings in the hands of different proponents. For example, for traditional therapists, neutrality denotes not taking sides in the patient's conflicts. Self psychologists claim that traditional therapists misuse the concept of neutrality to justify an attitude of austere aloofness. As was previously mentioned, for self psychologists the phrase *empathic understanding* takes on additional meanings that are significantly different from the meaning ascribed to it by traditional therapists.

---

*The case of Mrs. Radclyffe, discussed in Chapter 11, demonstrates that a patient's motivation to work in therapy can stem from a fear of rejection.

It is difficult to delineate a proper therapeutic attitude with a single adjective or a single set of adjectives. Indeed, during the course of treatment, the therapist's attitude toward the patient runs the full gamut of emotions. Most writers recognize this; the attitudes they recommend represent only an ideal. However, the notion of prescribing or recommending a proper therapeutic attitude is in itself problematical. Can an attitude really be prescribed? Some therapists who recommend warm acceptance are probably less warm and accepting than therapists who recommend neutrality. Attitudes, always the outcome of the interaction, are shaped by such factors as patient–therapist fit and the patient's and therapist's motivation and psychological-mindedness. In fact, the notion of a proper therapeutic attitude may unduly influence therapists to emulate the states of mind they have read about. Reaching for a contrived attitude may cause them to be less open to appreciating the many emotions the patient does in fact evoke in them. Interest in and fascination with the patient's material are widely accepted components of the therapist's attitude. However, these qualities represent only a baseline against which to measure one's reactions. Therapists need to be tuned in to all the subtle alterations in their emotional responses, whatever they may be. When interest and fascination wane, as they must, the therapist needs to examine the significance of this altered state. That a course of therapy is characterized by apparently unrelenting interest, fascination, and acceptance should in itself be a source of concern.

Sometimes, in writing about the proper therapeutic attitude, clinicians use the term *empathic* in conjunction with such adjectives as *warm* and *accepting* as if the terms were synonymous. The term *empathy* should be used only to denote experientially knowing another person's inner state. To link the term with a specific emotional attitude such as warmth and acceptance or, as Kohut and Wolf do, with specific explanatory powers (i.e., with the explanation that symptoms stem from the patient's once having experienced a lack of empathy) is to burden it with unnecessary assumptions. Limiting its definition widens its scope, making it possible to include in its purview the therapist's bearing with the patient's stories of both agency and victimization— that is, empathizing with the patient as a conflicted individual.

Furthermore, freeing the term from its association with a warm, accepting attitude makes it possible for therapists to consider the ways in which all their emotions—concern, criticism, hostile withdrawal, and envy, to name only a few—contribute to their understanding of the patient.

HEURISTIC ISSUES

Eagle and Wolitzky (1982) argue that some of the issues raised by the debate concerning curative factors (such as whether certain groups of patients would benefit more from interpretations focused specifically on extratherapeutic relationship difficulties than from other types of interpretations) should be subjected to rigorous studies. Such studies would necessitate classifying patients according to diagnostic criteria, developing well-defined categories of curative factors, and establishing measures for follow-up assessment that are more sophisticated than mere ratings of customer satisfaction.* These authors caution that the principles of dynamic psychotherapy that would evolve from such studies would be quasi-autonomous from theories of human development. For example, because some patients benefit from a warm, accepting attitude, it does not necessarily follow that they failed to receive warmth and acceptance as children. To use Eagle and Wolitzky's analogy, a patient suffering from headaches may benefit from aspirin; it doesn't necessarily follow that the patient is suffering from a lifelong aspirin deficiency.

Some of the issues raised by the debate can be circumvented by taking into consideration that, as mentioned earlier, in the clinical setting insight and relationship factors are intertwined; the therapist's position is a contradictory and often a conflicted one. On the therapeutic voyage of discovery, the therapist is at times the trailblazer, at times the follower. Therapists deal both

---

*The Menninger project (Kernberg et al. 1972) and the Columbia study (Weber et al. 1985) are examples of follow-up studies of psychoanalytic treatment and dynamic psychotherapy. Presumably, future psychotherapy outcome research, of which these studies are the vanguard, will become increasingly sophisticated.

with the here-and-now and with memories, with both extra-therapeutic relationship difficulties and transference–countertransference patterns. They pay attention to both content and process—that is, to interpretations as they reflect on the relationship and to the relationship as it influences interpretations. Furthermore, both the therapist and the patient are conflicted: conflicted about their personal wishes and about their desire to pursue self-inquiry. That subjectivity and conflict enter into the therapist's interpretations is often played down in theoretical discussions. Yet, as the cases presented throughout this book illustrate, subjectivity and conflict are ubiquitous elements of therapy. The patient is never simply provided with a correct interpretation. Indeed, the less formal term *intervention* was used for all the therapist's statements in the clinical section of this book to play down the notion of accuracy that is implicit in the term *interpretation*. Interpretations are merely hypotheses. Only with the patient's assistance is it possible to examine their significance.

However, that it is possible to do so makes it feasible to conceive of the clinical setting as a research laboratory. At one level, therapists take on the function of reader/editor of the patient's developing novel. At another level, to the extent that all human beings are similar, they are the confirmers, critics, and editors of established theoretical principles as well as the creators of new ones. Retrospectively, they wonder, for example, what steps were entailed in the patient's altering his memories concerning his parents or how such an altered conviction served to overcome a fear of traveling. They wonder why it is that a conflict concerning failure, a conflict that has been mulled over hundreds of times in therapy, suddenly falls into place for the patient (in a manner richer yet simpler than the therapist had postulated), profoundly altering the patient's day-to-day relationships.

As a laboratory, however, the clinical setting is fraught with obstacles. It is difficult to be both a participant in and an objective observer of a conflictual relationship. A therapist who has helped a patient by employing one set of theoretical principles may become overzealous in its use with other patients. To some extent, the therapist's own analysis, as well as participation in the ongoing dialogue between clinicians and theoreticians of various persuasions, reduces the tendency to develop blind spots and unfounded convictions.

SHARING THE PATIENT'S
PERSPECTIVE VERSUS INTERPRETING

The debate concerning the relative importance of relationship factors as opposed to interpretation and insight can be rephrased as follows. Is it ultimately beneficial to share the patient's perspective, thus providing a good experience or a feeling of being understood, or is it ultimately beneficial to help patients discover the ways in which their conflictual memories and convictions have been fashioned, thus moving them toward a more complex understanding of themselves? Is it preferable to provide a comforting experience, one that borders on denial, or to bring patients face to face with conflict and in turn with aspects of the antithetical nature of human existence? These questions trouble us all. They are exemplified in the ubiquitous intrapsychic conflict between the wish to pursue self-inquiry and the wish to avoid it. In this context, the contributors to the subject of curative factors can be approximately separated into those clinicians and researchers who place the soothing or sharing function ahead of interpretation and deeper understanding, and those clinicians and researchers who place deeper understanding ahead of soothing or sharing. This dichotomy can be depicted in the following metaphor. One side of this argument is represented by Dr. Frankenstein, the creator of new life in the form of a monster, the scientist who is driven by the desire to extend science beyond conventional limits. The other side is represented by that obligatory minor character in the cinematic version of the novel (does he personify public opinion?) who, having witnessed the havoc the monster created, finally cautions the audience that some issues are better left untouched.

Should therapists press forward to new frontiers, or should they let sleeping dogs lie? Some therapies, especially those that stress warmth, acceptance, and understanding the patient's predicament as it stands at the given moment, opt for the latter. As an ideal, dynamic psychotherapy opts for both. As observer on the scene, the therapist strives to comprehend the patient's predicament as it is understood at the given moment. As external observer, the therapist strives to expand the patient's self-understanding. Sometimes these opposing positions occur simultaneously and provide a close match between the patient's and the therapist's conflicts. The dynamic psychotherapist employs these dual perspectives to approximately comprehend the patient's subjectivity as well as warded-off contents. Occasionally, the therapist does need to make a choice between simply sharing the patient's perspective and pressing forward in new directions. In such instances, dynamic psychotherapists opt for deeper understanding—that is, for an explication of warded-off unconventional contents. It is the pursuit of *deeper* understanding that is the purely analytic component of dynamic psychotherapy.

To translate the effects of a fuller understanding of one's conflicts into a pragmatic concept of cure or a set of measurable attributes is a difficult task. Can fuller understanding be assessed in terms of contentment or more adaptive ways of functioning? Presumably, there is a link between these protean concepts. However, at present these issues are mainly the purview of the therapist's personal philosophy.

Fortunately, the ultimate choice of whether or not to press forward is the patient's. Indeed, patients choose the therapists and the therapies they prefer. It is the patient who sets the pace and who decides how far to press forward. A firmly entrenched resistance is usually stronger than a firmly imposed interpretation. That therapists employ a dual perspective and that they approach the patient tactfully and thoughtfully make it possible for the patient's own objectives to play a prominent role in the course and direction of therapy.

LONG-STANDING IMPROVEMENT

What is often insufficiently emphasized in theoretical discussions is that the concept of cure is itself uncertain. In the clinical setting, the most one can properly talk about is an improvement in the patient's symptoms or relationship difficulties or an adaptive alteration in behavior. Similarly, as mentioned earlier, the distinction between short-lived and long-standing change is also uncertain. These issues are considered in the following case discussion:

> Mrs. Snow's presenting complaint was a reading inhibition; whenever she picked up a book or a newspaper, her mind wandered and she was unable to concentrate. Mrs. Snow had matriculated from high school and wanted desperately to take a university course, but her symptom made it impossible to do so. A previous course of therapy had been helpful in relieving it. However, the symptom returned shortly after her termination, which had been her decision, not the therapist's.
>
> A newlywed in her midtwenties, Mrs. Snow had been born in South Africa. Her parents had separated when she was six. Her mother took off for Canada with her, and Mrs. Snow never saw her father again. As a student, Mrs. Snow did extremely well in some semesters, very poorly in others. Her relationship with her mother was stormy. At 16, unable to tolerate her mother's martyred outlook, she ran away from home. She lived in a boardinghouse and worked as a secretary until she married. Following her marriage, she reestablished contact with her mother.
>
> In the first months of therapy, Mrs. Snow's reading inhibition vanished. She attributed her symptom to a lack of encouragement from her mother, who always made her feel guilty and bad. At times, Mrs. Snow regarded the therapist as someone who encouraged her intellectual pursuits. Her previous therapist had done so as well. At other times, she regarded him as unsupportive. As therapy progressed, fantasies of her father emerged. Although Mrs. Snow's mother considered him a vagrant and believed that he had been unfaithful to her, he was an educated man, an intellectual. Mrs. Snow idealized her father, dreamed of being reunited with him, and believed that her symptom was caused by her mother's banishing him from the family.
>
> Her improvement, however, was temporary. Her reading inhibition returned whenever the therapist turned out to be

less than ideal. However, despite her complaints about him, she often fantasized running off with him to a South Sea island. Her behavior was understood as a wish to recreate a relationship with a supportive, idealized father. In the early stages, Mrs. Snow understood her conflicts in terms of victimization: She had been caught up in the war between a good father and a bad mother. With time, her perception of her parents became more complex. In part, her altered view stemmed from her attempts during the course of therapy to reestablish contact with her father, who was still living in South Africa. He turned out to be less receptive than she had imagined his being. She also came to see her mother as conflicted. Furthermore, her original view of herself as victim gave way, when she discovered a significant link between her perception of her mother as guilt-inducing and the wish to have her father for herself, to a view of herself as conflicted. When Mrs. Snow terminated therapy, she understood her difficulties in the context of a multitude of conflictual memories. Her ability to read was no longer dependent on her need to perceive the therapist as an idealized supporter. Indeed, her general need to regard the therapist as a perfect father (and her guilt over the wish to possess him) had become less urgent.

Two months following termination, Mrs. Snow sent an angry letter to the therapist's secretary claiming (incorrectly) that the therapist had overcharged her in his final billing. This action suggested that Mrs. Snow's conflicts had not been completely resolved. Nevertheless, two years later, the therapist learned from a colleague treating her niece that Mrs. Snow was successfully pursuing a university career and that her previous wide fluctuations in self-esteem were no longer apparent.

This summary of a course of therapy captures only the significant highlights of the case. Nevertheless, it illustrates that, although the patient's conflicts were not completely resolved (are conflicts ever completely resolved?), over the course of therapy she achieved an enhanced appreciation of her experiential state. This case also illustrates that patients go only as far as they wish to go. The reasons for Mrs. Snow's first termination were unclear, and her occasional accounts of her first course of therapy suggested that her two therapists were not significantly different. What is emphasized in this clinical example is that in dynamic psychotherapy the concept of *long-standing* change is associated not merely with relief from symptoms or an improvement in relationship difficulties but also with an altered appreciation from several perspectives of the stories that underlie the patient's patterns and convictions. To achieve this aim, the therapist needs to share the patient's perspective of the given moment but also to press beyond it. It is the appreciation of the link between long-standing change and an altered and more complex understanding of one's history that prompts therapists to consider it important to uncover warded-off contents.

SUMMARY

In this chapter, the degree to which empathy contributes to cure was discussed in the context of the debate concerning the relative importance of insight, interpretation, and working through as opposed to relationship factors. Although the arguments of some writers would appear to discount the usefulness of an accurate intervention, instead placing major importance on the patient's feeling of being understood, interventions should be accurate to the extent that they help bring out the stories and convictions that are significant to the patient. The notion of a proper therapeutic attitude (concerning which there is much disagreement) may inhibit therapists from appreciating the manner in which *all* their emotional states contribute to an understanding of the patient. Interest in and fascination with the patient's behavior and narrative provide a baseline against which to examine one's emotions. Empathy should be defined as experientially knowing the patient's inner state; it should not be confused with an attitude of warmth and acceptance or burdened with explanatory powers.

In the clinical setting, insight-generating factors and relationship factors are inseparable. The dual positions of observer on the scene and external observer make it possible for the therapist to understand the patient's present predicament yet to press forward to new levels of understanding. Although the concept of cure is itself unclear (in the clinical setting, all one can properly talk about is an adaptive alteration of the patient's symptoms or relationship difficulties), long-standing improvement is associated with patients' achieving an altered appreciation from many perspectives of the stories that underlie their convictions, symptoms, and behavioral difficulties.

Chapter Fourteen

Empathy in
Psychotherapy Supervision

Learning to empathize goes hand in hand with the acquisition of therapeutic skills. The methods of learning include lectures and seminars, reading (not simply technical papers but literature in general), one's personal analysis, and individual supervision. Supervision itself is a multifaceted process. It entails didactic instruction, discussing the case material the student presents and examining both the patient–therapist and the therapist–supervisor relationships from a psychodynamic perspective (Ekstein and Wallerstein 1958). Because supervision often occupies a midpoint between didactic teaching and a course of psychotherapy, some clinicians have described it as the psychoanalysis of a psychoanalysis, taking pains to distinguish it from the psychoanalysis of a *psychoanalyst* (Arlow 1963). When the case material is the major focus of attention, supervision takes the form of a tutorial. When the central concern is one or both of the two relationships of which the student is a significant participant (the patient–therapist and the therapist–supervisor relationships), it tends to resemble a therapeutic interaction. Because the student's level of expertise, capacity for self-awareness, and interactional patterns all need to be considered, the manner in which the supervisor listens is in many respects similar to the unfocused, evenly hovering attention Freud recommended for therapists. Thomas Mann's assertion that all learning is a form of self-realization is particularly true of the supervisory process when its focus is the conflictual component of learning.* Indeed, the learning that stems from the conflictual matrix contributes significantly to the therapist's ability to empathize. In this context, in the following sections some useful supervisory principles will be discussed.

THE CONFLICTUAL COMPONENT OF LEARNING

The oscillatory patterns experienced during learning parallel the oscillations that characterize the therapist's dual perspective (i.e., the back-and-forth movement between the positions of external observer and observer on the scene). These patterns will be examined in the context of two sets of responses that represent the extremes often observed in medical students during their first rotation in psychiatry: maintaining a distance from the patient and overidentification (Berger and Freebury 1973).

Maintaining a Distance from the Patient

When medical students have their first opportunity to study a patient's emotional response to medical illness, they acknowledge the presence of such symptoms as anxiety or depression but often question the value of looking for deeper significance. They buttress their views with such arguments as "Anyone would be upset under the circumstances," "The patient is reacting the way any normal person would react," and "But that's how I would behave if I were sick." Statements such as these indicate a need to distinguish normal behavior from mental illness

---

*Mann is quoted in Ekstein and Wallerstein (1958).

(i.e., individuals who function adaptively from those who require or could benefit from psychotherapy). They also indicate that students may be threatened by the notion that deeper or unconscious conflicts are part of their own repertory.

Medical students' requests to see hard core cases with diagnoses such as schizophrenia or cyclothymic disorder are further evidence of the need for distancing. The concept of hard core cases enables students to preserve the distinction between the disturbed patient and the normal doctor. A number of educators have decried the common procedure of exposing students, particularly psychiatric residents in their early years of training, to chronic hospitalized patients. However, one element that may make this procedure difficult to alter is that severely disturbed patients create a comfortable distance (comfortable for the physician) between the patient and the student.

Clearly, learning about patients and learning about oneself go hand in hand. Uncovering deeper conflicts in the patient leads students to the discovery of deeper conflicts in themselves. As students develop the capacity to regard others' conflicts less pejoratively, they become more open to recognizing conflict in themselves, and as they become less threatened by the notion of conflict in themselves, they become more open to looking for conflicts in others.

Residents in psychiatry and student therapists employ distancing defenses similar to the ones described in medical students. Such attitudes as overintellectualization and authoritarianism are often used to ward off discovering similarities between patients and oneself. Indeed, Merklin and Little (1967) consider distancing (e.g., deemphasizing the patient's psychological status and focusing on medical complaints) one of the symptoms of the Beginning Residents' Syndrome.

Overidentification

A difficulty in the opposite direction is that of overidentification with patients. Medical students sometimes worry about acquiring the diseases they study or are exposed to. The frame of mind engendered by such worries makes it difficult to be helpful. Student therapists as well are sometimes alarmed by the similarities they discover between patients and themselves. In the extreme, students may notice only the similarities and not the differences. Such concerns often generate a sense of ineptitude and excessive passivity. Merklin and Little also consider overidentification (e.g., hypochondriasis) to be one of the symptoms of the Beginning Residents' Syndrome.

The Oscillatory Pattern of Learning

The positions described in the foregoing paragraphs represent two poles of an axis along which oscillations (i.e., alternations between opposing perspectives) normally occur during learning. Similar oscillatory patterns also occur in the supervisory relationship and with respect to the therapist's interventions. For example, at times therapists comply or identify with the supervisor, but at other times they subtly or overtly adopt an adversarial position. Similarly, at times the therapist says too much to the patient, at times too little. Difficulties arise when the oscillations are extreme or when the therapist becomes fixated at one or another of the positions described. The supervisor's function is to monitor this pattern and, when necessary, to help the therapist become "unstuck" by providing interventions that enhance self-awareness. With time, the student, taking over the contemplative and introspective functions provided by the supervisor, develops the capacity for self-scrutiny. In this way, the ability to oscillate freely and to avoid extremes improves.

LEARNING THE PRINCIPLES OF PSYCHOTHERAPY

The supervisory functions of providing instruction, enhancing the therapist's self-awareness, and pointing out difficulties or conflicts that interfere with learning often overlap. In this section, some of the difficulties associated with learning the various principles of psychotherapy will be discussed.

The Role of Observer on the Scene

The student needs to be informed (as well as to discover) that the empathic function of sharing the patient's perspective is enhanced by encouraging the patient to expand on the setting, characters, and events that appear in the narrative. Simply hearing a complaint or a symptom reported in general terms by the patient makes placing oneself in the patient's shoes difficult. Expanding the material, on the other hand, facilitates this function.*

To an extent, that student therapists do not encourage patients to expand the narrative or neglect to empathize with the patient's predicament may be an artifact of supervision itself. Therapists want to report significant discoveries; they may feel that the supervisor will regard simply encouraging patients to expand on scenarios as superficial. This attitude is illustrated in the following vignette:

Miss Alcorn, a young businesswoman, arrived at a session with a cast on her left leg. She reported fracturing the leg two days earlier. Despite a show of concern, the therapist neglected to ask her to expand on the accident. In supervision, he wondered whether her injury had triggered a castration complex. The supervisor remarked that the therapist was pressing forward too hastily and that at times the course of events makes it necessary to stop and share the patient's perspective. Indeed, it is mainly through such exercises (enhanced by asking the patient to depict fully the circumstances of an event) that new significant material comes to light.

The therapist was initially disappointed that no new insights had emerged in this discussion of Miss Alcorn's case. Nevertheless, in the session following, by complying with the supervisor's advice, he was able to learn that Miss Alcorn had slipped on an icy patch of road on her way home at night from a coffee shop. After lying alone and frightened in the dark for what seemed an eternity, she was found by a passerby who called for an ambulance. This detailed description

---

*A detailed description of this principle was presented in Chapter 6.

made it possible for the therapist to appreciate her fear and humiliation.

The propensity not to share the patient's perspective via an expanded scenario often stems from the conscious or unconscious fear that the scenario will bring out the therapist's own conflicts. For example, at one stage, the therapist neglected to ask Miss Alcorn to expand on a scenario in which she described her mother's death. This lack of response stemmed from conflicts relating to his own mother's death.

The Role of External Observer

Some students find it easier to behave compassionately toward patients and to adopt the position of observer on the scene than to look for new significant themes. They accept the narrative only at face value. For example, in Miss Alcorn's case, the therapist, intent on appreciating her fear and humiliation, failed to notice until his supervisor mentioned it that the shame she experienced in the hospital exceeded her humiliation at lying neglected in the street. Furthermore, Miss Alcorn had instructed the nurses not to notify her brother, her closest relative in the city, of her accident. Despite her description of her brother as caring and thoughtful, she had kept her injury secret from him. This new piece of data later gave rise to a new significant theme: her irritation at needing to be comforted.

The Ability to Oscillate Freely

Difficulty in alternating between the two positions often stems from the assumption that a described incident actually happened in a given fashion, an assumption informed by the judgment that the patient was or was not in the right. For example, Miss Alcorn often described arguments with her employer. When she was overly demanding in therapy or when the therapist judged her to be unreasonable based on her own report, he moved toward the position of external observer—in this instance, a role tinged with disapproval—instead of sharing her perspective. When he was kindly disposed toward her or felt that her employer was unreasonable, he found it easier to adopt the more compassionate perspective of observer on the scene. Taking sides in reported disputes between patients and their relatives, friends, or colleagues is an inevitable aspect of the therapist's subjectivity, and it must be recognized that one consistently does so. Clearly, the neutrality therapists strive for is not a one-dimensional perspective but the product of both an awareness of one's own subjectivity and of one's capacity to adopt a precarious dual perspective of bearing with the patient's point of view yet moving beyond it.*

To an extent, employing the analogy of the novel-in-progress helps one develop the capacity to oscillate between positions, to use multiple perspectives. One needs to suspend one's disbelief, to immerse oneself in the patient/author's story while at the same time considering the factors and functions contributing to its creation.

Transference and Countertransference

Student therapists need to be informed and to discover that sooner or later they will be drawn into the patient's world and that they will play out a significant relationship in the patient's story. The oscillatory perspective necessary to appreciate transference–countertransference states is slightly different from the one necessary for transporting oneself into the patient's world. The scenario of note is the therapeutic relationship. The story is conveyed in the process, and the therapist's experiential state is altered by it. Moving back from the session in order to discern one's own patterns is integral to this perspec-

---

*Sharing the patient's perspective is the strictly empathic component of therapy. However, it is pressing forward to new themes that leads to a more complex empathic appreciation of the patient's experiential state. Indeed, it is the need to consider the latter function a significant component of the empathic process that makes the psychodynamic definition of empathy so complex.

tive. One also needs to wonder whether the role one has assumed is that of the patient as a child or that of a significant other
(e.g., parent, sibling, uncle), whether the pattern originated
mainly in the patient's conflicts or mainly in one's own, and
whether it resulted from taking on an assigned role or defensively warding it off.

> In Miss Alcorn's case, the discussion of her ambivalent atti-
> tude toward her brother prompted the therapist to remember
> that he had recommended she rest her leg on the coffee table
> in his office.
>
> "My offer flustered her," he said. "She turned it down."
>
> "What did you make of her behavior?" the supervisor
> asked.
>
> "I didn't give it a second thought. In the light of what we're
> talking about now, I should have considered its importance.
> At the time, I simply felt compassionate toward her . . . or
> did I? Were the two of us recreating her relationship with her
> brother? It's curious that I acted kindly toward her *after* she re-
> vealed that her brother's compassion irritated her. It may be
> that I was behaving defensively in order to ward off acknowl-
> edging her conflict. Perhaps I have the same need to be
> viewed as compassionate that her brother has."
>
> "Several explanations will turn out to be significant," the
> supervisor said. "No single pattern or story is sufficient to ex-
> plain one's behavior. At this stage, however, it's too early to
> know whether our assumptions are accurate. Keep them in
> mind, watch for the patterns to recur, and test out their signif-
> icance in the dialogue."

Therapists may also reenact (or defensively ward off) the roles
assigned to them by the patient in the supervisory session. For
example, the nervous or morose way the therapist presents the
case material may reveal that, without knowing he knows it, he
has sensed anxiety or a depressed state in the patient. At times,
the reenactment is obvious.* To examine the ongoing dynamic

---

*Arlow's vignette (1963) in which the therapist barged into the supervisor's
office the way the patient had barged into his (reported in Chapter 2) is an example of conflictual behavior originating in the therapeutic relationship and
spilling over into the supervisory situation.

between patient and therapist, the supervisor needs to pay attention to more than the narrative alone. Later in this chapter, the importance of considering the supervisory relationship (i.e., the therapist–supervisor interaction) will also be discussed.

Reenacting an assigned role in supervision does not in itself reflect a technical error. It is only the failure to appreciate the pattern's significance that interferes with therapy. The supervisor's primary aim is not to inhibit overidentification, acting out, or defensive behavior but to help therapists develop the introspective and contemplative skills necessary to recognize the significance of their behavior. As these capacities develop, as therapists learn to pay attention to details they don't know that they know, the tendency to move to such extremes as overidentification and defensive behavior will diminish. However, this tendency will never entirely disappear. At most, the therapist will appreciate enmeshments more quickly than before. The therapist's discovering, for example, that he resisted exploring Miss Alcorn's reaction to her mother's death because his own mother had recently died will help him appreciate the ubiquitous nature of unconscious conflict and will encourage him to look for conflicts in himself in the future.

The Commonality of Conflicts

Bringing attention to the relationship between the patterns patients exhibit and well-known literary and mythological themes is an important aspect of the supervisory function. Appreciating the universal component of a pattern brings patient and therapist closer together. It underlines that their conflicts stem from a common source: the dilemmas engendered by the human condition. The following case discussions illustrate this aspect of the supervisory function:

> After obtaining his degree in engineering, Mr. Webster had become depressed and began to experience a troubling fantasy involving his college roommate, Julian, a history scholar whose masculine lifestyle he admired. He was torn between the secret desire to have a homosexual relationship with Julian and the wish to have Julian teach him "the ways of

men." When he entered therapy, Mr. Webster was working as a waiter; he lacked the self-confidence to apply for a position commensurate with his training. The therapist's goals were to help Mr. Webster come to terms with his homosexuality and to enhance his self-confidence as an engineer. With the therapist's encouragement, Mr. Webster did in fact find temporary work preparing a report on sewerage systems for a local municipality. However, in the fifth month of therapy, the sessions lost their momentum. With the therapist's compliance, Mr. Webster reduced the sessions from twice- to once-weekly. The growing tediousness of the sessions finally prompted the therapist to discuss them with his supervisor.

Focusing on their latest session, the therapist reported that Mr. Webster had begun by expressing dissatisfaction with his job. His employer's demands were unreasonable; he was being pressured to work beyond his capacity.

"But you did overcome this feeling in college," the therapist said.

"Yes," said Mr. Webster, "but my professors were different. They knew just how much to expect. Their instructions were consistent. The inspector who draws up my schedule changes his mind from week to week."

Mr. Webster went on to talk about Julian, who was traveling through Europe. "I received a postcard from him yesterday. He slept with a prostitute in Rome. I don't mind him sleeping with women, but crazy as it may sound, I wish I were there, observing him in the act. I want to find out how he does it. Julian's mother was a lot like my own—cold and overbearing—but he doesn't have the same problems with women I do."

After a pause, Mr. Webster announced that he planned to take a vacation in two weeks.

"Isn't that when your report is due?" the therapist asked.

"I don't give a damn. My own welfare comes first. If the city chooses to fire me, I can always go back to my old job. Working as a waiter isn't as demeaning as some people think. Most customers treat you with respect."

The rest of the session was devoted to a tirade against his employer.

"How did you feel about the session?" the supervisor asked.

"I was puzzled by it," said the therapist. "Mr. Webster seems to be doing poorly at work."

"Let's examine the flow of the session as a whole."

"As a whole? . . I'm not sure . . . Well, I guess he's disappointed . . . in his job, in Julian . . . perhaps in me as well. My lack of confidence as a therapist may be showing. I'm probably as indecisive as his employer is."

"And you're disappointed in him. Isn't that the reason you're presenting his case to me?"

"Yes. The trouble is that Mr. Webster doesn't know what he wants: a masculine ideal, a homosexual lover, or something entirely different."

"If neither you nor he knows what he wants, why did you set so specific a goal for him as helping him come to terms with his homosexuality?"

"He seems to require direction."

"Is it possible that setting goals may be part of the countertransference? Do you think Mr. Webster may be avoiding setting goals for himself?"

"I think so. He still reads comic books and seems satisfied to take direction from others. As a child, he spent most of his time helping his mother—to the exclusion of other activities."

"He mentioned her in the session."

"Yes, he described her as cold and overbearing," said the therapist. "I wonder how his mother fits into the picture. Perhaps a part of him doesn't feel ready to grow up."

"That's very possible," said the supervisor. Sensing a judgmental note in the therapist's comments, he added, "But don't we all have conflicts growing up? Isn't that why Peter Pan appeals to us all?"

"I suppose so . . . would you mention Peter Pan to him?"

"Not at first. The main purpose of considering a literary or mythological theme is to remind myself that my own conflicts and the patient's conflicts have a common base. Whenever possible, I prefer to follow the patient's stories and associations rather than my own. For example, Mr. Webster may be more familiar with *The Picture of Dorian Gray* than with *Peter*

Pan. Both refer to a similar theme. Toward the end of therapy, as part of the summing-up process, I might bring in a well-known myth or work of fiction to expand on some of the themes that were discussed. . . . on the other hand, I was once so impressed by the similarity between the patient's story and the story of Cain and Abel that I introduced it immediately. . . . As a rule, I hold off."

"The more we talk, the less confident I feel about the direction to follow. I'm not sure how to proceed."

"Simply ask the patient to expand on scenarios — on an encounter with his employer, for example. Or point out general themes. In this session, you might have suggested that his disappointment with his job reflected a more general disappointment with himself, perhaps with you as well. Or you might have empathized with his struggle to clarify what it is he's searching for."

"How will that help him?"

"In the long term, it will help him appreciate more fully the complex nature of his conflicts. Discovering conflict is only the first step. All of us are conflicted. In many ways our conflicts are similar. On the other hand, the patient's stories were shaped by experiences different from the ones that shaped yours and mine. His solutions took a different turn from ours. What's useful as well as fascinating is to help the patient discover how his conflicts have been shaped by his unique history. Dynamic psychotherapy traces the history of our conflicts."

"Will he ever resolve them?"

"Let's hope he'll develop a more comprehensive understanding of them."

"In a way, I'm more puzzled than before."

"Good," said the supervisor, "so am I. I'm looking forward to hearing more about Mr. Webster."

Following a minor car accident, Mr. Horace, a draftsman for a construction company, developed anxiety, chest pain, and a phobia about driving. His traumatic neurosis failed to yield to medication, hypnosis, or suggestion. In fact, over a three-month period, his anxiety increased. When he was 5,

Mr. Horace had fallen from the roof of a cottage. He had been unconscious for several hours and spent two weeks in a hospital. The therapist postulated that the recent trauma dovetailed with the earlier one. "At times, Mr. Horace complains that his parents never set safe limits for him," the therapist said. "He blames them for his fall. Last week he was awakened on several occasions by dreams in which he fell from the cottage roof."

"I wonder why the earlier trauma should become prominent at this juncture?" the supervisor asked.

"I don't know. Recently his major concern had been the promotion he was offered at work. He can't make up his mind whether or not to accept it."

"The dangers of climbing the ladder of success?" the supervisor asked.

"Funny, I've been struggling to understand why this promotion bothered him. I didn't make the connection."

"In a sense you just did. It was your answer to my question that supplied the connection."

"Oh, . . . I see. . . . But you would think that receiving a promotion would be be less dangerous than climbing onto a roof."

In the session following, the therapist mentioned the possibility that climbing and receiving a promotion were similar. Mr. Horace immediately accepted this analogy. "The feelings they evoke are the same," he said, "exhilaration and fear." Mr. Horace also revealed that as a child he was an inveterate climber of trees. After a pause, he talked about his father who had never recovered from the Great Depression. Mr. Horace was ashamed of the used cars his father had always driven. Six months ago the patient had purchased an expensive new car of which he was proud.

In supervision, the therapist remarked that Mr. Horace's associations brought cars, car accidents, climbing, and receiving a promotion closer together.

"The imagery is centered on cars," said the supervisor, "yet my own thoughts lead me to the story of Daedalus and Icarus—the son's soaring too close to the sun, causing him to plunge to his death."

The therapist recalled that Mr. Horace often used the expression "Pride goeth before the fall" and that his father had died a year prior to the car accident. "I've never considered the father's role in the story," he said. "I suspect the themes we're talking about will make more sense to Mr. Horace than to me."

"As they should," said the supervisor. "In therapy the patient, not the therapist, decides what's significant. The conflict you're helping him sketch in is a universal one — the dangers entailed in the wish to soar and to outstrip others. However, the particular version of the story you're helping him uncover pertains to his own unique history."

With time, the therapist overcame his limited and distancing view of Mr. Horace as someone who, because he was suffering from a traumatic neurosis, was different from the therapist. Instead, he came to regard Mr. Horace as someone struggling with conflicts similar (but not identical) to his own. After twenty-two months of twice-weekly sessions, the details of Mr. Horace's conflictual history were sketched in more clearly and his generalized anxiety lessened significantly.

The Therapist's Interventions

When they strive to emulate the stereotypical silent psychoanalyst, student therapists say too little to patients. When they strive to be spontaneous, they sometimes say too much. Interventions are necessary if only to let the patient know someone is listening. However, the notion of spontaneity should be reserved for the capacity to experience fully the emotions evoked by the patient. Between the evoked emotion or the tentative hypothesis (the two often go hand in hand) and the intervention following, there should be an editorial pause containing such questions as "Will this intervention be unnecessarily hurtful to the patient?" and "To what extent does it harbor unnecessary personal or theoretical assumptions?" Pruning an intervention of assumptions makes it possible to say less than one intended to say. Unlike physicians, dynamic psychotherapists do not *provide* information. The patient and the therapist work together. Interventions are only half of the ongoing dialogue to which both patient and therapist contribute. The following vignette illustrates this principle:

> Mr. Matthews spent the first half of his session complaining about the impossible conditions at his new job. One of his co-workers informed him that the employee he had replaced had quit two months after being hired. In fact, no one had held this position for longer than six months. In the second half of the session, Mr. Matthews berated himself for not measuring up to his new employer's expectations.
>
> In supervision the therapist said, "I should have pointed out his masochistic tendencies."*
>
> "Masochistic tendencies?" the supervisor asked.
>
> "He's obviously angry at himself instead of at his boss," the therapist replied.
>
> "It's possible that his predecessors were all incompetent."
>
> "Well, yes . . . but that makes it hard to know what direction to take or what to interpret."
>
> "Why take any direction at all? Why not simply share the patient's perspective or step back to look at the general flow of the narrative and the emotions he evokes in you. Frankly, I'm not sure what you mean by interpret."
>
> "Inform him of the patterns that underlie his difficulties."
>
> "Your task is not to provide him with information but to help *him* discover significant patterns. To tell him he's masochistic is to introduce unwarranted assumptions, such as that there's a masochistic drive somewhere in his unconscious or that his employer is difficult to work for. Let's start by simply sharing Mr. Matthews' perspective."
>
> "Now I'm confused. I'm not sure which perspective to share, his view that his new job is impossible or his view that he's incompetent."
>
> "Good. As an external observer, you've discovered a discrepancy in his narrative, one that makes entering Mr. Matthews' world difficult. If you like, you can mention that to him."

---

*At this juncture, the supervisor wondered whether the therapist's self-critical style resembled the patient's.

"That I'm confused?"

"Not exactly. To tell him that might sound critical. He might take it to mean that he shouldn't confuse you. Since neither you nor he knows exactly where you're going, confusion and puzzlement are to be expected. Why not mention the discrepancy you've discovered—nonjudgmentally, of course, emphasizing that it may be significant, not that it's illogical or that you expect Mr. Matthews to explain it. You can't expect him to do that. At this stage he is as puzzled about himself as you are. All you can do is follow the narrative to see if your intervention has had an impact. Reik called it 'listening with a third ear.' "

"What would *you* say?"

"In this instance I might say, 'At first you talked about the job being impossible. Then you talked about feeling bad that you can't measure up to your new duties.' "

"Isn't that a critical statement?"

"A great deal depends on the music, on your tone of voice, on how you feel when you speak. What I'm emphasizing is that you should say something but not very much. The aim is to point out something you consider significant with the hope that indirectly the patient will take up the topic, confirm or deny its significance, and add something new in return."

SUPERVISION VERSUS PSYCHOTHERAPY

As mentioned earlier, the supervisor's scope includes the patient's disclosures, the reported interaction between patient and therapist, and the manner in which the presentation reveals aspects of the therapeutic relationship that therapists don't know that they know. In addition, supervisors pay attention to the supervisory relationship itself. They need to ask themselves whether the therapist's learning difficulties stem from a lack of knowledge, self-awareness difficulties (often grounded in personal conflicts), or their own (the supervisors') conflicts.

Learning also takes place through identification with the supervisor. For example, identifying with the supervisor's tolerance of conflict promotes tolerance toward themselves and others in therapists. Identification is characterized by the same oscillatory pattern apparent in the therapeutic relationship. At tims, therapists comply and identify with the supervisor. At times, they disagree or rebel. As mentioned earlier, the aim of supervision is not to eradicate such oscillations but to enhance the therapist's capacity to appreciate their significance.

When the focus of attention is self-awareness or relationship difficulties, the supervisor's work overlaps with that of the therapist. What distinguishes psychotherapy from supervision is that in the former, the therapeutic relationship is the pivotal topic; in supervision, the major focus is not the supervisory relationship but the reported patient–therapist interaction. Furthermore, whereas the therapist presses forward to uncover the stories and convictions that underlie the patient's conflicts or difficulties, the supervisor does not do so with the student but limits the discussion to the student's learning difficulties.

Despite these differences, the distinction between the two relationships is often negligible. Students commonly expand on their childhood conflicts, using supervision as if it were therapy. Indeed, without such discussion, countertransference, an essential topic in supervision, cannot be properly considered (Coin and Kline 1976). Although personal difficulties should be discussed only in the context of therapeutic practice (i.e., learning difficulties), the supervisor should not discourage the therapist from bringing them to light.

In addition to imparting the principles of psychotherapy, the supervisor should help therapists *discover* them in the course of their work. The supervisor's interventions should have the same allusive qualities that the therapist's interventions should have. These principles are illustrated in the following vignettes:

> Dr. Carlton, a young medical student, reported that his patient, who had recently suffered a myocardial infarction, was depressed. Under the circumstances, he considered it unnecessary to pursue a deeper understanding of the patient's psychological difficulties.
>
> "Wouldn't anyone who has severe heart disease be depressed?" he asked.
>
> "Have you noticed," the supervisor replied, "that some car-

diac patients become more depressed than others? Some become anxious rather than depressed."

"Yes, some deny their illness altogether. Isn't that attributable to individual differences?"

"I'm curious to know what you mean by that."

"Differences in genetic makeup . . . and other things, too. For example, this patient is a compulsive jogger. Much of his self-esteem comes from keeping fit. The first question he asked was whether the illness would interfere with his exercise routine; that worried him as much as any other aspect of his illness."

"Just as a surgeon would be concerned if he developed a tremor," the supervisor added.

"But if anyone under similar circumstances would become depressed," the student asked, "does this patient really need psychotherapy?"

"A better question would be 'Can the patient benefit from psychotherapy?' or 'Would he like to talk about his conflicts or difficulties?' Would you refuse to treat someone with pneumonia because anyone with a similar constitution exposed to the same bacteria would acquire a similar infection?"

"Am I balking at offering this patient psychotherapy because I consider it humiliating not to manage on one's own?"

"Possibly. At this juncture, however, the patient may not feel the same way you do."

"He did appreciate the opportunity of having me listen to him. It may be that I'm imposing my own views on the patient, wanting him to overcome his lassitude by himself, to manage on his own."

"You may also be denying that, if you were ill, you might appreciate having someone to talk to."

"Yes, that's possible. But there must be more to psychotherapy than simply listening."

"There is. In psychotherapy, patients learn more about the ways in which their convictions and stories, their personal histories (including aspects of their history of which they're not aware) influence their present state of mind. In a way, you and the patient are already engaged in psychotherapy. After all, you're helping him realize how his views on fitness are contributing to his depression."

"It's not a great revelation."

"Nevertheless, it's important. It's a small step, but it may lead to further disclosures. For example, you may help him discover the factors that caused him to emphasize fitness in the first place. Conceptualizing patients in this way is different from regarding them as normal or abnormal, disturbed or well. For example, recognizing that this patient's views on fitness play a role in his depression makes it possible to regard him not only as someone suffering from an illness but also as an individual whose plight makes sense. You can imagine yourself in his predicament. You can empathize with him. Psychotherapists take into account the similarities as well as the differences between themselves and patients."

"It does seem easier to acknowledge similarities and to imagine oneself in the patient's predicament if one puts aside the notion of abnormality. I'll try to use this approach the next time I talk to him."

Whenever the adolescent boy he was treating reported engaging in a clandestine homosexual involvement, Dr. Ross moved the narrative away from the subject at hand and toward a discussion of the patient's childhood relationship with his father. When the supervisor pointed out this pattern to him, Dr. Ross expressed concern that encouraging the patient to expand on his homosexual patterns might bring out too quickly the homosexual aspect of the transference. "Shouldn't interventions move the narrative away from the transference when the relationship becomes too intense?" Dr. Ross asked.

"It's a useful principle to employ when the patient has stopped talking," the supervisor said. "However, there are times when the therapist should simply listen. In this instance, you seem to be using this principle to avoid sharing the patient's homosexual concerns. Whenever you feel a strong urge to press forward or to move the narrative in one direction or another, you should question your motives. I

tend not to intervene when transference or countertransference feelings are at their height. It's easier to talk about feelings when both parties have calmed down. Moving the narrative to a new subject when feelings are intense may give the
patient the impression that you're afraid of them."

"I do get angry with the patient when he talks about homosexual encounters," Dr. Ross confessed. He went on to reveal
that the patient's mother resembled his own mother and to
describe childhood incidents that had caused him to question
his sexual orientation. "I guess I should be discussing these issues in my therapy, not in supervision," he said.

The supervisor shrugged. "Patients always evoke conflicts
in the therapist. It's true that they often perceive us as individuals who have resolved our conflicts. It's a useful myth—one
that I wouldn't dispel immediately. Some clinicians claim that
identification with the imaginary well-adjusted therapist is
the major curative factor. In my opinion, over the course of
therapy the patient gradually moves away from this myth toward the view of the therapist not as someone who has resolved his conflicts but as someone with the courage to face
up to them. Perhaps the patient identifies with the coura-
geous aspect of the therapist's work. Becoming a psychotherapist does require courage."

In the sessions following, Dr. Ross behaved less critically
toward his patient; the supervisor's nonjudgmental attitude
appeared to have carried over into the therapist's work.

Dr. Hartley presented the case of a single mother who complained that her daughter was unmanageable. During his presentation, the usually animated therapist sat rigidly in his
chair.

"How did you feel in the session?" the supervisor asked.

"It's hard to put into words," said Dr. Hartley. "Perhaps it's
because I don't have any strong feelings when I'm with her."

"It helps to consider how you feel during one session as
compared to another . . . or with one patient as compared
with another."

"I do tend to be more careful with this patient than with
others. I think twice before I speak."

"Oh."

"I don't want to upset her, to unleash her anger . . . she controls me with her moods."

"A significant feeling in the light of her complaint."

"Her complaint? . . . oh, that her daughter is unmanageable. . . . I guess the narrative *is* about control."

"Perhaps the patient is communicating an aspect of her relationship with her daughter in actions rather than words," the supervisor said.

"And I'm picking it up."

"In feelings rather than in conscious thoughts. In a sense, you didn't know that you knew it."

SUMMARY

Empathy, self-awareness, and an appreciation of the ubiquitous nature of conflict are enhanced by the supervisor's paying close attention to the student therapist's conflictual learning patterns. In this chapter, these patterns were examined in terms of several sets of oscillatory patterns. The opposing poles of these patterns are overidentification with the patient versus distancing, compliance or identification with the supervisor versus noncompliance, and maintaining a silence with patients versus overinterpretation. Although they are more extreme, the oscillatory patterns of learning parallel the oscillatory patterns between opposing positions and perspectives recommended for therapists.

As an auxiliary observing ego, the supervisor helps therapists develop the capacity to appreciate the significance of their oscillations. Identification with the supervisor's tolerant attitude and introspective skills enhances the therapist's capacity for observation and self-awareness. With time, the tendency to become fixated at one or another of the positions described diminishes, enabling the therapist to oscillate freely between them.

The scope of the supervisor's evenly hovering attention includes the patient's material, the patient–therapist interaction, the ways in which the presentation reveals what therapists don't know that they know, and the supervisory relationship. Not only do therapists take on (or defensively ward off) the roles assigned to them in the therapeutic setting by the patient, they also often reenact them in the supervisory situation. At times, supervision resembles psychotherapy. The supervisor should limit discussion of the therapist's difficulties to the ways in which they interfere with learning, taking pains to avoid a position that would inhibit the therapist from revealing them. In addition to imparting the principles of psychotherapy, the supervisor helps therapists *discover* these principles in their work.

Chapter Fifteen

Epilogue: The Fate of Empathy at Termination

Both the traditional and the self psychology models of empathy have been explored. It has been shown that a flexible approach involving multiple perspectives and the therapist's imaginative use of the patient's vivid imagery enhances empathic understanding. If all has gone well, the patient's story has been gradually expanded, and the possibility of termination arises. Clinicians base their decision to work toward termination on many factors, including intuition and countertransference. Their differences in conceptualizing the end phase of therapy stem from theoretical differences and from the subjective, nonquantifiable nature of the various indicators. Although no single criterion is in itself sufficient to demonstrate readiness for termination, the following are considered useful indicators:

1. Symptomatic improvement.
2. An improved capacity to work and to love.
3. The attainment of a new coherent narrative—that is, a more comprehensive appreciation of the stories underlying

one's symptoms and conflicts. To an extent, this attainment is encompassed in the phrase "where id was there shall ego be" (Freud 1933, p. 80).

4. A greater tolerance for anxiety, depression, and pleasure, especially pleasure unaccompanied by an oppressive sense of guilt.

5. The use of higher-level defenses.

6. An improved sense of autonomy.

7. The ability to use new-found insights to adaptively alter day-to-day functioning.

8. The resolution of the transference neurosis.

9. An enhanced facility for introspection and self−analysis.

10. Evidence that normal development has resumed (Firestein 1969, 1974; Shane and Shane 1984).

Some clinicians question the efficacy of any of the indicators listed. For example, Alexander (Alexander and French 1946) considers experimental, temporary interruptions the only useful test of the patient's readiness to terminate. Of the criteria listed, symptomatic improvement is generally considered the least reliable. In fact, once the patient and the therapist have agreed upon a termination date, patients often experience a recrudescence of symptoms.

Most terminations coincide with an alteration in the patient's situation (e.g., marriage, divorce). It should be noted, however, that Ticho (1972) has advised therapists not to confuse therapeutic goals with life goals. Fleming recommends terminating while the therapist is engaged in practice, not in conjunction with a regular prolonged recess such as a summer vacation (Firestein 1969). She believes that the knowledge that the therapist is now involved with a new patient facilitates separation.

Clinicians commonly view termination as a distinct phase of therapy with its own characteristic patterns and aims. For example, as specific transference distortions begin to play a reduced role in the patient's perception of the therapist, the latter often experiences a new sense of spontaneity in the relationship (Reich 1950b). Hurn (1971) has proposed that the primary consideration during this phase should be the giving up of the therapeutic alliance. He contends that perceiving the therapist as a person in his own right should be the goal not only of the terminal phase but of therapy as a whole. In his view, the need for therapists to alter their behavior and to present themselves as 'real' in the final stages is a sign that, in its overall thrust, therapy has fallen short of the mark. Most clinicians believe that the therapist should not veer from a therapeutic stance. Termination entails mourning the loss of the therapeutic relationship, and the conflicts it evokes (in the patient and the therapist) should be discussed. The therapist's capacity to tolerate separations (including the termination of one's own analysis) strongly influences the manner in which patient and therapist take leave of each other. In the sections following, the fate of empathy at termination in terms of the therapeutic relationship and the narrative will be discussed.

THE FATE OF THE THERAPEUTIC RELATIONSHIP

Although both participants experience a similar sense of accomplishment at the conclusion of therapy, the difficulties and frustrations they experience and should discuss are also similar. One obstacle that the patient needs to overcome is the unwillingness to give up a relationship with an empathic other whose attention is focused mainly on the patient. Because the therapist, limited by subjectivity, has in many instances failed to empathize with or to fully comprehend the patient's predicament, it is also necessary for the patient to give up the hope of ever being completely understood.

The therapist is more than an empathizer, more than an observer who helps patients discover new significant convictions and stories that motivate them. As a significant participant in the therapeutic relationship, the therapist is also the object of the patient's conflictual desires, the one upon whom the patient's hopes for affection, attention, and significance have been placed. The therapist's failure to live up to the patient's expectations—that is, the failure to fulfill the role of omnipotent provider and lover—also needs to be lamented and discussed.

The difficulties confronting the therapist are similar to those confronting the patient. Therapists, too, need to overcome an unwillingness to separate, to give up the exalted roles the patient has assigned to them of idealized empathizer and omnipotent parent, provider, and lover. They, too, need to endure sadness, the patient's disappointment in them, and their own disappointment in themselves and in the patient. Although therapy ends with an expanded appreciation of the stories and convictions that motivate the patient, in many respects it also ends on the same conflictual note on which it began—with expressions of ambivalence and a recounting of successes and failures.

At the same time, however, the therapeutic relationship never truly ends. In the minds of the participants, the dialogue continues forever. They continue to mull over the things they have said and done to each other, provided and failed to provide, or accomplished and failed to accomplish. As with all significant experiences, over time the therapeutic relationship is altered in memory and recreated anew, attaining the status of a new, memorable story to add to all the others. Similarly, the therapist becomes a new permanent transference figure for the patient, receiving a place alongside parents, siblings, teachers, and all others who have attained this status.

Clearly, the course of termination is influenced by the work that preceded it. In addition, however, the more patient and therapist discuss their feelings, their successes and failures, their gratitudes and disappointments, and the realistic and unrealistic hopes they have placed in each other, the more the patient will have benefited from the therapeutic experience.

THE FATE OF THE NARRATIVE

The finite yet enduring therapeutic relationship has provided a more comprehensive set of motives, convictions, and stories in which to imbed the patient's yearnings and conflicts. The yearnings and conflicts themselves are not renounced, nor are they relegated to the distant past as merely fictional themes that have been replaced by a tighter grip on objective reality. The use of the terms *narrative* and *story* may give this impression initially, but in fact the conflictual yearnings for love, passion, omnipotence, and immortality persist. Only their context is altered. Their insertion into a new, more comprehensive set of stories and explanations (into which the old stories and convictions have been telescoped and contained) alters their significance, giving rise to a new subjectivity.

For example, a patient becomes aware through therapy of a link between her fear of letting her child out of her sight and her conviction (fashioned by her history) that her leaving home resulted in her father's death. She is then able to step back from the frame of events that grip her and to contemplate the patterns or stories in a new light. This process can be conceptualized as one in which an unconscious metaphor, equating the patient's relationship with her son and that with her father, has come to light. The patient is then able to move back from her conviction and to examine it from a new perspective. She is able to consider the ways in which it does and does not make sense. Every metaphor, after all, is inaccurate. When we say that A equals B, we are turning our backs on reality. A and B are never the same thing. They are similar in some respects and different in others. Once the patient has come to appreciate the unconscious link or metaphor in her behavior (one might call it her mistake), she is able to say, "I have felt or behaved as if my relationship with my son and my relationship with my father were identical. Now that I'm aware of this, I can see that they are similar in some respects and different in others." In this two-step process, an unconscious metaphor has been transformed into a conscious one. By the patient's contemplating its significance, it is then turned into a more flexible simile.

This process can be conceptualized in its opposite form. In a sense, the patient discovers a link where none had existed before. However, whether one starts with the notion of unconscious metaphor (absolute identity) or of absence of metaphor (absolute nonidentity), the end point is the same: a heightened awareness of simile (the introduction of the words *like* or *as if*).

Although the bond of significance between one story and another is altered, it is never entirely relinquished. Furthermore, the underlying issues—fears of dying or abandonment, concern for the welfare of one's children—are never completely erased. Although the stories the patient uncovers may be as fantastic as the *Tales of the Arabian Nights,* they are also as serious as Scheherazade's purpose in telling them: Her very existence depends on the king's enthrallment with them.

The fate of the relationship and the narrative, and the serious life-and-death issues that underlie them both, are illustrated in the following case discussions:

Mrs. Woolf, a middle-aged divorcée, complained of outbursts of uncontrollable anger and unilateral headaches and attributed her symptoms to her previous therapist's ill-advised interventions. Two years ago, he had persuaded her to leave her husband. Following the separation, Mrs. Woolf was discovered to have carcinoma of the breast.

"My husband had many affairs, and we used to argue all the time when we were together," she said, "but when you're sick you need someone . . . anyone. When I moved out of the house, my daughters sided with my husband. If I'd have known it would turn out so badly, I wouldn't have left him."

Whether or not her daughters had been alienated by Mrs. Woolf's decision to separate from her husband or by long-standing relationship difficulties was uncertain. Mrs. Woolf described her life as one of interminable conflict, especially conflict with men. "My father was no better than my husband. I fought with him for as long as I can remember. He wasn't very nice to my mother."

She had suffered from headaches for more than four months. Because her anger extended to her medical doctors, who "always looked glum" and "never answered my questions," she was now refusing to consult them.

The therapist suspected that the headaches were in fact due to physical causes. He also postulated that Mrs. Woolf's motivation for undergoing further psychotherapy stemmed in part from a wish to deny the seriousness of her medical condition, from a wish to believe that all her symptoms were psychological in origin. To an extent, her anger stemmed from her failure to find an omnipotent other, someone who could predict the course of events and advise her accordingly, or who could provide her with a favorable medical prognosis. The therapist chose not to confront her denial. Instead, difficult as it was for him, he empathized with her predicament, commenting on how disappointing it was not to be able to find someone who could make things better.

Mrs. Woolf greeted such statements with derision. Nevertheless, of her own accord she expanded on her stories. She confessed, for example, that all her married life she and her daughters had competed for her husband's attention and that she felt herself fated to discover failings in every man she met. After several sessions, her relationship with her daughters improved. In addition, she decided to consult her medical doctor. As the therapist had suspected, the tests revealed metastatic carcinoma of the brain. Although her doctor insisted on putting her in the hospital, she gave the therapist permission to visit her there.

The therapist met with her twice in hospital. The bedside visits were characterized by the same contradictory combination of bitterness and conciliatory behavior that had characterized her office appointments. She would complain that the visits were pointless.

"What makes you think you're so smart? Doctors also have to die." Moments later she would apologize for her angry remarks and proceed to talk about herself.

"I should have been kinder to my daughters," she said. "Do you think they'll ever think about me?"

"I'm sure they will."

"Not very kindly."

"None of us go through life without accomplishments or without disappointments and regrets."

The morning following the second hospital visit, Mrs. Woolf died. Two weeks later the therapist received a phone call from her husband. "Before she died, my wife asked me to pay for your sessions. She told me you helped more than anyone else did. Could you send me a bill for the visits?"

The indirect criticism of her husband contained in the message did not escape the therapist's attention. Mrs. Woolf's ambivalence toward men had persisted to the end. And although the message contained gratitude, the therapist couldn't help noting that he, too, had ultimately failed to help her.

In her initial interview, Mrs. Montez, a middle-aged house-wife with three small children, complained of a generalized anxiety whose cause was a mystery to her. "I have no reason to be upset," she said, "yet everything troubles me." She was afraid that her children would be attacked on their way to and from school, that her husband would be involved in a car accident, that someone would break into their home. Because she required constant companionship, her husband had arranged to have his sister stay with her during the day.

Mrs. Montez' narrative consisted of an endless catalogue of fears grounded in day-to-day activities. As therapy progressed, her intense anxiety persisted and no new themes emerged. After two puzzling months of twice-weekly sessions, the young therapist who met with her consulted with his supervisor who advised instituting a trial of anxiolytic medication. However, Mrs. Montez refused to take medication, preferring instead to continue talking about her fears, her own faith in the process being apparently greater than the therapist's. The sessions continued unaltered; the therapist continued experiencing the same puzzlement that he had experienced at the start. In the fourth month, however, Mrs. Montez suddenly arrived for her session in a new frame of mind. Her symptoms had vanished overnight, and thanking the therapist, she informed him that she no longer required his assistance.

Puzzled, the therapist asked how the sessions had helped her.

"Do I have to explain it?"

"Not if you prefer not to," the therapist replied, "but it would help me to understand."

Reluctantly, Mrs. Montez confessed that she had known all along what was troubling her. "I couldn't bring myself to tell you what it was. It has to do with my superstitious nature."

When the therapist emphasized that he would nonetheless appreciate hearing her story, Mrs. Montez went on to explain that her own mother had died on her forty-eighth birthday while her father was away on a fishing trip. For many years, Mrs. Montez believed that she, too, would die on her forty-eighth birthday. "I first came to see you a few months before my birthday. I didn't want it to happen while I was alone. . . . The truth is that I believed I could stop it from happening if someone was always with me. Well, my birthday came last week . . . it came and it went . . . and I didn't die. Now I feel fine. You must have been puzzled by our discussions. I'm sorry I couldn't tell you."

"Yes, I was *very* puzzled," said the therapist.

"I desperately needed someone to talk to, yet I couldn't tell you what was troubling me. . . . Well, now it's over."

At this juncture, Mrs. Montez decided not to continue her sessions. She left therapy optimistic that her anxiety would not recur.

The cases of Mrs. Woolf and Mrs. Montez illustrate the dual but overlapping roles the therapist assumes with patients. As observer on the scene, both as expander of the patient's scenarios and as significant participant in the conflictual relationship, the therapist assumes the role of empathizer and/or illusory, omnipotent other. Oscillating between the positions of observer on the scene and external observer moves the narrative forward. In Mrs. Woolf's case, the therapist's major function was to empathize with her predicament. This stance both permitted the relationship to continue until her death and expanded her appreciation of the significance of her anger. The therapist's role of provider, albeit provider who failed her and against whom she could rail, also, although in a minor way, fueled the relationship.

Mrs. Montez, on the other hand, relied almost totally on the magical aspects of therapy, on the therapist as omnipotent other. She persistently thwarted his attempts to empathize with her or to move the story forward. In the end, her understanding of herself remained unaltered.

In Mrs. Woolf's case, the therapist did allude to his helplessness (and to Mrs. Woolf's disappointment in him) in the face of her incurable illness. In Mrs. Montez' case, his admission of puzzlement did lead her to clarify what had transpired. The preceding case examples do not, however, provide a clear illustration of the benefits of discussion with the patient the ways in which therapy ultimately succeeded and failed or of the intricate and prolonged course termination often follows. What they do illustrate is the inevitable incompleteness of the termination process. Disappointment in the therapist (as in Mrs. Woolf's case) or an irrepressible view of the therapist as omnipotent (as in Mrs. Montez' case) are attitudes that often persist long after termination.

These examples, furthermore, illustrate the serious nature of the patient's stories and convictions. Mrs. Woolf's and Mrs. Montez' stories cannot be transformed into light-hearted fictions. The yearnings and conflicts that underlie such stories never lose their significance. At best, they are augmented by a more comprehensive conflictual subjectivity, making it possible for patients to live more adaptively.

INTROSPECTION, FASCINATION, AND CURIOSITY

As Margulies (1984) has asserted, the self-understanding that patients exhibit at the conclusion of therapy often outstrips the therapist's comprehension of the patient's experiential state. Nevertheless, at best only a fraction of the available stories, convictions, and explanations that influence the patient's behavior are uncovered. The incompleteness of our theories makes such an outcome inevitable. To an extent, this shortfall is a source of disappointment (to both therapist and patient). At the same time, it should also provide a source of continued curiosity and interest. Continued interest in the human condition, evoked by the discovery that one's own motives are complex and that self-understanding is necessarily incomplete, is in itself a life-generating force, a wellspring of narcissism (i.e., positive regard for oneself as an individual). Therapy in the form of introspection, contemplation, and wonder often continues long after the sessions have ended. The ongoing dialogue may take the form of imagined discussions and arguments with one's own therapist or with other significant individuals in one's life.

Because the story it uncovered falls well beyond the purview of the established psychologies, the following case example illustrates starkly the incompleteness of our theories. It also illustrates the vitalizing quality of wonder.

Mrs. Reilly, a 32-year-old housewife, was referred for consultation by an orthodox rabbi. She had originally contacted the rabbi regarding her intention to convert to Judaism. In the session, she explained that recent discussions with Jewish neighbors had influenced her decision. Both her neighbors and the rabbi, however, were puzzled by her sudden wish to convert, and Mrs. Reilly's background provided no clues to explain it. She had been born on a farm in Alberta, and her Anglican family had attended church regularly. When she was 18, she had moved to the city, where she had shared an apartment with her three older sisters and worked as a secretary for a utility company. She had met her husband, an industrial engineer, at a company picnic. At age 20 she married. Her first major contact with Jews and Judaism occurred when she and her husband moved to a suburb. Religion had never been discussed in her home, and Mrs. Reilly herself was at a loss to understand the motives underlying her decision. Her husband and family were also at a loss to understand them.

Mrs. Reilly agreed to the consultation, not for reasons related to the conversion but because her life was in turmoil. Two months prior to the referral, she had discovered that her husband had had an affair, and she had decided to leave him. The affair and her decision to leave were not discussed at home; in fact, she and her husband rarely talked. On her own, she had signed up for courses to upgrade her secretarial skills. In addition, her 10-year-old son had recently experienced a brief episode of school phobia, which Mrs. Reilly attributed to the strained atmosphere of the home. With the help of a school counselor, he had overcome it. Mrs. Reilly also complained of anorexia and suicidal ideation.

In the course of her therapy, Mrs. Reilly discovered significant links between her conflictual relationship with her husband and her childhood relationships. Her mother's unavailability and conflicts with her father and one older brother came to light. Her conflictual relationships with men in general consistently colored the therapeutic relationship. Ultimately, she did separate from her husband and found a new career with a marketing firm. Over time, her anorexia abated and her suicidal ideation disappeared. In the end, both she and the therapist considered her five years of therapy a rewarding experience.

In her second year of therapy, Mrs. Reilly did in fact convert to Judaism. Despite her son's decision not to do so, she felt comfortable with her new affiliation. Originally, the rabbi had postulated that Mrs. Reilly's unsettled state played a role in her wish to convert, a possibility she herself had entertained. Indeed, she had made every effort to study her family background and had scoured her mind for conflictual memories of references to Judaism but could not discover any trace of a connection. Nor was there any evidence to link her childhood conflicts with issues of religious significance. In the end, the psychological origins of her conversion remained a mystery.

In the third year of therapy, however, an episode did come to light that touched on the subject of Judaism—but not in a manner explicable in terms of psychology. Following her conversion, Mrs. Reilly had spent two weeks vacationing in Jamaica. There, on the beach, she had met another tourist, an elderly Englishman.

"He was a very likable gentleman," she said. "He thought deeply about things."

To her surprise, she discovered that the stranger's surname was identical to her own maiden name.

"My maiden name is S———," she explained to the therapist. "Have I mentioned it to you before? Its origin has always been a mystery to me. My father believed it came from the Gaelic "S———." I'd never met anyone with the same name before."

The Englishman had explained to Mrs. Reilly that the name originated in an unmistakable source. It was the name assumed by a number of Marrano Jews, who during the Spanish Inquisition had converted to Catholicism. He himself was a Catholic who, intrigued by his strange-sounding name, had researched its origin.

"Can you believe it?" she said to the therapist. "It made me feel eerie – as if I were a character in a ghost story."

This episode and Mrs. Reilly's conversion came up for discussion again in the end phase of therapy.

"Some of the themes and incidents we discussed in therapy," she said, "made me realize how complicated our lives are. So many factors contribute to the simplest action or mood. Of course, the episode in Jamaica is the strangest of them all. I still think about the Englishman I met on the beach. Could such distant ancestry really have played a role in my conversion? I'll probably wonder about it until the day I die."

"We only scratch the surface," said the therapist.

"That's true, but scratching the surface makes you realize how much there is to know. It makes you want to go on thinking and wondering . . . not only in a self-centered way but generally . . . about others as well as yourself. The more you think about things, the more foolish and petty the notion of suicide becomes."

Mrs. Reilly's case illustrates not only the incompleteness of our theories (and hence of the therapeutic process) but that the contemplation and self-inquiry that therapy often sets in motion are themselves generative forces.

SUMMARY: THE BOOK AS METAPHOR OF PSYCHOTHERAPY

Throughout this text, the therapeutic process has been compared to the reading or editing of a novel or drama. In many respects, therapy also ends the way books do. Indeed, the metaphor of termination as epilogue of a book is useful and apt. Both mark the end of a dialogue and of a relationship. Like the therapist–patient interaction, the author–reader interaction has been grounded in two subjectivities. Both participants bring their personal histories and convictions into the relationship. As the author writes, he carries on a conversation and a debate with his many teachers and colleagues; so does the reader as he reads. And although disagreement between reader and author is less immediately apparent than it is between patient and therapist, sooner or later it will come out in critiques, reviews, and rebuttals.

The author, like the patient, must overcome the unwillingness to give up the relationship in which the reader's attention has been centered on the text, to give up the hope of being totally understood or of the reader's registering total agreement. Sadly, he must, like the therapist, renounce the illusory but flattering role of instructor, recognizing that his words have fallen short of the mark. Many questions have remained unanswered. The boundaries of empathy, fashioned by the moods and assumptions of the era, theoretical preferences, and the goals intrinsic to dynamic psychotherapy, are still uncertain. Although the capacity to empathize has been linked with the ability to tolerate puzzlement and dilemma and to oscillate freely between conflicting or paradoxical positions (e.g., between the positions of observer on the scene and external observer, between intellectually contemplating and emotionally experiencing), it has been shown to be an inexact capacity, limited by one's conflictual subjectivity. Our present understanding of empathy and its relationship to understanding is impeded by the incompleteness of our theories and our uncertainty as to what constitutes cure in dynamic psychotherapy. The various facets of empathy require further research and discussion. In addition, the author has omitted or only briefly touched on many important therapeutic principles—for example, those pertaining to dream interpretation. The reader also needs to come to terms with the shortcomings of the book and to renounce the hope of its answering all the questions it raises.

Indeed, as with therapy, the success of a book can be measured only in relative terms. If it has carried the subject forward and has enhanced both the reader's and the author's appreciation of the subject (both in agreement with and in opposition to the views expressed) then the paired endeavor can be considered worthwhile. The book's shortcomings, however, (although a source of disappointment) should also be a spur for both author and reader to carry the subject forward into new arenas. At their best, books and articles should spawn new books and articles, just as the discoveries patients make in therapy should whet their appetites for further quests and discoveries. Both books and therapy are part of the dialogue that expands on the significance of our thoughts. The bells E. M. Forster wrote about, the bells that tell novelists when to stop, mark beginnings as well as endings. Although books and therapy come to an end, the dialogue continues.

References

Alexander, F., and French, T. (1946). *Psychoanalytic Therapy*. New York: Ronald Press.

Allison, A. W., Barrows, H., Blake, C. R., Carr, A. J., Eastman, A. M., English, Jr., H. M., eds., (1983). *The Norton Anthology of Poetry*. 3rd ed. New York: W. W. Norton.

American Psychiatric Association (1980). *Diagnostic and Statistical Manual of Mental Disorders*. 3rd ed. Washington, DC: American Psychiatric Association.

Arlow, J. A. (1963). The supervisory situation. *Journal of the American Psychoanalytic Association* 11:576–594.

―――― (1969). Unconscious fantasy and disturbances of conscious experience. *Psychoanalytic Quarterly* 38:1–27.

―――― (1985). The concept of psychic reality and related problems. *Journal of the American Psychoanalytic Association* 33:521–535.

Bach, S. (1984). Perspectives on self and object. *Psychoanalytic Review* 71:145–168.

Bachrach, H., Mintz, J., and Luborsky, L. (1971). On rating empathy and other psychotherapy variables: an experience with the effects of training. *Journal of Consulting and Clinical Psychology* 36:445.

Bachrach, H. M. (1976). Empathy: we know what we mean, but what do we measure? *Archives of General Psychiatry* 33:35–38.

Bakan, D. (1965). *Sigmund Freud and the Jewish Mystical Tradition*. New York: Schocken.

Balint, A., and Balint, M. (1939). On transference and countertransference. *International Journal of Psycho-Analysis* 20:223–230.

Balint, M. (1968). *The Basic Fault: Therapeutic Aspects of Regression*. London: Tavistock.

Balter, L., Lothane, Z., and Spencer, Jr., J. H. (1980). On the analyzing instrument. *Psychoanalytic Quarterly* 49:474–504.

Basch, M. F. (1976). The concept of affect: a re-examination. *Journal of the American Psychoanalytic Association* 24:759–777.

—— (1980). *Doing Psychotherapy*. New York: Basic Books.

—— (1981). Psychoanalytic interpretation and cognitive transformation. *International Journal of Psycho-Analysis* 62:151–175.

—— (1983a). Affect and the analyst. *Psychoanalytic Inquiry* 3:691–703.

—— (1983b). Empathic understanding: a review of the concept and some theoretical considerations. *Journal of the American Psychoanalytic Association* 31:101–125.

Basch-Kahre, E. (1984). On difficulties arising in transference and countertransference when analyst and analysand have different socio-cultural backgrounds. *International Review of Psycho-Analysis* 11:61–67.

Bate, W. J. (1964). Negative capability. In *Keats: A Collection of Essays*. ed. W. J. Bate, pp. 51–58. Englewood Cliffs, NJ: Prentice-Hall.

Becker, E. (1975). *Escape from Evil*. New York: Free Press.

Begley, S. (1979). Probing the universe. *Newsweek*, March 12.

Bemporad, J. (1982). Change factors in the treatment of depression. In *Curative Factors in Dynamic Psychotherapy*, ed. S. Slipp, pp. 317–336. New York: McGraw-Hill.

Beres, D. (1957). Communication in psychoanalysis and in the creative process: a parallel. *Journal of the American Psychoanalytic Association* 5:408–423.

—— (1960). The psychoanalytic psychology of imagination. *Journal of the American Psychoanalytic Association* 8:252–269.

—— (1962). The unconscious fantasy. *Psychoanalytic Quarterly* 31:309–328.

Beres, D., and Arlow, J. A. (1974). Fantasy and identification in empathy. *Psychoanalytic Quarterly* 43:26–50.

Berger, D. M. (1971). Hysteria: in search of the animus. *Comprehensive Psychiatry* 12:277–286.

—— (1984). On the way to empathic understanding. *American Journal of Psychotherapy* 38:111–119.

Berger, D. M., and Freebury, D. R. (1973). The acquisition of psychotherapy skills: a learning model and some guidelines for instructors. *Canadian Psychiatric Association Journal* 18:467–472.

Bion, W. R. (1963). *Elements of Psychoanalysis*. New York: Jason Aronson.

Blum, M. H. (1972). Obstacles to the teaching of empathy. Paper presented to the American Psychiatric Association, New Orleans.

Book, H. (1984). Personal communication.

Brenner, C. (1973). *An Elementary Textbook of Psychoanalysis.* New York: International Universities Press.

———— (1974). On the nature and development of affects: a unified theory. *Psychoanalytic Quarterly* 43:532–556.

———— (1982). *The Mind in Conflict.* New York: International Universities Press.

Brice, C. W. (1984). Pathological modes of human relating and therapeutic mutuality: a dialogue between Buber's existential relational theory and object relations theory. *Psychiatry* 47:109–123.

Brown, J. J. (1984). The response to self development: on the necessity of parallel development in analyst and patient. *Psychoanalytic Review* 71:105–121.

Browning, R. (1895). *The Complete Poetic and Dramatic Works of Robert Browning.* Boston: Houghton Mifflin.

Buie, D. H. (1981). Empathy: its nature and limitations. *Journal of the American Psychoanalytic Association* 29:281–307.

Burlingham, D. (1967). Empathy between infant and mother. *Journal of the American Psychoanalytic Association* 15:764–780.

Cohen, M. B. (1952). Countertransference and anxiety. *Psychiatry* 15:231–243.

Coin, M. K., and Kline, F. (1976). Countertransference: a neglected subject in clinical supervision. *American Journal of Psychiatry* 133:41–44.

Coleridge, S. T. (1802). Letter to William Sotheby, July 13, 1802. In *Collected Letters of Samuel Taylor Coleridge.* (1956), ed. Earl Leslie Griggs. Oxford: Oxford University Press.

———— (1817). *Biographia Literaria.* (1907), ed. J. Shawcross. Oxford: Clarendon Press.

Derrida, J. (1977). *Of Grammatology* Trans. G. C. Spivak. Baltimore: Johns Hopkins University Press.

Deutsch, F., and Madle, R. A. (1975). Empathy: historic and current conceptualizations measurement and a cognitive theoretical perspective. *Human Development* 18:267–287.

Deutsch, H. (1926). Occult processes occurring during psychoanalysis. In *Psychoanalysis and the Occult* (1970), ed. G. Devereaux, pp. 133–146. New York: International Universities Press.

Dilthey, W. (1894). Ideen uber eine beschreibende und Zergliedernde Psychologie. In *Wilhelm Diltheys Gesammelte Schriften*, vol. 5, pp. 139–240. Leipzig–Berlin: Teubner 1921–1934.

Eagle, M., and Wolitzky, D. L. (1982). Therapeutic influences in dynamic psychotherapy: a review and synthesis. In *Curative Factors in*

Dynamic Psychotherapy, ed. S. Slipp, pp. 349–378. New York: McGraw-Hill.

Edelheit, H. (1973). Discussion: "Development and distortions of empathy" by T. Shapiro. 585th Meeting of the New York Psychoanalytic Society, New York, February 13.

Eissler, K. R. (1968). The relation of explaining and understanding in psychoanalysis. *Psychoanalytic Study of the Child* 23:141–177.

Ekstein, R., and Wallerstein, R. S. (1958). *The Teaching and Learning of Psychotherapy.* New York: Basic Books.

Fenichel, O. (1941). *Problems of Psychoanalytic Technique.* New York: Psychoanalytic Quarterly.

———— (1953). Identification. In *The Collected Papers of Otto Fenichel, First Series,* pp. 97–112. New York: W. W. Norton.

Ferenczi, S. (1928). The elasticity of psychoanalytic technique. In *Final Contributions to the Problems and Methods of Psychoanalysis,* pp. 87–101. London: Hogarth Press.

Ferreira, A. J. (1961). Empathy and the bridge function of the ego. *Journal of the American Psychoanalytic Association* 9:91–105.

Firestein, S. K. (1969). Panel: Problems of termination in the analysis of adults. S. Firestein, reporter. *Journal of the American Psychoanalytic Association* 17:222–237.

———— (1974). Termination of psychoanalysis of adults: a review of the literature. *Journal of the American Psychoanalytic Association* 22:873–894.

Fliess, R. (1942). The metapsychology of the analyst. *Psychoanalytic Quarterly* 11:211–227.

———— (1953). Countertransference and counteridentification. *Journal of the American Psychoanalytic Association* 1:268–284.

Frank, J. (1978). *Psychotherapy and the Human Predicament.* New York: Schocken.

Freud, A. (1946). *The Ego and the Mechanisms of Defense.* New York: International Universities Press.

Freud, S. (1899). Screen memories. *Standard Edition* 3:301–322.

———— (1900). The interpretation of dreams. *Standard Edition* 4/5:1–621.

———— (1905). Fragment of an analysis of a case of hysteria. *Standard Edition* 7:3–124.

———— (1907). Delusions and dreams in Jensen's *Gradiva. Standard Edition* 9:3–96.

———— (1909). Analysis of a phobia in a five-year-old boy. *Standard Edition* 10:3–149.

———— (1911). Formulations on the two principles of mental functioning. *Standard Edition* 12:213–226.

_____ (1912). Recommendations to physicians practising psycho-analysis. *Standard Edition* 12:109–120.

_____ (1913). On beginning the treatment. *Standard Edition* 12:123–144.

_____ (1914a). Remembering, repeating, and working through. *Standard Edition* 12:145–156.

_____ (1914b). The Moses of Michelangelo. *Standard Edition* 13:211–236.

_____ (1915). Observations on transference-love. *Standard Edition* 12:157–171.

_____ (1921). Group psychology and the analysis of the ego. *Standard Edition* 18:67–143.

_____ (1930). Civilization and its discontents. *Standard Edition* 21:59–145.

_____ (1931). Female sexuality. *Standard Edition* 21:221–243.

_____ (1933). New introductory lectures on psycho-analysis. *Standard Edition* 22:3–182.

_____ (1939). Moses and monotheism. *Standard Edition* 23:3–137.

Friedman, L. (1969). The therapeutic alliance. *International Journal of Psycho-Analysis* 50:139–153.

Frye, N. (1963). *The Educated Imagination.* Toronto: Canadian Broadcasting Corporation.

_____ (1982). *The Great Code.* New York: Harcourt Brace Jovanovich.

Furer, M. (1967). Some developmental aspects of the superego. *International Journal of Psycho-Analysis* 48:277–280.

Gardner, M. R. (1983). *Self Inquiry.* An Atlantic Monthly Press Book. Boston: Little, Brown.

Gedo, J. E. (1981). On the use and abuse of empathy in psychoanalysis. In *Advances in Clinical Psychoanalysis,* pp. 160–184. New York: International Universities Press.

Gitelson, M. (1952). The emotional position of the analyst in the psychoanalytic situation. *International Journal of Psycho-Analysis* 33:1–10.

Goldberg, A. (1973). Psychotherapy of narcissistic injuries. *Archives of General Psychiatry* 28:722–726.

_____ (1974). On the prognosis and treatment of narcissism. *Journal of the American Psychoanalytic Association* 2:243–254.

_____ (1978). *The Psychology of the Self: A Casebook,* ed. A. Goldberg. New York: International Universities Press.

Gray, P. (1973). Psychoanalytic technique and the ego's capacity for viewing intrapsychic activity. *Journal of the American Psychoanalytic Association* 21:474–495.

Greene, M. A. (1984). The self psychology of Heinz Kohut. *Bulletin of the Menninger Clinic* 48:37–53.

Greenson, R. R. (1960). Empathy and its vicissitudes. *International Journal of Psycho-Analysis* 41:418–424.

———— (1965a). The working alliance and the transference neurosis. *Psychoanalytic Quarterly* 34:155–181.

———— (1965b). The problem of working through. In *Drives, Affects and Behavior*, vol. 2, ed. M. Schur, pp. 277–314. New York: International Universities Press.

Hamilton, N. G. (1981). Empathic understanding. *Psychoanalytic Inquiry* 1:417–422.

Handelman, S. A. (1982). *The Slayers of Moses*. Albany, NY: State University of New York Press.

Hartmann, H. (1927). Understanding and explanation. In *Essays in Ego Psychology*, (1964), pp. 369–403. New York: International Universities Press.

Havens, L. L. (1973). *Approaches to the Mind*. Boston: Little, Brown.

———— (1982a). The choice of clinical methods. *Contemporary Psychoanalysis* 18:16–41.

———— (1982b). The risks of knowing and not knowing. *Journal of Social Biological Structure* 5:213–222.

Hollender, M. H. (1965). *The Practice of Psychoanalytic Psychotherapy*. New York: Grune & Stratton.

Holt, R. (1972). Freud's mechanistic and humanistic images of man. In *Psychoanalysis and Contemporary Science*, ed. R. Holt and E. Peterfreund, pp. 3–24. New York: Macmillan.

Hurn, H. (1971). Toward a paradigm of the terminal phase. *Journal of the American Psychoanalytic Association* 19:332–348.

Jacobson, E. (1954). The self and the object world. *Psychoanalytic Study of the Child* 9:75–127.

Kaplan, H. B., and Bloom, S. W. (1960). The use of sociological and social-psychological concepts in physiological research: a review of selected experimental studies. *Journal of Nervous and Mental Disease* 131:128–134.

Katan, M. (1950). Schreber's hallucinations about the 'little men.' *International Journal of Psycho-Analysis* 31:32–35.

Kernberg, O. F. (1974). Contrasting viewpoints regarding the nature and psychoanalytic treatment of narcissistic personalities: a preliminary communication. *Journal of the American Psychoanalytic Association* 22:255–267.

———— (1980). *Internal World and External Reality*. New York: Jason Aronson.

_____ (1982). The theory of psychoanalytic psychotherapy. In *Curative Factors in Dynamic Psychotherapy*, ed. S. Slipp, pp. 21–43. New York: McGraw-Hill.

Kernberg, O. F., Appelbaum, A., Burnstein, E. D., Coyne, L., Horwitz, L., and Voth, H. (1972). Psychotherapy and psychoanalysis: final report of the Menninger Foundation Psychotherapy Research Project. *Bulletin of the Menninger Clinic* 36:3–275.

Kline, P. (1972). *Fact and Fantasy in Freudian Theory*. London: Methuen.

Knight, R. P. (1940). Introjection, projection and identification. *Psychoanalytic Quarterly* 9:334–341.

Koff, R. H. (1957). The therapeutic Man Friday. *Journal of the American Psychoanalytic Association* 5:424–431.

Kohut, H. (1959). Introspection, empathy and psychoanalysis: an examination of the relationship between mode of observation and therapy. *Journal of the American Psychoanalytic Association* 7:459–483.

_____ (1966). Forms and transformations of narcissism. *Journal of the American Psychoanalytic Association* 14:243–272.

_____ (1971). *The Analysis of the Self*. New York: International Universities Press.

_____ (1977). *The Restoration of the Self*. New York: International Universities Press.

_____ (1979). The two analyses of Mr. Z. *International Journal of Psycho-Analysis* 60:3–27.

_____ (1982). Introspection, empathy, and the semi-circle of mental health. *International Journal of Psycho-Analysis* 63:395–407.

_____ (1984). The role of empathy in psychoanalytic cure. In *How Does Analysis Cure? Contributions to the Psychology of the Self*, ed. A. Goldberg and P. Stepansky, pp. 172–191. Chicago: University of Chicago Press.

Kohut, H., and Seitz, P. (1963). *In the Search for the Self*. New York: International Universities Press.

Kohut, H., and Wolf, E. S. (1978). The disorders of the self and their treatment: an outline. *International Journal of Psycho-Analysis* 59:413–425.

_____ (1982). The disorders of the self and their treatment. In *Curative Factors in Dynamic Psychotherapy*, ed. S. Slipp, pp. 44–59. New York: McGraw-Hill.

Kris, E. (1950). On preconscious mental processes. *Psychoanalytic Quarterly* 19:540–560.

_____ (1956). The recovery of childhood memories in psychoanalysis. *Psychoanalytic Study of the Child* 11:54–88.

Langs, R. (1978-1979). Some communicative properties of the bi-personal field. *International Journal of Psychoanalytic Psychotherapy* 7:87-135.

_____ (1982). Countertransference and the concept of cure. In *Curative Factors in Dynamic Psychotherapy*, ed. S. Slipp, pp. 127-152. New York: McGraw-Hill.

Leavy, S. (1973). Psychoanalytic interpretation. *Psychoanalytic Study of the Child* 28:305-330.

Leider, R. J. (1983). Analytic neutrality – a historical review. *Psychoanalytic Inquiry* 3:665-674.

Lichtenberg, J. D. (1981). The empathic mode of perception and alternative vantage points for psychoanalytic work. *Psychoanalytic Inquiry* 1:329-355.

_____ (1983). *Psychoanalysis and Infant Research*. The Analytic Press, pp. 233-234. Hillsdale, NJ: Lawrence Erlbaum Associates.

Little, M. (1951). Counter-transference and the patient's response to it. *International Journal of Psycho-Analysis* 32:32-40.

_____ (1957). "R" – the analyst's total response to his patient's needs. *International Journal of Psycho-Analysis* 38:240-254.

Loewald, H. W. (1960). On the therapeutic action of psycho-analysis. *International Journal of Psycho-Analysis* 41:16-33.

_____ (1970). Psychoanalytic theory and the psychoanalytic process. *Psychoanalytic Study of the Child* 25:45-68.

Low, B. (1935). The psychological compensations of the analyst. *International Journal of Psycho-Analysis* 16:1-8.

Mahler, M., Pine, F., and Bergman, A. (1975). *The Psychological Birth of the Human Infant: Symbiosis and Individuation*. New York: Basic Books.

Mailer, N. (1955). *The Deer Park*. New York: G. P. Putnam's.

Margenau, H. (1949). Einstein's conception of reality. In *Albert Einstein: Philosopher–Scientist*, ed. P. A. Schilpp, pp. 244-268. Menasha, WI: Banta.

Margulies, A. (1984). Toward empathy: the uses of wonder. *American Journal of Psychiatry* 141:1025-1033.

Margulies, A., and Havens, L. L. (1981). The initial encounter: what to do first? *American Journal of Psychiatry* 138:421-428.

Marmor, J. (1982). Change in psychoanalytic treatment. In *Curative Factors in Dynamic Psychotherapy*, ed. S. Slipp, pp. 60-70. New York: McGraw-Hill.

Meissner, W. W. (1971). Notes on identification: II. Clarification of related concepts. *Psychoanalytic Quarterly* 40:277-302.

———— (1972). Notes on identification: III. The concept of identification. *Psychoanalytic Quarterly* 41:244–260.

Merklin, L., and Little, R. B. (1967). The beginning psychiatry training syndrome. *American Journal of Psychiatry* 124:193–197.

Michels, R. (1985). Introduction to panel: perspectives on the nature of psychic reality. *Journal of the American Psychoanalytic Association* 33:515–519.

Modell, A. H. (1976). "The holding environment" and the therapeutic action of psychoanalysis. *Journal of the American Psychoanalytic Association* 24:285–307.

Moore, B. E., and Fine, B. D. (1968). *A Glossary of Psychoanalytic Terms and Concepts*, 2nd ed. New York: The American Psychoanalytic Association.

Newman, K. (1980). Defense analysis and self psychology. In *Advances in Self Psychology*, ed. A. Goldberg, pp. 263–278. New York: International Universities Press.

Novick, J., and Kelly, K. (1970). Projection and externalization. *Psychoanalytic Study of the Child* 25:69–95.

Noy, P. (1982). A revision of the psychoanalytic theory of affect. *Annual Review of Psychoanalysis* 10:139–186.

Nunberg, H. (1955). *Principles of Psychoanalysis*. New York: International Universities Press.

Olden, C. (1953). On adult empathy with children. *Psychoanalytic Study of the Child* 8:111–126.

———— (1958). Notes on the development of empathy. *Psychoanalytic Study of the Child* 13:505–518.

Olinick, S. L. (1969). On empathy and regression in service of the other. *British Journal of Medical Psychology* 42:41–49.

Ornstein, P. H., and Ornstein, A. (1977). On the continuing evolution of psychoanalytic psychotherapy: reflections and predictions. In *The Annual of Psychoanalysis* 5:329–370.

Orr, D. W. (1954). Transference and countertransference: a historical survey. *Journal of the American Psychoanalytic Association* 2:621–670.

Piaget, J. (1954). *The Construction of Reality in the Child*. New York: Basic Books.

Poland, W. S. (1984). On the analyst's neutrality. *Journal of the American Psychoanalytic Association* 32:283–299.

Popper, K. (1968). *The Logic of Scientific Discovery*. New York: Harper & Row.

Post, S. L. (1980). Origins, elements and functions of therapeutic empathy. *International Journal of Psycho-Analysis* 61:277–293.

Racker, H. (1957). Contribution to the problem of psycho-pathological stratification. *International Journal of Psycho-Analysis* 38:223–239.

Rapaport, D. (1959). The structure of psychoanalytic theory: a systemizing attempt. In *Psychology: A Study of a Science,* vol. 3, ed. S. Koch. New York: McGraw-Hill.

Rapaport, D., and Gill, M. M. (1959). The points of view and assumptions of metapsychology. *International Journal of Psycho-Analysis* 40:153–161.

Reich, A. (1950a). On counter-transference. *International Journal of Psycho-Analysis* 31:25–31.

———— (1950b). On the termination of analysis. *International Journal of Psycho-Analysis* 31:179–183.

———— (1953). Narcissistic object choice in women. *Journal of the American Psychoanalytic Association* 1:22–44.

———— (1966). Empathy and countertransference. In *Psychoanalytic Contributions* (1970), pp. 344–368. New York: International Universities Press.

Reik, T. (1948). *Listening with the Third Ear.* New York: Grove Press.

Rothstein, A. (1980). Toward a critique of the psychology of the self. *Psychoanalytic Quarterly* 49:423–455.

Roustang, F. (1980). *Psychoanalysis Never Lets Go.* Baltimore: Johns Hopkins University Press.

Rubinstein, B. (1972). On metaphor and related phenomena. In *Psychoanalysis and Contemporary Science,* vol. 1, ed. R. R. Holt and E. Peterfreund, pp. 70–108. New York: Macmillan.

Sander, L. (1980). New knowledge about the infant from current research: implications for psychoanalysis. L. Sander, reporter. *Journal of the American Psychoanalytic Association* 28:181–198.

Sandler, J., and Rosenblatt, B. (1962). The concept of the representational world. *Psychoanalytic Study of the Child* 17:128–144.

Sandler, J., Dare, C., and Holder, A. (1973). *The Patient and the Analyst: The Basis of the Psychoanalytic Process.* New York: International Universities Press.

Sawyier, F. H. (1975). A conceptual analysis of empathy. *The Annual of Psychoanalysis* 3:37–47.

Schafer, R. (1959). Generative empathy in the treatment situation. *Psychoanalytic Quarterly* 28:342–373.

———— (1978). *Language and Insight.* New Haven: Yale University Press.

———— (1983). *The Analytic Attitude.* New York: Basic Books.

Scharfman, M. A., and Blacker, K. H. (1981). Insight: clinical conceptualizations. *Journal of the American Psychoanalytic Association* 29:659–671.

Schimek, J. G. (1975). The interpretations of the past: childhood trauma, psychical reality and historical truth. *Journal of the American Psychoanalytic Association* 23:845–865.

Schlesinger, H. J. (1981). The process of empathic response. *Psychoanalytic Inquiry* 1:393–416.

Schwaber, E. (1980). Self psychology and the concept of psychopathology: a case presentation. In *Advances in Self Psychology*, ed. A. Goldberg, pp. 215–242. New York: International Universities Press.

_____ (1983a). Construction, reconstruction, and the mode of clinical attunement. In *The Future of Psychoanalysis*, ed. A. Goldberg, pp. 273–291. New York: International Universities Press.

_____ (1983b). A particular perspective on analytic listening. *Psychoanalytic Study of the Child* 38:519–546.

Scott, W. C. (1962). Symposium: A reclassification of psychopathological states. *International Journal of Psycho-Analysis* 42:344–350.

Segal, H. (1980). *An Introduction to the Work of Melanie Klein*. New York: Basic Books.

Shane, M., and Shane, E. (1984). The end phase of analysis: indicators, functions and tasks of termination. *Journal of the American Psychoanalytic Association* 32:739–772.

Shapiro, T. (1974). The development and distortions of empathy. *Psychoanalytic Quarterly* 43:4–25.

_____ (1981). Empathy: a critical reevaluation. *Psychoanalytic Inquiry* 1:423–448.

_____ (1984). On neutrality. *Journal of the American Psychoanalytic Association* 32:269–282.

Sharpe, E. F. (1950a). The analyst. In *Collected Papers on Psycho-Analysis*, pp. 9–21. New York: Brunner/Mazel.

_____ (1950b). The psychoanalyst. In *Collected Papers on Psycho-Analysis*, pp. 109–122. New York: Brunner/Mazel.

Silverman, L. H., and Lachmann, F. M. (1985). The therapeutic properties of unconscious oneness fantasies: evidence and treatment implications. *Contemporary Psychoanalysis* 1:91–119.

Simon, B. (1981). Confluence of visual image between patient and analyst: communication of failed communication. *Psychoanalytic Inquiry* 1:471–488.

Spitz, R. (1965). *The First Year of Life: A Psychoanalytic Study of Normal and Deviant Development of Object Relations*. New York: International Universities Press.

Steingart, I. (1983). *Pathological Play in Borderline and Narcissistic Personalities*. New York: Spectrum Publications.

Sterba, J. (1934). The fate of the ego in analytic therapy. *International*

Journal of Psycho-Analysis 15:117–126.

Stolorow, R. D., Brandchaft, B., and Atwood, G. E. (1983). Intersubjectivity in psychoanalytic treatment with special reference to archaic states. *Bulletin of the Menninger Clinic* 47:117–128.

Sullivan, H. S. (1953). *The Interpersonal Theory of Psychiatry.* New York: W. W. Norton.

Szalita, A. B. (1976). Some thoughts on empathy. *Psychiatry—Journal for the Study of Interpersonal Processes* 39:142–152.

Tansey, M. H., and Burke, W. F. (1985). Projective identification and the empathic process. *Contemporary Psychoanalysis* 21:42–69.

Taylor, G. J. (1984). Alexithymia: concept, measurement, and implications for treatment. *American Journal of Psychiatry* 141:725–732.

Thompson, C., trans. (1965). *The Colloquies of Erasmus.* Chicago: University of Chicago Press.

Thomson, P. (1980). On the receptive function of the analyst. *International Review of Psycho-Analysis* 7:183–205.

Ticho, E. (1972). Termination of psychoanalysis: treatment goals, life goals. *Psychoanalytic Quarterly* 41:315–333.

Truax, C. B. (1966). Influence of patient statements on judgments of therapist statements during psychotherapy. *Journal of Clinical Psychology* 22:335–337.

Truax, C. B., Wargo, D., Frank, J. D., Imber, D., et al. (1966). Therapist empathy, genuineness, and warmth and patient therapeutic outcome. *Journal of Consulting Psychology* 30:395–401.

Tuchman, B. (1979). In search of history. *Radcliffe Quarterly,* March, pp. 33–37.

Tuttman, S. (1982). Regression: curative factor or impediment in dynamic psychotherapy. In *Curative Factors in Dynamic Psychotherapy,* ed. S. Slipp, pp. 177–198. New York: McGraw-Hill.

U'Ren, R. C. (1980). *The Practice of Psychotherapy: A Guide for the Beginning Therapist.* New York: Grune & Stratton.

Volkan, V. D. (1982). Identification and related psychic events. In *Curative Factors in Dynamic Psychotherapy,* ed. S. Slipp, pp. 153–176. New York: McGraw-Hill.

Wallerstein, R. S. (1985). The concept of psychic reality: its meaning and value. *Journal of the American Psychoanalytic Association* 33:555–569.

Weber, J. J., Bachrach, H. M., and Solomon, M. (1985). Factors associated with the outcome of psychoanalysis: report of the Columbia Psychoanalytic Center Research Project (II). *International Review of Psycho-Analysis* 12:127–141.

Weiss, J., Sampson, H., Gaston, J., Silberschatz, G., and Gassner, S.

(1977). Research on the psychoanalytic process. *Bulletin No. 3*, December 1977. The Psychotherapy Research Group, Department of Psychiatry, Mount Zion Hospital and Medical Center.

Weiss, J., Sampson, H., Gassner, S., and Gaston, J. (1980). Further research on the psychoanalytic process. *Bulletin No. 4*, June 1980. The Psychotherapy Research Group, Department of Psychiatry, Mount Zion Hospital and Medical Center.

Wetzler, S. (1985). The historical truth of psychoanalytic reconstructions. *International Review of Psycho-Analysis* 12:187-197.

Winnicott, D. W. (1958). Transitional objects and transitional phenomena. In *Collected Papers — Through Paediatrics to Psycho-Analysis*, pp. 229-242. New York: Basic Books.

―――― (1965). Ego distortion in terms of true and false self. In *The Maturational Processes and the Facilitating Environment*, pp. 140-152. New York: International Universities Press.

―――― (1967). The location of cultural experience. *International Journal of Psycho-Analysis* 48:368-372.

―――― (1971). The use of an object and relating through identifications. In *Playing and Reality*, pp. 86-94. New York: Methuen.

Wolf, E. S. (1976). Recent advances in the psychology of the self: an outline of basic concepts. *Comprehensive Psychiatry* 17:37-46.

―――― (1980). On the developmental line of selfobject relations. In *Advances in Self Psychology*, ed. A. Goldberg, pp. 117-130. New York: International Universities Press.

―――― (1983a). Aspects of neutrality. *Psychoanalytic Inquiry* 3:675-689.

―――― (1983b). Empathy and countertransference. In *The Future of Psychoanalysis*, ed. A. Goldberg, pp. 309-326. New York: International Universities Press.

Yankelovich, D., and Barrett, W. (1970). *Ego and Instinct: The Psychoanalytic View of Human Nature*, rev. ed. New York: Random House.

Zetzel, E. R. (1956). Current concepts of transference. *International Journal of Psycho-Analysis* 37:369-376.

Index

Abstinence, 7
  in self psychology, 52–53
Affect
  communication of, 25–26
  and ideation, 67–68, 89
Alexander, F., 260
Allison, A. W., 102
Analyzing instrument, 27–28, 36
Antithetical issues, 12–15,
    139–140
Arlow, J. A., 20, 28, 33–34, 56, 91,
    237, 244
Atwood, G. E., 15, 75

Bach, S., 150
Bachrach, H. M., 3
Bakan, D., 87
Balint, A., 33
Balint, M., 33, 218
Balter, L., 27
Barrett, W., 82

Basch, M. F., 7, 10, 19, 25–26, 31,
    37, 57, 63, 97, 117
Basch-Kahre, E., 39
Bate, W. J., 85–86
Becker, E., 12, 13
Begley, S., 70
Bemporad, J., 226
Beres, D., 20, 28, 91–92
Berger, D. M., 76, 238
Bergman, A., 53, 55
Bibring, E., 218
Bion, W. R., 85
Blacker, K. H., 219
Bloom, S. W., 26n
Blum, M. H., 36
Book, H., 35
Brandchaft, B., 15, 75
Brenner, C., 8, 56, 67
Brice, C. W., 21n
Brown, J. J., 31
Browning, R., 65

DEMCO